Eurasia's Regional Powers Compared – China, India, Russia

Taking a long view, and a wide perspective, this book by Japan's leading scholars on Asia and Eurasia provides a comprehensive and systematic comparison of the three greatest powers in the region and assesses how far the recent growth trajectories of these countries are sustainable in the long run. The book demonstrates the huge impact of these countries on the world. It examines the population, resource and economic basis for the countries' rise, considers political, social and cultural factors, and sets recent developments in a long historical context. Throughout, the different development paths of the three countries are compared and contrasted, and the new models for the future of the world order which they represent are analysed.

Shinichiro Tabata is Professor in the Slavic-Eurasian Research Center at Hokkaido University, and specializes in comparative economic systems and studies of the Russian economy.

Routledge Advances in Asia-Pacific Studies

1. Environment, Education and Society in the Asia-Pacific
Local traditions and global discourses
David Yencken, John Fien and Helen Sykes

2. Ageing in the Asia-Pacific Region
David R. Phillips

3. Caring for the Elderly in Japan and the US
Practices and policies
Susan Orpett Long

4. Human Rights and Gender Politics: Asia-Pacific Perspectives
Edited by Anne Marie Hilsdon, Martha Macintyre, Vera Mackie and Maila Stivens

5. Human Rights in Japan, South Korea and Taiwan
Ian Neary

6. Cultural Politics and Asian Values
The tepid war
Michael D. Barr

7. Social Policy in East and Southeast Asia
Education, health, housing and income maintenance
M. Ramesh

8. Sino–Japanese Relations
Facing the past, looking to the future?
Caroline Rose

9. Directors of Urban Change in Asia
Edited by Peter J. M. Nas

10. Education Reform and Education Policy in East Asia
Ka Ho Mok

11. The Strong and the Weak in Japanese Literature
Discrimination, egalitarianism, nationalism
Fuminobu Murakami

12. Civilization, Nation and Modernity in East Asia
Chih-Yu Shih

13. Diminishing Conflicts in Asia and the Pacific
Robin Jeffrey, Edward Aspinall and Anthony Regan

14. Health Transitions and the Double Disease Burden in Asia and the Pacific
Histories of responses to non-communicable and communicable diseases
Edited by Milton J. Lewis and Kerrie L. MacPherson

15. Film Censorship in the Asia-Pacific Region
Malaysia, Hong Kong and Australia compared
Saw Tiong Guan

16. Asian and Pacific Cities
Development patterns
Edited by Ian Shirley and Carol Neill

17. Eurasia's Regional Powers Compared – China, India, Russia
Edited by Shinichiro Tabata

Eurasia's Regional Powers Compared – China, India, Russia

Edited by
Shinichiro Tabata

LONDON AND NEW YORK

First published 2015
by Routledge

2 Park Square, Milton Park, Abingdon, Oxfordshire OX14 4RN
711 Third Avenue, New York, NY 10017

Routledge is an imprint of the Taylor & Francis Group, an informa business

First issued in paperback 2017

Copyright © 2015 selection and editorial material, Shinichiro Tabata; individual chapters, the contributors

The right of Shinichiro Tabata to be identified as author of the editorial material, and of the individual authors as authors of their contributions, has been asserted by them in accordance with sections 77 and 78 of the Copyright, Designs and Patents Act 1988.

All rights reserved. No part of this book may be reprinted or reproduced or utilised in any form or by any electronic, mechanical, or other means, now known or hereafter invented, including photocopying and recording, or in any information storage or retrieval system, without permission in writing from the publishers.

Notice:
Product or corporate names may be trademarks or registered trademarks, and are used only for identification and explanation without intent to infringe.

British Library Cataloguing in Publication Data
A catalogue record for this book is available from the British Library

Library of Congress Cataloging in Publication Data
Eurasia's regional powers compared : China, India, Russia / edited by Shinichiro Tabata.
    pages cm. – (Routledge advances in Asia-Pacific studies ; 17)
Summary: "Taking a long view, and a wide perspective, this book by Japan's leading scholars on Asia and Eurasia provides a comprehensive and systematic comparison of the three greatest powers in the region and assesses how far the recent growth trajectories of these countries are sustainable in the long run. The book demonstrates the huge impact of these countries on the world. It examines the population, resource and economic basis for the countries' rise, considers political, social and cultural factors, and sets recent developments in a long historical context. Throughout, the different development paths of the three countries are compared and contrasted, and the new models for the future of the world order which they represent are analysed"– Provided by publisher.
Includes bibliographical references and index.
    1. Geopolitics–Eurasia. 2. Eurasia–Foreign relations. 3. Eurasia–Foreign economic relations. 4. China–Foreign relations. 5. China–Foreign economic relations 6. India–Foreign relations. 7. India–Foreign economic relations. 8. Russia (Federation)–Foreign relations. 9. Russia (Federation)–Foreign economic relations. I. Tabata, Shin'ichiro, 1957- editor of compilation.
    DK293.E765 2015
    327.5–dc23
                    2014027179

ISBN: 978-1-138-78294-5 (hbk)
ISBN: 978-0-8153-5796-4 (pbk)

Typeset in Times New Roman
by Taylor & Francis Books

Contents

List of illustrations	ix
Notes on contributors	xi
Introduction	1
SHINICHIRO TABATA	

PART I
Economic development 7

1 Industrialization in the process of economic reform: comparative
analysis of China, Russia and India 9
AKIRA UEGAKI

2 A comparison of trade policy reform in China, India and Russia 28
TOMOO MARUKAWA AND YUGO KONNO

3 Emergence of regional powers in the international financial system 47
SHINICHIRO TABATA

PART II
Political systems and diplomacy 65

4 Power and limitations of dominant party control: United Russia,
the Indian National Congress and the Chinese Communist
Party compared 67
ATSUSHI OGUSHI AND YUKO ADACHI

5 Client, agent or bystander? Patronage and village leadership in
India, Russia and China 85
FUMIKI TAHARA

viii *Contents*

6 Loss of political leadership and passive 'triple transformation' in the
former Soviet Union: a comparison with China's reform strategy 106
LIANG TANG

7 The political consequences of peace: China's retreat for
survival, 1988–91 120
YOSHIFUMI NAKAI

8 India's pragmatic diplomacy with major powers: a comparative
study of the strategic partnership with the US, China, and Russia 137
TORU ITO

PART III
History 153

9 Autonomous regions in the Eurasian borderlands as a legacy of the
First World War 155
YOSHIRO IKEDA

10 Empires and shari'a: a comparison of colonial Islamic legal systems 171
JUN AKIBA

PART IV
Culture and society 189

11 Delineating contours: portrayal of regional powers in British Asian
immigrant literature 191
HISAE KOMATSU

12 Illusion and mirror: images of China in contemporary
Russian literature 205
GO KOSHINO

13 UNESCO World Heritage and the regional powers: changing
representations of religious cultural heritage 222
SANAMI TAKAHASHI, NORIKO MAEJIMA, AND HIROSHI KOBAYASHI

Index 240

List of illustrations

Tables

1.1	Export share, IPD, and ISD: China in 1985	19
1.2	Export share, IPD, and ISD: China in 2002	20
1.3	Export share, IPD, and ISD: Russia in 2003	21
1.4	Export share, IPD, and ISD: India in 1993–1994	22
1.5	Export share, IPD, and ISD: India in 2003–2004	23
2.1	Trade openness index	38
2.2	Actual and Predicted net export of Russia, China and India (percent of GDP)	40
3.1	Factors contributing to the increase in foreign reserves in China, Russia and India, 2000–2012	50
3.2	Savings and investment balance by institutional sector in China, Russia and India	52
4.1	Typology of dominant parties	70
4.2	Characteristics of dominant parties in Eurasian regional powers	70
4.3	Number of United Russia members in Murmansk	78
5.1	People's representatives of Indian research sites	87
5.2	People's representatives of Russian research sites	89
5.3	Correlation between party politics and village leadership	100
7.1	China's diplomatic relations 1989–1997	129
8.1	Image of relations with the US, China and Russia from the Indian viewpoint in 2012	147

Figures

2.1	China's average import tariff rate and the rate of import tariff burden	33
2.2	India's average import tariff rate and the rate of import tariff burden	34
2.3	Russia's average import tariff rate and the rate of import tariff burden	35

x   *List of illustrations*

3.1	Nominal exchange rates of three currencies against the dollar, monthly average in percent	48
3.2	International reserves, PBC bills and money supply (M2) in China, 2001–2013	54
3.3	International reserves, stabilization fund and money supply (M2) in Russia, 2001–2013	55
3.4	International reserves, MSS bonds and money supply (M2) in India, 2001–2013	55
4.1	Results of regional elections (proportional representation part) 2005–March 2011	77
5.1	Typology of village leadership	85
5.2	Winning party in AP, Orissa MLA elections	91
7.1	FDI in China actual	133
9.1	Grand Duke Nikolai Nikolaevich	159
9.2	Central Asia region (1922)	163
9.3	Outer Mongolia and Tuva	164

Notes on contributors

Yuko Adachi is Associate Professor in the Department of Russian Studies, Sophia University, and specializes in Russian political economy. Publications include *Building Big Business in Russia: The Impact of Informal Corporate Governance Practices*, London and New York: Routledge, 2010; and 'Subsoil law reform in Russia under the Putin administration', *Europe-Asia Studies*, 61 (8), 2009, pp. 1393–1414.

Jun Akiba is Associate Professor in the Faculty of Letters, Chiba University, specializing in the history of the Ottoman Empire. Publications include 'The local councils as the origin of the parliamentary system in the Ottoman Empire', in T. Sato, ed., *Development of Parliamentarism in the Modern Islamic World*, Tokyo: Toyo Bunko, 2009, pp. 176–204; 'Preliminaries to a comparative history of the Russian and Ottoman Empires: Perspectives from Ottoman studies', in K. Matsuzato, ed., *Imperiology: From Empirical Knowledge to Discussing the Russian Empire*, Sapporo: Slavic Research Center, 2007, pp. 33–47; and 'A new school for Qadis: Education of shari'a judges in the late Ottoman Empire', *Turcica: Revue d'études turques*, 35, 2003, pp. 125–63.

Yoshiro Ikeda is Associate Professor in the Graduate School of Humanities and Sociology at the University of Tokyo, and specializes in modern Russian history. Published work includes 'The reintegration of the Russian Empire and the Bolshevik views of "Russia": The case of the Moscow Party organization', *Acta Slavica Iaponica* 22, 2005, pp. 120–40; *The Republic and the Nation in Revolutionary Russia*, Tokyo: Yamakawa Shuppansha, 2007 (in Japanese); and 'A new horizon of Soviet imperiology', *Study of World History*, 234, 2013, pp. 1–12 (in Japanese).

Toru Ito is Associate Professor in the Graduate School of Security Studies at the National Defense Academy. He specializes in international relations in South Asia and India's diplomacy. His published work includes '"China threat" theory in Indo-Japan relations', in T. Horimoto and L. Varma, eds, *India-Japan Relations in Emerging Asia*, New Delhi: Manohar, 2013, pp. 113–31; and 'The approach to Indian diplomacy: How to establish alternative IR rooted in

India', paper presented to the Annual Convention of the Indian Association of International Studies, December 2012, India International Center.

Hiroshi Kobayashi is a Post-Doctoral Research Fellow at the, Japan Society for the Promotion of Science, specializing in Chinese society and culture. Publications include 'Traditional environmental knowledge in Hakka vernacular architecture' (with H. Kawai), paper presented to the forum on 'Hakka tulous: Lessons to be Learned, Past, Present and Future' at the launch of the International Hakka Tulou Alliance (IHTA), June 24, 2009, Xiamen University, Fujian, China (in Mandarin and English); and 'Regeneration of Hakka culture from the perspective of Fujian tulous', in M. Segawa and N. Iijima, eds, *Generation and Regeneration of Hakka*, Tokyo: Fukyosya, 2012, pp. 97–127 (in Japanese).

Hisae Komatsu lectures in the Faculty of International Liberal Arts at Otemon Gakuin University, and specializes in Hindi literature and Indian cultural studies. Her published work includes 'Women of virtue; A case study of Janakidevi Bajaj (1892–1979)', in U. Sachidanand and T. Sakata, eds., *Imaging India – Imaging Japan: A Chronicle of Reflections on Mutual Literature*, New Delhi: Manak, 2005; 'Tell me what love is: A study of "love" in early twentieth century Indian women's narratives', in T. Mochizuki and S. Maeda, eds, *India, Russia, China: Comparative Studies on Eurasian Culture and Societ,* (Comparative Studies on Regional Powers no. 11), Sapporo: Slavic Research Center, 2012, pp. 131–39; and 'Speaking about Desi; The sense of belonging in contemporary British-Asian writers', in T. Mochizuki and G. Koshino, eds., *Orient on Orient: Images of Asia in Eurasian Countries* (Comparative Studies on Regional Powers no. 12), Sapporo: Slavic Research Center, 2013, pp. 97–107.

Yugo Konno is Senior Economist at Mizuho Research Institute Ltd, specializing in the Russian economy. Publications include 'Analysis of structural changes in Russia's trade with CIS countries', *Slavic Studies*, 55, 2008, pp. 29–59 (in Japanese); and 'Comparison of trade liberalizations in Russia, China, and India', in T. Sato, ed., *The BRICs as Regional Economic Powers in the Global Economy* (Comparative Studies on Regional Powers, no. 10), Sapporo: Slavic Research Center, 2012, pp. 1–13.

Go Koshino is Associate Professor in the Slavic-Eurasian Research Center at Hokkaido University, specializing in Russian and Belarusian literature. Publications include 'Image of Empire and Asia in the contemporary science fictions of Russia', *Acta Slavica Iaponica*, 26, 2009, pp. 177–90; and (co-edited with T. Mochizuki) *Orient on Orient: Images of Asia in Eurasian Countries* (Comparative Studies on Regional Powers no. 13), Sapporo: Slavic Research Center, 2012.

Noriko Maejima is Assistant Professor in Nagoya University Graduate School of Environmental Studies and specializes in Regional sociology, urban sociology, and studies of Buddhist sacred places in India. Published work includes: 'Decline of the traditional rule and social change in BodhGaya: An approach to the local context of social change', *The Sociological Review of Nagoya University*, 27, 2007, pp. 83–104 (in Japanese); 'The significance of local context for the formation of "sacred place": the social formation of "sacred place" in Bodh Gaya, India', *The Annals of Japan Association for Urban Sociology*, 28, 2010, pp. 167–81 (in Japanese); and 'The sphere of "sacred place": social construction of "sacred place" with local society', *The Annals of Association for Regional and Community Studies*, 2011, pp. 67–81 (in Japanese).

Tomoo Marukawa is a Professor at the Institute of Social Science, University of Tokyo, and specializes in the Chinese economy. Publications include 'Why Japanese multinationals failed in the Chinese mobile phone market: A comparative study of new product development in Japan and China', *Asia Pacific Business Review*, 15 (3), 2009, pp. 411–31; 'Why are there so many automobile manufacturers in China?' *China: An International Journal*, 11 (2), 2013, pp. 171–86; and 'Japan's high-technology trade with China and its export control', *Journal of East Asian Studies*, 13 (3), 2013, pp. 483–501.

Yoshifumi Nakai is a Professor in the Department of Political Studies at Gakushuin University, and specializes in Chinese politics and international relations. His publications include 'The return of the learned politician: Abe's security strategy', *Tamkang Journal of International Affairs*, Taiwan, forthcoming; *How can China live in harmony? Empire, sovereignty, and discourse*, Chinese University of Hong Kong Press, forthcoming; and 'Japan's perspective on U.S.-China-Taiwan relations', in C. Lin and D. Roy, eds, *The Future of United States, China, and Taiwan Relations*, New York: Palgrave, 2011, pp. 189–208.

Atsushi Ogushi is Associate Professor in the Faculty of Law at Keio University, and specializes in Russian and post-Soviet politics. Publications include *The Demise of the Soviet Communist Party*, Abingdon: Routledge, 2008; *Post-Communist Transformations: The Countries of Central and Eastern Europe and Russia in Comparative Perspective*, Sapporo: Slavic Resaerch Center, 2009, edited with T. Hayashi; and 'Russian bureaucratic elites: Patrimonial or technocratic?' paper presented to the VIII World Congress of the International Council for Central and East European Studies (ICCEES), July 27, 2010, City Conference Centre Stockholm, Sweden.

Shinichiro Tabata is Professor in the Slavic-Eurasian Research Center at Hokkaido University, and specializes in comparative economic systems and studies of the Russian economy. His publications include *The Elusive Balance: Regional Powers and the Search for Sustainable Development* (Comparative Studies on Regional Powers, no. 2), Sapporo: Slavic Research Center, 2010, edited with A. Uegaki; and 'Growth in the International Reserves of Russia, China, and India: A Comparison of xiv *Notes on contributors*

Underlying Mechanisms', *Eurasian Geography and Economics*, 52 (2), 2011, pp. 409–427.

Fumiki Tahara is Associate Professor in the Department of Area Studies, Graduate School of Arts and Sciences, University of Tokyo. He specializes in community studies and contemporary China studies. Publications include *Rural Leaders in China: Connection, Cohesion and Agrarian Politics*, Jinan: Shandong People's Press, 2012, (in Chinese); and 'Principal, agent or bystander? Governance and leadership in Chinese and Russian villages', *Europe-Asia Studies*, 65 (1), 2013, pp. 75–101.

Sanami Takahashi is an Assistant Professor in Slavic-Eurasian Research center, Hokkaido University, and specializes in the cultural history of Soviet Russia and Russian religious studies. Publications include 'Church or museum? The role of state museums in conserving church buildings, 1965–85', *Journal of Church and State* (Oxford University Press), 51 (3), 2009 pp. 502–17; 'Religion as an object of science in atheistic society: The function of the Historical Museum of Religion and Atheism in late socialist Russia', in T. Mochizuki and S. Maeda, eds, *India, Russia, China: Comparative Studies on Eurasian Culture and Society* (Comparative Studies on Regional Powers no. 11), Sapporo: Slavic Research Center, 2012, pp. 11–18; and 'Religious practices in Latgale (Eastern Latvia) during the Soviet era: Catholicism, the old believers, and "the socialist new rituals"', paper presented to BASEES/ ICCEES, European Congress 2013: 'Europe: Crisis and Renewal', April 5–8, 2013, Cambridge.

Liang Tang is a Professor in the School of Political Science and Economics, Waseda University, and specializes in contemporary Chinese politics. His publications include *The Party-Government Relationship in Communist China*, Tokyo: Keio University Press, 1997 (in Japanese); *Transformation of Politics and Society in the Post-Mao China*, Tokyo: Tokyo University Press, 2001 (in Japanese); and *Contemporary Chinese Politics: the authoritarian developmentalism and its future.* Tokyo: Iwanami-Shinsho, 2012 (in Japanese).

Akira Uegaki is a Professor in the Faculty of Economics at Seinan Gakuin University. Professor Uegaki specializes in comparative economic systems, and studies of Russian, Romanian and other East European economies. Publications include 'Development in the global economy: China since Deng Xiaoping and Russia since Gorbachev', *The Economic Review of Seinan Gakuin University*, 46 (1–2), 2011, pp. 99–121; *The Elusive Balance: Regional Powers and the Search for Sustainable Development* (edited with S. Tabata) (Comparative Studies on Regional Powers, no. 2), Sapporo: Slavic Research Center, 2010; and 'Russia and China in global imbalances: Analysis in open-macro framework', European Association for Comparative Economic Studies, the 12th Biannual Conference, September 7, 2012, University of the West of Scotland.

Introduction

Shinichiro Tabata

In this book, while the USA, EU and Japan are regarded as 'core' players that lead the contemporary world, China, India and Russia are designated as 'regional powers' which have emerged as challengers to the core countries or the existing world order.[1] These regional powers may represent developing countries or provide a certain model for developing countries. We think that by focusing on these three countries, we can understand the contemporary world more deeply and consider the future world more appropriately. In other words, the present world is not represented or controlled exclusively by core countries in the sphere of politics, economics and culture. Neither can it be understood sufficiently in the context of a dichotomy between developed and developing countries. The three countries may be an intermediary layer through which we can see the world completely differently.

The three countries have emerged as major regional powers since the beginning of this century. Historically, these regional powers have formed empires and civilizations in Eurasia. This is another reason that we focus on them and why we believe that we are able to understand the contemporary world and various international issues more deeply by doing so. It is safe to say that without properly placing these regional powers in the world system, we cannot sufficiently grasp the characteristics of the contemporary and future world system.

Our first approach is to compare these regional powers in order to distinguish their commonalities and differences so that we can analyze the sustainability of these states as regional powers in the future. In other words, we are seeking any obstacles that may constrain them from developing further as such powers.

This book includes the most distinguished accomplishments of our project, entitled 'Comparative Research on Major Regional Powers in Eurasia', which was adopted by the Ministry of Education and Science, Japan, at the end of 2008 as a Grant-in-Aid for Scientific Research on Innovative Areas, that is a special grant for the development of new research areas, and carried out until March 2013. This project, headed by Shinichiro Tabata, involves more than fifty Japanese specialists on China, India and Russia. We intended to make a comprehensive, systematic, and multidisciplinary comparison of major regional powers.

2   Introduction

This book is composed of four parts: economic development; political systems and diplomacy; history; and culture and society. Part I analyzes the emergence of regional powers in the world economy. Since the seventeenth century, when China, India and Russia governed Eurasia as empires, economic development in these areas has been outstripped by Europe and the USA, and later by Japan as well. As one of the important commonalities of China, India and Russia, they had opened up and liberalized their economies from the late 1970s till the beginning of the 1990s in order to fill the gap with developed countries.

Akira Uegaki compares the process of economic reforms in the three countries in Chapter 1, interpreting the liberalization reforms of these countries as an attempt towards industrialization or modernization of industrial power of the latecomers. He argues that Deng Xiaoping's China has succeeded in becoming a factory of the world by pursuing anti-Gerschenkron-type industrialization, while the Soviet Union and Russia have intermittently pursued and abandoned Gerschenkron-type industrialization and Russia remains a monopoly economy. Uegaki explains the differences in industrialization policies and their consequences among these countries by the relationship between the domestic economy and the external economy. In China, the leading export sectors have been transferred from labor-intensive industries with weak power of ripple effect to moderately capital-intensive industries with high power of ripple effect. In Russia there have been no such dynamic processes until today, while India has shown a unique type of industrialization, which can be called post-modern-type industrialization.

In Chapter 2, Tomoo Marukawa and Yugo Konno compare the economic opening policies implemented by China, India and Russia during the 1980s and 1990s. The comparison suggests that the sequence of economic opening has influenced their outcomes. China started from a partial opening, made full use of the dual trade system to promote exports and protect infant industries at the same time, and finally achieved a high level of openness. Russia started from a radical opening, and it failed to promote exports except for those of oil and gas, and also failed to protect its infant industries. Russia ended up creating a rather closed economy, because of the inefficiency of its customs procedures. In many respects, India stands in between these two extreme cases.

Chapter 3, written by Shinichiro Tabata, shows that China, India and Russia emerged as regional powers in the international financial system in the 2000s by accumulating huge foreign reserves. This is one of the consequences of the opening-up policies of the three countries. The new Bretton Woods system was said to be set up, where emerging economies represented by regional powers have re-established the United States as the center of the world economy through their commitment to maintaining an undervalued exchange rate. The global imbalance, which was another side of the revived Bretton Woods system, led to the global financial crisis in 2008. The author concludes that although the latter crisis has changed the mechanisms of foreign reserve accumulation in regional powers considerably, their presence in the international financial system will remain large in the future as well.

Part II deals with the political aspects of the emergence of regional powers. Together with the enhancement of their economic presence, their political clout has increased as well. China, India and Russia, however, have common problems due to the largeness of their countries. A serious problem is how to integrate diversities of nationalities, religions, languages, and cultures while maintaining statehood or nationhood. In this context, we reveal that the political system, including election and party systems both at the national and local levels, plays a crucial role.

In Chapter 4, Atsushi Ogushi and Yuko Adachi argue that one of the keys to establishing a stable political order is the role of the dominant party, which works as an integrating mechanism in such huge, developing, and changing countries. While all dominant parties in China, India and Russia (the Chinese Communist Party, Indian Congress, and United Russia) have contributed to creating a political order, each party has a distinct mechanism. By advancing conceptual ideal types of dominant parties that help to reveal the peculiarities of the three parties, this chapter also demonstrates the limitations of each party's controlling power.

Chapter 5, authored by Fumiki Tahara, focuses on village leadership. In particular, he examines the patronage networks of village leaders in three regional power states in Eurasia. Employing two indices, the inclination toward electoral patronage and selectivity of patrons, the author argues that the characteristics of today's village leaders can be conceptualized as the 'competitive client' in India, the 'faithful agent' in Russia, and as either the 'principal' or the 'bystander' in China. These four village leadership types are byproducts of different forms of patronage networks as determined by the structure of party politics and competitiveness in the national and local elections of each of the three countries.

In Chapters 6 and 7, Liang Tang and Yoshifumi Nakai compare China's political reform strategy with that of the former Soviet Union, respectively. Tang analyzes the interaction between dominant political power and political reform strategy in the two countries. He concludes that China has been able to maintain a steady conservative approach to political reforms characterized by slow-paced liberalization, while aiming at economic development as the primary goal. In contrast, the former USSR started with moderate reform, but ended up with radical democratization, marketization, and restructuring of the sovereign state.

In Chapter 7, Nakai concentrates on the crucial period from 1988 through 1991. He argues that the abandonment of political reform during 1988–91 saved the Chinese Communist Party (CCP) from collapse. While the Soviet Union and its Communist Party headed toward dissolution, China and the CCP remained intact. China's retreat to its pre-reform position brought peace and stability, which made economic development possible. The political consequences of this peace, however, were grave. China turned into an economic

4   *Introduction*

giant without political modernization. He concludes that while today's Russia is a post-empire, today's China looks increasingly like an empire, seeking prosperity without political reform.

We analyze the emergence of regional powers in international politics as well. We can say that, until the end of the Cold War, not only Russia, but also China and India had prepared for their emergence as regional powers in Eurasia. In Chapter 8, written by Toru Ito, relationships between regional powers and relations between regional powers and core countries are discussed with special emphasis on India. He shows that India has established strategic partnerships with almost all the major and emerging powers in the world today. The author highlights the different types of India's strategic partnerships with the US, China and Russia. This chapter concludes that India has no reliable and powerful cooperative partner and as a result, India has adopted 'omnidirectional strategic partnership' as pragmatic diplomacy in today's world. The analysis here may symbolize today's multipolar world.

Part III examines the regional powers from a much longer time horizon. If we start with the world around the seventeenth century when China, India and Russia ruled over Eurasia as respective empires, Eurasian history since then may be well described as the history of the relationships of these three empires and post-empires. In other words, comparison of these empires may give a new and deep insight into Eurasian history. In this part, comparison of various empires is made, which has contributed to the development of a new discipline, i.e., comparative imperiology (see Kimitaka Matsuzato, ed., *Comparative Imperiology*, Sapporo: Slavic Research Center, Hokkaido University, 2010 (Slavic Eurasian Studies, 22)).

The First World War brought about the downfall of a series of empires. In Chapter 9, Yoshiro Ikeda examines the 'autonomous region' system which was a key institution that supported the integrity of these empires and obtained a new significance afterward. In some places, they contributed to the reintegration of the post-imperial sphere, while their existence may also serve as a destabilizing factor in the borderlands. This chapter traces the development of the autonomous regions in Europe and Eurasia from the early nineteenth century through World War I to the 1920s. Since the collapse of the Soviet Union, its autonomous republics have been inherited by Russia and other former states of the USSR. Furthermore, the Soviet nationalities policy gave inspiration to China as well, though Beijing did not grant any kind of statehood to its ethnic minorities. The author emphasizes that the practice and idea of the autonomous republic is still essential today in understanding the problem of stability in the Eurasian borderlands. The former Soviet autonomous republics or regions and their counterparts on the Chinese periphery, including Crimea, Abkhazia, and Xinjiang, are serving as a destabilizing factor for international relations.

Chapter 10, written by Jun Akiba, sheds light on the issue of the shari'a or Islamic law in nineteenth-century empires. Confronted with a Muslim society, these empires generally incorporated the existing Islamic legal system into their governmental institutions, which resulted in the imperial powers' involvement in defining what the 'proper' shari'a was. The author takes examples from British India, the Volga-Ural regions in Russia, Russian Turkestan, and French-ruled Algeria to investigate the shari'a politics in each region between the late eighteenth and early twentieth centuries and examine their connections. The author also refers to the legal and judicial reforms in the Ottoman Empire, and argues that colonial shari'a politics after the late nineteenth century can be understood in the context of the encounter between 'Ottoman shari'a' and 'colonial shari'a'.

The final part, Part IV, is engaged in comparison of the cultures and societies of the regional powers. We pay special attention to the fact that China, India and Russia represented respective civilizations in the past. Through a comparison of the cultural aspects of the three countries that may challenge the cultural dominance of the USA and Europe in the contemporary world, we may obtain a deep insight into present and future world culture. In this part, we make a comparative analysis of some cases of representation, perception and self-consciousness illustrated in literature and cultural activities.

In Chapters 11 and 12, Indian and Chinese images in British and Russian literature are discussed, respectively. Chapter 11, written by Hisae Komatsu, examines British Asian migrant literature. She argues that in the 2000s, especially after September 11, 2001, British Asian literature garnered much attention in British literary world as it 'reveals the hidden worlds that shine in the darkness'. This chapter investigates the literary works of several authors of Indian descent who are second generation migrants living in contemporary Britain, and examines their sense of belonging, which is inherent in their work, as well as how they position and represent their roots.

Chapter 12, authored by Go Koshino, sheds some light on Chinese images in Russia today, mainly analyzing contemporary fantasy novels in which a remarkable role is allocated to the eastern neighbor. Vladimir Sorokin, Viktor Pelevin, Kholm van Zaichik and other contemporary writers create a kind of mirror image, intentionally reversing and grotesquely distorting traditional representations of the Celestial Empire. The author observes a sense of inferiority or superiority toward the West (or even toward the East), a 'megalomaniac' self-image of Eurasian power, a homophobic machismo mentality, anxiety over an energy-dependent economy, and various other aspects of Russian culture and society, reflected in the fantastic mirrors of China.

In the final chapter (Chapter 13), Sanami Takahashi, Noriko Maejima and Hiroshi Kobayashi compare three World Cultural Heritage Sites in China, India and Russia respectively, and discuss the problems arising from a discrepancy in the understanding of cultural heritage between these regions and the World Heritage Committee that recognizes the 'universal value' of the sites. They argue that religious heritage, inscribed on the World Cultural Heritage List, provides a prime example of fusion of traditional sacredness and modern mass consumer culture. By exploring cultural issues of their representation and management, they found several opposing and competing

6   *Introduction*

stakeholders, giving contradictory accounts of the significance of each site. They conclude that UNESCO's seemingly neutral evaluation makes it more difficult to create a balance between preservation, economic stake and spiritual significance.

As a whole, we show that it is essential for these regional powers, i.e., China, India and Russia, to maintain huge country status in terms of population and territory, since they have regained their importance in the world economically, politically and culturally, and enjoy substantial benefits due to the expansiveness of their repective territories. If we look at per capita indicators, these countries are not among the top countries in the world. In this sense, they do not lead the world and they do not provide attractive models for the world, including the developed countries.

China, India and Russia have invented specific means or institutions in order to exploit the size of their countries and to integrate large territories containing divergent nationalities, religions, languages and cultures. These means and institutions include, for instance, a specific dominant party system, a state-dominant economic system, the institution of autonomous regions, and a specific ideology or nostalgia integrating the country. We have to admit that some of these institutions have not been regarded as normal or desirable by the current international standard created by the core countries. This may be attributed to the costs involved in maintaining regional powers. It should be noted that among developed countries, only the USA has maintained big country status in the contemporary world. We should take these Chinese, Indian and Russian institutions seriously, since they are playing an important role in the increasing world presence of these countries, and some of them may be regarded as models for other developing countries.

We believe that, as the importance of these regional powers increases, the significance of our study, i.e. the comparison of these regional powers, increases as well. And we are proud that our research is the very first attempt of this kind in the world.

I would like to express my deep appreciation for the support of the Ministry of Education and Science, Japan by noting that this is one of the major results of the Grant-in-Aid for Scientific Research on Innovative Areas entitled 'Comparative Research on Major Regional Powers in Eurasia', carried out in 2008–13. I would also like to thank the Slavic-Eurasian Research Center, Hokkaido University, for supporting the activities of this big research project. Special thanks go to Masanori Goto of the Slavic-Eurasian Research Center for helping me with the editorial work.

Note

1 We do not argue that China is still a regional power and not a global power. We just define regional powers as such countries as are challengers to the existing world order.

Part I
Economic development

1 Industrialization in the process of economic reform

Comparative analysis of China, Russia and India

Akira Uegaki

Liberal reforms as industrialization process in China, Russia and India

There are common features in the recent historical process of China, Russia (and the Soviet Union) and India in that they had begun liberal reforms from the late 1970s till the beginning of the 1990s, abandoning the socialist or quasi-socialist systems extant until then. The reforms include Deng Xiaoping's reforms in China from 1978, Gorbachev's reforms in the Soviet Union from 1985, and the New Economic Policy in India from 1991. As time goes by, however, a clear contrast has appeared, at least between China and Russia. China has become 'a factory of the world', whereas Russia remains a mono-cultural country exporting oil and gas. Why has such a contrast appeared during the last twenty years? Where can we locate India along the spectrum between China and Russia? This paper will examine these problems based on the idea that the liberal reforms of these three countries can be interpreted as an attempt at the industrialization or modernization of industrial power of the latecomers in today's high-technology context. In the following, the second section compares the processes of industrialization of China, Russia (or the USSR) and India from the perspective of Gerschenkron's theory. The third section clarifies the preconditions for the industrialization of these three countries, while the fourth section examines those processes of industrialization by using trade statistics and IO data.

China, Russia (the USSR), and India from the perspective of Gerschenkron's theory

Six propositions of Gerschenkron and China

Alexander Gerschenkron made six propositions concerning the characteristics of industrialization of backward economies. He says (Gerschenkron, 1962, pp. 353–54):

1 The more backward a country's economy, the more likely was its industrialization to start discontinuously as a sudden great spurt proceeding at a relatively high rate of growth of manufacturing output.

10 Economic development

2 The more backward a country's economy, the more pronounced was the stress in its industrialization on the large size of both plant and enterprise.
3 The more backward a country's economy, the greater was the stress upon producers' goods as against consumers' goods.
4 The more backward a country's economy, the heavier was the pressure upon the levels of consumption of the population.
5 The more backward a country's economy, the greater was the part played by special institutional factors designated to increase supply of capital to the nascent industries and, in addition, to provide them with less decentralized and better informed entrepreneurial guidance; the more backward the country, the more pronounced was the coerciveness and comprehensiveness of those factors.
6 The more backward a country, the less likely was its agriculture to play any active role by offering to the growing industries the advantages of an expanding industrial market based in turn on the rising productivity of agricultural labor.

Gerschenkron extracted these propositions from experiences of European economic history. They are not imperative advice for backward countries, but epistemological statements concerning the industrialization of backward countries. If we apply this epistemology to the economic history of China after Deng Xiaoping, we will find some contradictions between the propositions and the facts in China.

In the 'open/reform policies' of Deng Xiaoping, economic growth began after the initial rapid increase in investment policy was replayed by milder investment policy (against proposition 1) (Wu and Fan, 2010, p. 246; Bramall, 2009, pp. 334–35). The industrialization was launched by small-scale enterprises (township and village enterprises or TVEs) (Nakagane, 1999, pp. 105–7) (against proposition 2). The industrialization was promoted by light industries and consumer goods industries (Minami and Makino, 2012, p. 53; Bramall, 2009, pp. 409–11) (against proposition 3). Deng did not deny people's desire to be rich and to consume more[1] (against proposition 4). There were no strong institutions that could allocate capital to special industries; rather, the government tried to attract FDI to Special Economic Zones directly for export-oriented industrialization (Bramall, 2009, pp. 366–68). The mono-bank system was abolished at the beginning of industrialization (Wu, 2005, pp. 154–57) and the initiatives of regional governments and rural economic units were encouraged so as to raise capital for industrialization within their own territories (Kueh, 2008, pp. 63–71) (all these are against proposition 5). There is no room for doubt that Chinese agriculture has been playing a decisive role in its industrialization (against proposition 6).

It is true that investment has had priority in the course of Deng's reform process in comparison with experiences in developed economies and, in this sense, we can evaluate the process as Gerschenkron-type development, as it emphasizes the production of capital goods[2] (according to proposition 3). It is not easy to decide whether there was forced suppression of people's consumption in Deng's China. On the one hand, it is said that the labor distribution rate in the

Industrialization in the reform process   11

agriculture, trade and restaurant service sectors increased rapidly in China in the 1980s (Nakagane, 1999, p. 147).[3] On the other hand, other research indicates that the distributed income was not used for their consumption but poured into investment. No matter how generous to the people Deng might have been, we cannot disagree with the statement that there was virtual consumption suppression in China (according to proposition 4).

Consequently, although there were some aspects in China that coincide with Gerschenkron's propositions, it is more important that the main features of the policies after Deng Xiaoping are against the propositions. We call the economic process from 1978 until today in China *anti-Gerschenkron-type industrialization*.

Gorbachev's reform from Gerschenkron's perspective

Compared with the case of China, the economic process in the Soviet Union and Russia after Gorbachev is far more complicated. First of all, Gorbachev's attempt to modernize the Soviet Union cannot be called 'industrialization of a backward country', because the society of the Soviet Union just before Gorbachev had a rather industrialized economic structure as a result of forced industrialization by and after Stalin. Notwithstanding, Gorbachev's strategy of modernizing society has some aspects that Gerschenkron formalized in the six propositions. First, Gorbachev propelled the so-called acceleration policy at the first stage of his reform (according to proposition 1). Second, what was emphasized in his 'acceleration policy' was promotion of a large-scale machine-building industry with high technology (Ellman and Kontorovich, 1998, pp. 110–12, 126–29) (according to propositions 2 and 3). Third, there is no evidence to show that the leaders of that era tried to contrive a new financial method to raise capital for industrialization other than the old centralized system[4] (according to proposition 5). Fourth, agriculture did not play a decisive role in driving the Soviet economy forward, though Gorbachev tried to release peasant initiatives during Perestroika (Brown, 1996, pp. 142–45) (according to proposition 6).

It is true that Gorbachev did not deny the increase in the production of consumer products and people's desire to consume more (against propositions 3 and 4). The supply of consumer goods, however, stagnated against growing wages because of confusion of the economic order under Perestroika, which deprived Gorbachev of the people's political support (Ellman and Kontorovich, 1998, p. 156). It is also true that Gorbachev tried to activate small-scale enterprises including cooperatives (Brown, 1996, pp. 145–47) (against proposition 2). Here again, however, quasi-free economic activities of small-scale enterprises under Perestroika could not lead to growth in the economy as a whole, because of the lack of radical ownership reform. Consequently, we can look upon Gorbachev's policies as *Gerschenkron-type industrialization*.

Gorbachev's policies were fully frustrated by the end of the 1980s and his assignments had to be handed over to a new independent Russia. Yeltsin in the first years of his power did not try to change the industrial structure of

12   *Economic development*

Russia deliberately. We see some kind of laissez-faire attitude all over society. Too liberalized a trade system forced domestic light industries into decline, whereas only the oil and gas industry developed as a strong sector in Russia. After the inauguration of Putin, the attitude of the state leaders turned towards intentional industrial policy again, that is, governmental assistance for the development of nanotechnology and building of the Skolkovo Innovation Centre (Mizoguchi, 2007, pp. 261–66, *Skolkovo*). This strategy seems to revive Gerschenkron-type industrialization from above, instead of inventing a new method of modernization in the new era.

If we compare the industrialization in China since Deng Xiaoping with the industrialization in the Soviet Union and Russia since Gorbachev, anti-Gerschenkron-type industrialization has been continuously pursued since the 1980s until today in China, whereas Gerschenkron-type industrialization has been adopted and abandoned intermittently since the mid-1980s until today in the Soviet Union/Russia.

China vs. Russia

Now, we are confronted with a problem: Why did the anti-Gerschenkron-type industrialization in China achieve a wealthier result than the intermittent adoption of Gerschenkron-type industrialization in the Soviet Union/Russia? Paul Gregory and Kate Zhou wrote an article with the straightforward title of 'How China Won and Russia Lost'. They attribute the reason to the fact that the Chinese leaders tacitly permitted private semi-legal economic initiatives from below, which had already appeared just before Deng's reform. They assert that this tacit policy has brought about intense competition among economic units all over the country (Gregory and Zhou, 2009). This is a persuasive argument and can give a clear account of the rapid economic development in China until today. Gregory and Zhou's argument, however, does not examine another important point that would also explain the growth of the Chinese economy: the aspect of international economic relations.

It is noteworthy that Gerschenkron's theory also lacks an international aspect[5] except in the case where he referred to the problem of technology transfer from advanced to backward countries. As a matter of course, he anticipated the importance of neither FDI nor international financial transactions today. According to Gerschenkron, even backward countries can be industrialized by such strong policies as formalized in the six propositions. Industrialization is possible because they can enjoy the so-called advantages of backwardness (Gerschenkron, 1962, p. 51). This idea is now criticized by many writers. Akira Suehiro[6] criticizes Gerschenkron in that the experiences of Germany, the USA, and Japan of having introduced technologies do not fit Gerschenkron's theory, because they have not necessarily introduced the latest technologies that the most advanced countries had at that time. Suehiro asserts that Gerschenkron missed the significance of the 'disadvantages of backwardness' (Suehiro, 2000, pp. 37–41). Suehiro's criticism would lead us to the conclusion

Industrialization in the reform process 13

that the problem to be solved by backward countries today is how to lose the 'disadvantages of backwardness' by combining primitive, standard, and advanced technologies that fit the country concerned.

Why has China's development strategy been successful even though it stepped out of the ordinary line of Gerschenkron's industrialization? In the following sections we will answer this question by referring to the fact that China has been successfully changing the relationship between the domestic and the external economy.

India

How can we locate the industrialization of India between China and Russia? As is well known, India after World War II attached greater importance to heavy industry with a version of economic planning under the strong influence of the Soviet Union and Marxism. The industrialization strategy based on the theory of P. C. Mahalanobis was an Indian version of Gerschenkron-type industrialization in the sense that it placed greater priority on production of capital goods than production of consumer goods. Indira Gandhi's administration after the death of J. Nehru strengthened this line by pursuing a nationalization policy of enterprises. This line was abolished in 1991 after the preliminary liberalization policy of Rajiv R. Gandhi, and India pushed forward with liberalization policies such as fiscal stabilization, privatization, deregulation, liberalization of foreign trade, capital movement, and international finance, all of which were the main contents of the IMF's structural adjustment program (Esho, 2008, pp. 15–122; McCartney, 2009, p. 105). This is a movement more similar to the policies under Yeltsin's administration from 1992 (abolishment of Gerschenkron-type industrialization) rather than those of Gorbachev's Soviet Union. The difference between India after 1991 and Russia after 1992 lies in the fact that in India a new sector has emerged in a liberalized environment: the service sector. On the other hand, a new structure where the domestic economy could grow hand in hand with its international economic relations was not established, as is witnessed in the case of China. We evaluate that India has been pursuing a unique type of industrialization, which is similar to neither Gerschenkron-type industrialization nor anti-Gerschenkron-type industrialization.

In the following, we will examine the differences in the industrialization processes among the three countries, based on economic statistics. First of all, let us compare the initial conditions of industrialization.

Initial conditions of industrialization

Composition of the workforce

The initial conditions of Deng's China are totally different from those of the Soviet Union around the advent of Gorbachev. A simple but very important

14   *Economic development*

fact was the difference in composition of the workforce between the two countries. The proportion of the primary sector of industry (agriculture, fishery and forestry) in China's workforce was 70.5 percent in 1978, whereas that of the Soviet Union in 1985 was only 14.7 percent.[7] In China in the following ten years, it fell by ten percentage points, and the ratio of people working in the secondary and tertiary sectors grew rapidly. In 2000, the ratio of the primary sector fell to less than 50 percent. China in the first years of Deng's reform stood far behind the Lewisian turning point[8] and was still advancing towards that point (Yan, 2008, pp. 30–40).

On the other hand, the proportion of the workforce in the primary sector in the Soviet Union was 14.5 percent in 1980 and 13.9 percent in 1989. This suggests that the Soviet Union passed the Lewisian turning point far before the appearance of Gorbachev.

This contrast shows us a clear difference in the tasks of the leaders of the two countries. The task of Deng Xiaoping at the start of the reform was to transfer agricultural people to modern industrial sectors smoothly. By the transfer, he could automatically expect a rise in the whole nation's productivity and a growth in GDP. The problem that Gorbachev faced was more complicated. His task was to raise the productivity of the secondary and tertiary sectors whose workforce was already overwhelming at that time. The task could be achieved only by radical reorganization of old industries and ineffective service sectors (including the banking sector) into modern, effective ones. This, however, might be difficult because the Soviet economy was entwined with a lot of vested interests.

Openness of the economy

Another difference between the two countries is the setting of international economic relations. If we consider 'export volume/GDP' or 'import volume/GDP' as a degree of openness, these statistics for China were 4.60 percent and 5.14 percent in 1978 respectively, and they since have grown to 7.35 percent and 7.07 percent in 1983.[9] Deng's reform was a process in which the openness of the Chinese economy started at a low level and grew gradually. In the 1990s, the openness increased rapidly, reaching 20 percent for 'export volume/GDP' and 19 percent for 'import volume/GDP' in 2000. In 2006, the figures were 36.6 percent and 29.9 percent respectively.[10] These figures reveal that China had much room for radical industrial transformation at the beginning of Deng's reform.

In the Soviet Union, while the openness ratios were 9.35 percent and 8.94 percent respectively in 1985, they fell to 6.08 percent and 7.07 percent in 1990. According to these figures, Gorbachev did not pursue an opening-up policy (*VES*, 1990, pp. 20–21). Interestingly, the openness of the economy jumped in Russia after the collapse of the Soviet Union, especially since the mid-1990s. The ratio of export volume per GDP was 44.1 percent in 2000.[11] This structural change, however, does not have the same character as in the case of China, because it was caused by a soaring of oil and gas prices in the world market. In fact, the share of 'minerals' (most of them are oil and gas) in Russia's exports was 54.2 percent in 2000 and it grew to 66.3 percent in 2006.[12] It was attained by over-representation of the comparative advantages of the country in the past.

Gerschenkron-type industrialization and initial conditions

Summing up, China had much room for radical transformation in the sphere of the composition of the working population and international economic relations at the beginning of the reform. On the other hand, the Soviet Union had reached a stabilizing or stagnating stage of development and had a structure that was very difficult to alter.

If we consider this contrast in our framework of Gerschenkron-/anti-Gerschenkron-type industrialization, it will lead us to an interesting conclusion. China had the opportunity to some extent to carry out Gerschenkron-type industrialization policies based on the six propositions, because the main implication of the propositions is for the government and other large-scale institutions to allocate excess resources and to pursue high-speed accumulation. Notwithstanding this, China did not carry out such policies. As for the Soviet Union and Russia, there was only a little room to employ policies based on the six propositions. Gorbachev, however, did try them, and they proved to be an anachronism.

How can we evaluate the contrast between the two countries, if we consider another aspect of Gerschenkron's theory, 'advantages of backwardness', whose main message is that the borrowing of the latest technologies by backward countries is not difficult? Here, we must clarify what the 'latest technologies' are today and how backward countries can borrow them (Hayami, 1995, pp. 287–89). It is true that China borrowed the latest technologies from abroad and used them as the driving force for industrialization. This process was, however, not so easy a task. The borrowing process was accompanied by the cultivation of poor peasant-origin workers, transforming of the composition of trade goods, experiments with Special Economic Zones, acceptance of FDI, involvement in international financial transactions, etc. To use Suehiro's terminology, it can be called a process of overcoming the 'disadvantages of backwardness'. On the other hand, Gorbachev does not seem to have examined the proper arrangement of domestic materials and human resources and tried to borrow the latest technologies when he initiated the so-called acceleration strategy in Perestroika.

India's initial conditions

The share of workers in the primary industry in India was rather high immediately after the inauguration of the New Economic Policy (61.68 percent in 1993–94).[13] This figure is higher than that of China in the same period. It is also interesting that the share did not decrease rapidly during the next ten

16   *Economic development*

years (54.02 percent in 2003–04). Besides, it is worth noting that the share of the workers in the tertiary industries was higher than that for the secondary industries, already reaching 22.60 percent in 1993–94. We cannot easily find a general trend of modern economic development in India, in which the workforce has been steadily transferred from agriculture to industry. We see a post-modern situation in India in which the service sector is playing a decisive role in the economy, and we do not know when they passed the Lewisian turning point in its economic history.[14]

As for the openness of the Indian economy, the export volume per GDP was 6.81 percent and the import volume per GDP was 7.80 percent in 1991, figures that were a little bit higher than those of China at the beginning of Deng's reform. They have been increasing to the level of 15.93 percent and 26.39 percent respectively in 2008.[15] It is important that a solid structure had already been established at the beginning of the reform in which trade deficits are usually recorded in its international transactions. The trade deficits must be offset by inflows of some financial resources, and in the case of India, what functioned as offsets were inflows of FDI, portfolio investments, inflows as deposits, and workers' remittances from Indians living abroad. In 2010, India was the number one country in the world for receiving workers' remittances (*M&R*, p. 13). Gerschenkron could not imagine that there could be a developing country where workers' remittances are the main route to counterbalancing trade deficits.

Considering the characteristics of the initial conditions and the subsequent development process, the industrialization of India can be called neither the Gerschenkron-type nor the anti-Gerschenkron-type.

International competitiveness and domestic industrial structure of export sectors

RCA

Balasa's revealed comparative advantage (RCA) is a statistical indicator that shows the export competitiveness of a commodity of a country.[16] The author calculated the RCAs of China, the Soviet Union and Russia, and India for commodity groups classified by the SITC classification of the UN[17] since the beginning of the reforms.[18] First, as for China, it is worth noting that the RCA of 'mineral fuels, lubricants, and related materials (SITC 3)' was higher than 1 until the end of the 1980s.[19] It means that mineral fuels, etc. had relatively strong competitiveness in the composition of China's export commodities in the first years of the reform. At least in this respect, the export structure of China was similar to that of the Soviet Union.

This structure, however, began to change gradually in the 1990s. What recorded high RCA marks in 1990s China was 'manufactured goods classified chiefly by material (SITC 6)' and 'miscellaneous manufactured articles (SITC 8)'. We must note that the group of SITC 8, which mostly includes labor-intensive goods, has recorded an RCA of always higher than 2 since 1990. This indicates that the export of goods made by cheap labor had been growing in the 1990s.

More interesting is the movement of the RCA of 'machinery and transport equipment (SITC 7)'. While it showed trivial figures in the 1980s, it began to grow in the 1990s and it reached a level higher than 1 at last in 2005. Examining more detailed data (two-digit data of SITC[20]), we can find China to be an 'advanced industrial country'. For example, the RCA of 'office machines and automatic data-processing machines (SITC 75)' was 0.84 in 1985 and it experienced a big rise in the next twenty-three years to a level of 3.37 in 2008. Here, we can realize that China has been changing its competitive structure from one based on cheap labor to one based on the latest technologies. According to Gerschenkron's strategy, China should have borrowed the latest technologies from abroad from the beginning, but this was not the case. The international economic relations of China, especially in the sphere of comparative advantage structure, have been experiencing strong and dynamic transformation.

As for the Soviet Union and Russia, the movement of the RCA was totally different from that of China. The RCA of 'mineral fuels, lubricants, and related materials (SITC 3)' has recorded the highest mark among other commodity groups in the last thirty years. The figure has been growing steadily through the historic events of Perestroika, the collapse of the Soviet Union, and the independence of Russia. In 2010, SITC 3 is the only commodity group in Russia whose RCA is higher than 1.[21] The RCA of the commodity group 'machinery and transport equipment (SITC 7)' always slumped during the period of the Soviet Union and after the independence of Russia. It fell to 0.08 in 2010. Generally speaking, the movement of RCA there has been stagnating and is unchangeable.

As for India, its RCAs do not show a clear trend, at least at the one-digit level of SITC. If we examine data at the two-digit level of SITC, however, we will find some interesting features in the Indian trade structure. For example, while the RCA of 'iron and steel (SITC 67)' was 0.49 in 1990, it grew to 2.01 in 2003 and is still keeping a level of 1.78 in 2010 (chart 3). This shows a distinct contrast to the case of Russia, which has shown a falling tendency since 1996.[22] The movement of the RCA of 'articles of apparel and similar clothing accessories (SITC 84)' is also interesting. Although the index for India was 4.23 in 1990 and 4.51 in 2000, it fell to 2.15 in 2010. It is true that India is still competitive in SITC 84 in the world market, using cheap labor, but this competitiveness has begun to weaken. Here, we see a similar tendency in the case of China.

When we examine one-digit-level data on the RCA of India, we cannot see such a dynamic trend as we see in the case of China. If we follow two-digit-level data, however, we realize that India has also experienced significant changes in export competitive structure.

18 *Economic development*

Domestic input–output structure of export sectors

In the following, we analyze the domestic industrial structure of each country by using input-output tables and investigate the relations between the domestic industrial structure and export structure. Tables 1.1 to 1.5 show Rasmussen's IPD (index of power of dispersion) and ISD (index of sensitivity of dispersion) with data on the export share of the industries concerned (classified according to IO tables, including the service sector). IPD is defined as:

$$\text{IPD}_j = \frac{\sum_i B_{ij}}{1/n\left(\sum_j \sum_i B_{ij}\right)},$$

where B_{ij} is factor ij of the Leontiev inverse matrix of n rows by n columns. And ISD is defined as:

$$\text{ISD}_i = \frac{\sum_j B_{ij}}{1/n\left(\sum_i \sum_j B_{ij}\right)}.$$

IPD_j shows by how much the production of the whole economy is increased through inter-industrial ripple effects if the product of sector j is increased by one unit. If the IPD of sector j is more than 1, it means that the degree of ripple effect of sector j on the whole economy is more than the average. It is meaningless to compare one country's IPD_j with another country's IPD_j directly. ISD_i shows how sector i increases its production when each of all the sectors of the whole economy increases its production by one unit. It is also expressed as a ratio to the average of the whole industries.

Table 1.1 indicates that the main leading export sectors of China in 1985 had a low IPD. This tells us that the exports of China at that time did not have a strong impact on the domestic economy. These sectors were, however, a labor-intensive part of the economy and were fit for the factor endowment of China at that time. Among them, the three sectors 'textiles, sewing, and leather and fur products', 'agriculture', and 'mining and quarrying' were producers of export commodities of SITC 0, 3, and 8, which recorded relatively high RCAs in the early years of the reform. It is also important that these exports functioned as earners of financial resources for imports of machines and equipment for further industrialization. The industrialization of China began slowly by producing competitive export commodities using an abundant labor force.

Table 1.2 shows that this structure has changed dramatically over seventeen years. Among six leading export sectors, five had strong IPD figures (higher than 1) in 2002. These sectors had a close connection with the domestic economy and their growth would have led to an increase of the whole economy through inter-industrial ripple effects. We also see that four of the six sectors had high ISD figures (higher than 1). This means that when the whole

Table 1.1 Export share, IPD, and ISD: China in 1985 (from the IO table 1985)[1]

Sector	Export Share[2] (%)	Index of Power of Dispersion	Index of Sensitivity of Dispersion
Textile, Sewing, Leather and Fur Products	19.31	1.118	1.189
Agriculture	12.41	0.603	1.670
Wholesale and Retail Trades, Hotels, and Catering Services	11.37	0.333	0.827
Transportation, Postal and Telecommunications Services	10.32	1.357	1.124
Mining and Quarrying	8.58	0.817	1.065
Foodstuff	8.15	1.723	1.086
Machinery and Equipment	7.48	3.708	2.762
Other Manufacturing	5.89	0.823	0.753
Coking, Gas, and Petroleum Refining	4.03	0.538	0.531
Other Services	2.67	1.699	1.308
Metal Products	2.41	0.691	1.093
Banking and Insurance	2.15	0.086	0.324
Chemical Industry	1.27	1.914	0.639
Building Materials and Non-metal Mineral Products	0.93	1.159	0.807
Production and Supply of Electric Power, Heat Power, and Water	0.01	0.276	0.518
Construction	0.00	0.186	0.079
Real Estate, Leasing, and Business Services	0.00	0.129	0.079

Notes: [1] = According to a "non-competitive import type" model. Calculated at producers' prices.
[2] = "Export Share" means export value of a given sector divided by the total export.
Source: CIOT, pp. 45–46; p. 166 (the author re-compiled 106 x 106 table into 17 x 17 table).

economy of China grows at high speed, these sectors will grow at a higher speed than average. Here, we see a form of virtuous cycle of the Chinese economy. At the beginning of the new century, China was no longer a country whose growth strategy mainly depended on exporting labor-intensive commodities based on cheap labor.

On the other hand, the overwhelmingly leading export sector of Russia in 2003 was a sector with a low IPD figure: 'products of the oil and gas industry' (Table 1.3). The exports of oil and gas had relatively insufficient strength to be able to pull up the whole Russian economy. It is also a common phenomenon in other countries that the IPD of the oil and gas industry is low, but the problem is that this sector has been the leading export sector recently (Kuboniwa, 1999, pp. 100–101).

If we look back to the beginning of the 1970s, however, we see a different situation (table not shown). For example, among the exports of the Soviet Union in 1968–72, 'mineral fuels, lubricants, and related materials (SITC 3)'

20   *Economic development*

Table 1.2 Export share, IPD, and ISD: China in 2002 (from the IO table of 2002)[1]

Sector	Export Share[2] (%)	Index of Power of Dispersion	Index of Sensitivity of Dispersion
Machinery and Equipment	33.75	1.452	2.452
Textile, Sewing, Leather, and Fur Products	17.76	1.349	0.676
Wholesale and Retail Trades, Hotels, and Catering Services	9.33	0.792	1.218
Chemical Industry	7.03	1.288	2.009
Other Manufacturing	6.72	1.112	0.933
Metal Products	4.93	1.316	1.755
Transportation, Postal and Telecommunications Services	4.69	0.883	1.047
Other Services	3.89	0.806	0.333
Real Estate, Leasing, and Business Services	3.24	0.719	0.751
Foodstuff	2.89	1.016	0.448
Agriculture	1.53	0.643	1.160
Mining and Quarrying	1.45	0.712	1.624
Building Materials and Non-metal Mineral Products	1.35	1.093	0.324
Coking, Gas, and Petroleum Refining	0.85	1.148	0.696
Construction	0.34	1.327	0.133
Production and Supply of Electric Power, Heat Power, and Water	0.17	0.797	0.824
Banking and Insurance	0.07	0.547	0.620

Notes: [1] = According to a "competitive import type" model. Calculated at producers' prices.
[2] = "Export Share" means export value of a given sector divided by the total export.
Source: CSY, 2007, pp. 89–91.

was the largest but its share was only 20 percent. Among them, the share of 'petroleum, petroleum products, and related materials (SITC 33)' in its exports was 13 percent in 1972. At the same time, 'iron and steel (SITC 67)', 'metalworking machinery (SITC 73)', 'non-ferrous metals (SITC 68)', 'road vehicles (SITC78)', 'textile fibers and their waste (SITC 26)', and 'machinery specialized for particular industries (SITC 72)' accounted for no small part of the export (3.5 to 9.5 percent).[23] This situation reflected two factors. One is the timing; that is, the fact that 1972 was the year before the emergence of the first oil shock. The other is the existence of the COMECON market. Gorbachev, like Brezhnev before him, could not take the initiative to raise the real bottom line of competitiveness.

As for India, we can use the IO table of 1993–94. According to the table, we see both high IPD commodities and low IPD commodities in the leading export goods (Table 1.4). The industrialization of India is not similar to that of China. We see a type of Gerschenkron industrialization because some of the driving forces of Indian industrial growth are the automobile and steel

Industrialization in the reform process 21

Table 1.3 Export share, IPD, and ISD: Russia in 2003 (from the IO table of 2003)[1]

Sector	Export Share[2] (%)	Index of Power of Dispersion	Index of Sensitivity of Dispersion
Products of Oil and Gas Industry	46.53	0.799	1.665
Precious Metal	9.87	1.112	1.437
Machines and Equipment, Metal-Processing Products	8.77	1.286	1.738
Ferrous Metal	7.14	1.223	1.257
Chemical and Oil-chemical Industry	5.71	1.388	1.276
Services of Transportation and Communication	4.32	0.773	2.624
Products of Wood, Timber-Processing, Cellulose, and Paper Industry	3.50	1.169	0.796
Products of Food Industry	2.96	1.311	0.634
Commerce-Intermediary Services	1.38	0.466	3.678
Buildings	1.20	0.898	0.563
Other Industrial Products	1.15	1.188	0.377
Coal	1.14	1.222	0.470
Agricultural Products, Services for Agriculture, and Products of Forestry	0.95	0.737	0.888
Products of Light Industry	0.82	1.387	0.778
Electric and Heat Energy	0.34	0.919	1.787
Products of Other Types of Activities	0.32	0.648	0.275
Construction Materials	0.31	1.129	0.455
Services of Financial Intermediary, Insurance, Administration, and Social Associations	0.21	0.671	0.367
Services of Sciences, Geology, Investigation of Underground Resources, Surveying, and Meteorological Water-Supply Work	0.20	0.906	0.538
Services of Health, Sports, Social Security, Education and Culture, and Art	0.14	0.627	0.041
Services of Housing and Public Economy, and Non-Productive Type of People's Welfare	0.08	0.752	0.328
Oil Shale and Peat	0.01	1.346	0.028

Notes: [1] = According to a "competitive import type" model. Calculated at basic prices.
[2] = "Export Share" means export value of a given sector divided by the total export.
Source: STZV, pp. 14–19; pp. 112–114.

industries based on a huge domestic market (Esho, 2008, pp. 145–82).[24] We, however, see another aspect of the industrialization in India. It is the fact that one of the driving forces of Indian economic growth is the service sector (Rakshit, 2009, pp. 140–78). A striking feature of Indian trade at the beginning of the 1990s was the large share of service exports, whose IPDs were relatively low. This structure has not been weakened in the new century, but strengthened (Table 1.5). Especially since 2000, the IT service sector (for example, the software industry) has grown rapidly, and is regarded as a

22 Economic development

Table 1.4 Export share, IPD, and ISD: India in 1993–1994

Sector	Export Share[2] (%)	Index of Power of Dispersion	Index of Sensitivity of Dispersion
Textile, Sewing, Leather, and Fur Products	16.63	1.863	1.14
Wholesale and Retail Trades, Hotels, and Catering Services	16.49	0.260	0.98
Machinery and Equipment	14.74	3.770	2.15
Metal Products	10.80	1.320	1.56
Transportation, Postal and Telecommunications Services	10.02	0.410	1.02
Chemical Industry	7.77	1.980	1.89
Other Services	7.75	0.630	0.71
Agriculture	6.48	2.32	2.51
Foodstuff	5.42	1.060	0.60
Mining and Quarrying	1.27	1.000	1.05
Coking, Gas, and Petroleum Refining	1.16	0.540	0.46
Other Manufacturing	0.69	0.620	0.55
Banking and Insurance	0.50	0.270	0.72
Production and Supply of Electric Power, Heat Power, and Water	0.25	0.360	1.21
Building Materials and Non-metal Mineral Products	0.20	0.320	0.17
Construction	0.00	0.160	0.20
Real Estate, Leasing, and Business Services	0.00	0.120	0.08

Notes: [1] = According to a "non-competitive import type" model. Calculated at producers' prices.
[2] = "Export Share" means export value of a given sector divided by the total export.
Source: IOT India (the author re-compiled 130 x 130 table into 17 x 17 table).

'super-export-oriented' sector (Esho, 2008, pp. 135–44). The industrialization in India can be considered as neither the Gerschenkron type nor the anti-Gerschenkron type. If we call a type of industrialization based on large-scale production of industrial goods and their export 'modern-type industrialization', we cannot call the Indian industrialization modern. We should call it 'post-modern-type industrialization' based on growth of the service sector and on international financial resource circulation including workers' remittances.

Are the problems ahead different?

Deng Xiaoping's China has succeeded in being 'a factory of the world' by pursuing anti-Gerschenkron-type industrialization. The Soviet Union/Russia has intermittently pursued and abandoned Gerschenkron-type industrialization policies, and still cannot break away from a traditional 'monopoly' economy based on oil and gas exports. The difference has arisen from the relationship between the domestic economy and the external economy. In

Industrialization in the reform process   23

Table 1.5 Export share, IPD, and ISD: India in 2003–2004

Sector	Export Share[2] (%)	Index of Power of Dispersion	Index of Sensitivity of Dispersion
Other Services	16.57	0.630	0.65
Textile, Sewing, Leather, and Fur Products	13.57	1.410	0.74
Wholesale and Retail Trades, Hotels, and Catering Services	9.46	0.230	0.98
Building Materials and Non-metal Mineral Products	8.94	0.450	0.28
Chemical Industry	8.86	1.760	1.86
Machinery and Equipment	8.36	3.630	2.19
Transportation, Postal and Telecommunication Services	7.13	0.760	1.25
Mining and Quarrying	6.34	0.910	0.89
Metal Products	6.06	1.090	1.35
Agriculture	4.49	2.720	2.54
Foodstuff	4.08	1.000	0.57
Coking, Gas, and Petroleum Refining	3.43	0.560	1.11
Real Estate, Leasing, and Business Services	1.44	0.470	0.38
Banking and Insurance	0.80	0.260	0.73
Other Manufacturing	0.44	0.560	0.45
Production and Supply of Electric Power, Heat Power, and Water	0.02	0.400	0.77
Construction	0.00	0.150	0.27

Notes: [1] = According to a "non-competitive import type" model. Calculated at producers' prices.
[2] = "Export Share" means export value of a given sector divided by the total export.
Source: IOT India (the author re-compiled 130 x 130 table into 17 x 17 table).

China, the leading export sectors have been transferred from labor-intensive industries with weak power of ripple effect to moderately capital-intensive[25] industries with high power of ripple effect. What has stimulated this transformation is a dynamic process of conquering the 'disadvantages of backwardness' including cultivation of workers, change of trade goods, experiments with Special Economic Zones, acceptance of FDI, and active involvement in international financial transactions. We have not seen this dynamic process in Russia until today. India shows a unique type of industrialization where the domestic automobile industry and the iron and steel industry have developed based on a huge domestic market, along with an increase in service exports, which we call 'post-modern-type industrialization'. We do not assert here that the leaders of China were cleverer than those of Russia. The results are interconnected effects of the domestic and international environments.

We have emphasized the differences among the three countries. So, do the three countries stand in different places now and are their problems ahead

24 *Economic development*

different? This is not the case. Although there are many points that make the three countries different, we also find some important common features. As for the prospects for the industrial development of the three countries in the near future, a common problem that they face now is the fact that they have constituted a similar domestic economic system that is vulnerable to fluctuations in the international economy and to changes in the framework of the international economic system. Chinese exports are vulnerable to changes in the exchange rate system, changes to the WTO regime, and fluctuations in the level of foreign reserves. The diversification of the industrial structure of Russia, the most important task of its government, can be realized by export revenues that depend on a fluctuating oil price (Kuboniwa, 2011, p. 54). India's service exports and revenues from workers' remittances are very sensitive to the ups and downs of the world economy itself. In order to alleviate their vulnerability, they all need growth based on domestic demand and continuous increase in TFP on the supply side. The problems that face the three countries now are not necessarily greatly different. Considering the presence of the three countries in the world economy, the solution of their problems would help stabilize the world system as a whole.

Notes

1 Deng said that those for whom it was possible should be rich first, and then they were advised to help others. See Minami and Makino (2012, pp. 27, 272).
2 This is connected with the problem of low efficiency of investment. See Wu and Fan (2010, p. 257).
3 Minami and Makino point out that the savings rate of the Chinese people was already pretty high in 1980 (rural family: 15.2 percent, city family: 13.7 percent), and that it grew to a level much higher than that of Spain, which is considerably high among developed countries (China in 2009: rural family: 22.5 percent, city family: 28.6 percent; Spain in 2010: national average: 16.9 percent). See Minami and Makino (2012, pp. 169–72).
4 In fact, they did not discuss seriously how to raise money for the 'acceleration policy'. See Ellman and Kontorovich (1998 pp. 128–9).
5 Here, we must also note that Gerschenkron's theory is totally different from Gregory and Zhou's argument.
6 A Japanese economist specializing in Southeast Asia.
7 Concerning the statistical comparisons of China and Russia (and the Soviet Union), we use data from *CSY* and *NKh*, and the figures that the author calculated from these statistical books.
8 However, there is a dispute about whether an infinite labor supply was possible even in Deng's time. See Marukawa (2003, p. 34). The main message of the author here is that the room for labor movement from villages to towns was larger in China than in the Soviet Union/Russia.
9 The figures are calculated by the author using the sources of note 22.
10 The author calculated using the data of *CSY*, 2009.
11 The author calculated this figure using the data of *IFS*. The ratio of import volume per GDP was not very high, reaching the highest point of 27.5 percent in 1998.
12 The figures are calculated using data from *TAMOZH*.

13 As for the composition of the workforce of India, the author calculated it from *Databook India*, p. 49.
14 A. Panagariya of Columbia University, however, points out that the following argument is hopelessly flawed: 'It is natural for India to grow rapidly in services, skip industrialization, and leapfrog into the services stage. To put it dramatically, India need not become South Korea on the way to the United States.' See Panagariya (2008, p. 286).
15 The author calculated these figures from the data of *IFS*.
16 To be exact, the RCA of commodity i of country $j = (X_{ij} / X_j) / (X_{iw} / X_w)$, where X_{ij} = export of commodity i of country j, X_j = total export of country j, X_{iw} = export of commodity i in the world, and X_w = total export of the world.
17 Standard International Trade Classification of the United Nations.
18 The author calculated these figures mainly based on the data of *UN Comtrade* and his original database on the Soviet and Russian trade statistics.
19 This fact is not based on the author's calculation but is according to Yeats (1991, p. 16).
20 SITC rev. 3.
21 Excluding the figures of SITC 9. The figures of SITC 9 can be calculated only as residuals and they show abnormal values.
22 As for Russia, two-digit data of SITC are available only after 1996.
23 According to the author's calculation based on his own database.
24 The export competitiveness of these industries also increased.
25 In China, full-scale capital intensiveness is not observed everywhere. A characteristic feature there is a subtle merger of the capital-intensive setting with labor-intensive efforts, as in the case of the mobile phone sector. See Marukawa, 2007.

References

Bramall, Chris (2009) *Chinese Economic Development*, London and New York: Routledge.
Brown, Archie (1996) *The Gorbachev Factor*, London: Oxford University Press.
Ellman, Michael and Vladimir Kontorovich (1998) *The Destruction of the Soviet Economic System: An Insiders' History*, Armonk, NY and London: M. E. Sharpe.
Esho, Hideki (2008) *Ririku shita Indo keizai: kaihatsu no kiseki to tenbo* [The Indian Economy Has Taken Off: Locus and Prospect of Development], Kyoto: Mineruva Shobo (in Japanese).
Gerschenkron, Alexander (1962) *Economic Backwardness in Historical Perspective: A Book of Essays*, Cambridge, MA: Belknap Press of Harvard University Press.
Gregory, Paul and Kate Zhou (2009) 'How China Won and Russia Lost', *Policy Review*, no. 158, Hoover Institution (www.hoover.org/publications/policy-review/article/5469).
Hayami, Yujiro (1995) *Kaihatsu keizaigaku: syokokumin no hinkon to tomi* [Development Economics: Poverty and Wealth of Nations], Tokyo: Sōbunsha (in Japanese).
Kuboniwa, Masaaki (1999) Sangyo kozo no hendo [Changes of Industrial Structure], in M. Kuboniwa and S. Tabata, eds, *Tenkanki no Roshia keizai: shijo keizai iko to tokei shisutemu* [The Russian Economy at a Crossroads: Transition to Market and SNA], Tokyo: Aoki Shoten (in Japanese).
——(2011) *Roshia keizai no seicho to kozo: sigen izon keizai no shinkyokumen* [Growth and Structure of the Russian Economy: New Phase of Resource-dependent Economy], Tokyo: Iwanami Shoten (in Japanese).
Kueh, Y. Y. (2008) *China's New Industrialization Strategy: Was Chairman Mao Really Necessary?* Cheltenham and Northampton, MA: Edward Elgar.

26 Economic development

Marukawa, Tomoo (2003) *Rodo shijo no chikaku hendo* [Chinese Economy Today, vol. 3, Diastrophism of Labor Market], Nagoya: University of Nagoya Press (in Japanese).

——(2007) *Gendai Chugoku no sangyo: bokko suru Chugoku kigyo no tsuyosa to ayausa* [Industries in Today's China: Strength and Vulnerability of Rising Chinese Enterprises], Tokyo: Chuokoron Shinsya (in Japanese).

Minami, Ryoushin, and Humio Makino, eds, (2012) *Chugoku keizai nyumon: sekai dainii no keizai taikoku no zento* [A Guide to the Chinese Economy: Economic Development in China], 3rd edition, Tokyo: Nippon Hyoron Sha (in Japanese).

McCartney, Matthew (2009) *India: The Political Economy of Growth, Stagnation and the State, 1951–2007*, London and New York: Routledge.

Mizoguchi, Shuhei (2007) 'Roshia no nanotekunoroji shinkosaku' [Promotion of Nanotechnology in Russia], *Gaikoku no rippo*, no. 234, pp. 261–66, National Diet Library (in Japanese).

Nakagane, Katsuji (1999) *Chugoku keizai hatten ron* [Chinese Economic Development], Tokyo: Yuhikaku (in Japanese).

Panagariya, Arvind (2008) *India: The Emerging Giant*, New York: Oxford University Press.

Rakshit, Mihir (2009) *Macroeconomics of Post-reform India*, New Delhi: Oxford University Press.

Suehiro, Akira (2000) *Kyatchiappu gata kogyoka ron: Ajia keizai no kiseki to tenbo*, [Catch-Up-type Industrialization: Locus and Prospect of Asian Economy], Nagoya: University of Nagoya Press (in Japanese).

Wu, Jinglian (2005) *China's Long March Toward a Market Economy*, San Francisco, CA: Long River Press.

Wu, Jinglian and Fan Shitao (2010) 'Beyond the East Asian Miracle: Looking Back and Future Prospects for China's Economic Growth Model', in Cai Fang, ed., *Transforming the Chinese Economy*, Leiden and Boston, MA: Brill.

Yan, Shanping (2008) 'Chugoku keizai wa Luisu no tenkanten wo koetaka' [Has China Reached the Lewisian Turning Point?], *Toa*, no. 498, pp. 30–42, Kazankai Foundation (in Japanese).

Yeats, Alexander J. (1991) *China's Foreign Trade and Comparative Advantage: Prospects, Problems, and Policy Implications*, World Bank Discussion Paper no. 141, Washington, DC: World Bank.

Abbreviations of statistical books and websites

CSY: National Bureau of Statistics of the People's Republic of China, *China Statistical Yearbook* (various years, printed version and web version).

Databook India: The Planning Commission, Government of India, *Databook for Deputy Chairman* (November 1, 2011).

CIOT: Institute of Developing Economies, *China Input–Output Table 1985* (Institute of Developing Economies, Tokyo, 1991).

IFS: The IMF, *International Financial Statistics* (various issues, CD-ROM version).

IOT India: Ministry of Statistics and Programme Implementation, Government of India, *Input Output Table of India* (http://mospi.nic.in/Mospi_New/upload/ftest10: this site can be logged in through http://mospi.nic.in/Mospi_New/Admin/Login.aspx).

M&R:	The World Bank, *Migration and Remittances Factbook 2011: Second Edition* (Washington, DC, 2001).
NKh:	Tsentral'noe statistical upravlenie SSSR, *Narodnoe Khoziaistvo* (various years).
Skolkovo:	Website of the Skolkovo Innovation Centre (www.sk.tu/en/).
STZV:	Rosstat, *Sistema tablits zatraty – vypusk Rossii za 2003 god* (Moscow, 2006).
TAMOZH:	Gosudarstvennyi tamozhennyi komitet Rossiiskoi Federatsii, *Tamozhennaia statistika vneshnei torgovli Rossiiskoi Federatsii, Godovoi sbornik* (various issues).
UN Comtrade:	Trade Statistics Branch, United Nations Statistics Division, *UN Comtrade Database* (internet version) (http://comtrade.un.org/).
VES:	Tsentral'noe statisticheskoe upravlenie SSSR, *Vneshnie ekonomicheskie sviazi SSSR v 1990*.

2 A comparison of trade policy reform in China, India and Russia

Tomoo Marukawa and Yugo Konno

Introduction

China, India, and Russia created a command economy system and restricted their trade and investment relationships with other countries during the latter half of the twentieth century. During the 1980s and 1990s, however, they launched an economic opening and liberalization policy, which created economic structures that depend a great deal on foreign trade and inward foreign direct investment. The entry of these countries into the global flow of trade and investment has changed the course of global economic development.

Before the opening policy, China, India and Russia/Soviet Union had somewhat similar industrial structures, though the level of industrialization was not the same. But after the opening, the three nations developed very different industrial and trade structures. China made great progress in industrialization, exceeding the United States in the added value of the manufacturing sector in 2011 and becoming the world's largest manufacturing powerhouse. The share of manufactured goods in China's total exports increased from 46 percent in 1978 to 95 percent in 2012. Russia's exports, on the other hand, were concentrated in mineral fuels (HS27), such as petroleum and natural gas, whose share in Russia's exports increased from 43 percent in 1996 to 70 percent in 2012. With the appreciation of the ruble caused by the exports of mineral fuels, domestic industries were damaged by the surge of imports, transforming the economy into an oil-cum-gas monoculture (Tabata, 2008). India stood in the middle of China and Russia, with manufactured goods exports accounting for 67 percent of its total exports in 2012. What characterized India's exports was the fact that 25 percent of its merchandise and service exports was contributed to by the IT-BPO (information technology and business process outsourcing) industry in the fiscal year 2012.[1] The IT-BPO industry, which includes software, accounting services, and call centers, accounted for 7.5 percent of India's GDP in the same year. While China's export structure is heavily inclined toward the exports of manufactured goods and that of Russia leans toward the exports of mineral products, India has a relatively balanced export structure.

The reason that the three nations developed different export structures can be partially explained by the difference in their factor endowments, but these are not enough to explain the divergence between China and India. Both of them had abundant labor forces at the beginning of economic opening, and yet they developed very different export structures. We hypothesize that the sequencing of the economic opening policy has also influenced the export structure. The sequence reflects the country's strategy of minimizing the shock of opening felt by domestic industries and placing the country in a favorable position in the world economy. It is also influenced by the negotiations with their trading partners and international organizations such as the World Trade Organization (WTO) and International Monetary Fund (IMF). The sequence is important because most industries in a command economy, especially the manufacturing sector, are inefficient, and a certain period of protection is necessary to make them competitive in an open environment. A precipitate opening may strangle infant industries in their cradle.

The chapter aims to prove this hypothesis by comparing the respective economic opening processes of China, India and Russia. The first section describes the commonalities and differences in the process of economic opening. The second section measures the openness of the three nations by employing an 'outcome-based measure of trade openness'. The third section compares the policies of protecting the infant industries of the three countries.

A comparison of the economic opening policies

The reason for starting economic opening

Nations implementing a closed command economy will hesitate to open their economy because that will cause damage to the domestic industries. They will launch economic opening only when it is needed as a means to overcome an economic crisis. China, India and Russia were indeed facing economic crises when they started their opening.

In 1977 and 1978, China signed contracts with Japanese and other Western companies to buy many manufacturing plants with cash, in order to modernize its heavy industries. This reckless spending led to a sharp decrease in its foreign reserves to US$1.56 billion, which was equivalent to the 1.7-month import value, at the end of 1978. The only way to avoid default for China was to cancel the contracts with Western companies. However, the Japanese government persuaded the Chinese government not to do so, and proposed to offer loans from government and private banks (Kojima, 2012). The United Kingdom and France also pledged to provide credit to China in order to avoid the cancellation of plant contracts. The acceptance of loans from Japanese and other Western banks was the first move made by China towards economic opening. In 1979, China decided to accept ODA (official development assistance) loans from Japan, to establish special economic zones, and to promulgate laws on Sino-foreign joint ventures.

30 *Economic development*

India launched a full-fledged opening policy in 1991, after a long preparation period (Ito and Esho, 1995). India had created a command economy system in the 1950s, in which state-owned enterprises monopolized steel, shipbuilding, coal and power generation industries, and private enterprises were obliged to acquire licenses from the government when they built new plants or expanded their production capacity. During the mid-1960s, when the country faced a shortage of foreign exchange and inflation, the government tried to overcome this crisis by borrowing money from the World Bank. The World Bank required economic liberalization in exchange for the provision of loans, and India therefore devalued its currency, decreased its import tariffs on some items, and relaxed some of its licensing requirements in 1966. In January 1991, being influenced by the Gulf War, India again faced an economic crisis which caused its foreign reserves to fall to only US$700 million. India asked the IMF to provide loans, and the IMF required India to stabilize its economy by cutting budget deficits as a condition for providing those loans. India rapidly launched economic opening measures from that time. Its currency was devalued, and foreign exchange with regards to current account transactions was liberalized. The government increased the number of items which could be imported without acquiring licenses. Restrictions on inward foreign direct investment were greatly relaxed.

Russia's economic crisis, which was related to its political crisis that led to the collapse of the Soviet Union, was far deeper than the cases of China and India. Soviet Communist Party Secretary Gorbachev launched an economic reform policy in 1985, but it achieved little. With the decrease in income from petroleum exports, the Soviet economy faced a serious crisis at the end of the 1980s. Net foreign debt increased from US$14.2 billion at the end of 1984 to US$56.5 billion at the end of 1991, and foreign reserves fell to only US$100 million at the end of 1991 (Aslund, 1995). Consumer goods were in shortage and inflation became rampant. In August 1991, the Soviet Union collapsed and Yeltsin's Russia declared independence. Yeltsin's rapid liberalization policy was launched during this political turmoil. The plan to solicit financial aid from the West in exchange for market reform and democratization was first proposed when Gorbachev was still in power, and it developed into a comprehensive reform plan under the Yeltsin administration. In November 1991, a presidential decree declared that all kinds of enterprises were now permitted to engage in foreign trade, which had previously been reserved for state trading enterprises. The Russian ruble was made convertible to foreign currency for current account transactions, and Russian citizens were even allowed to have foreign currency deposits and to buy foreign securities (Uegaki, 2001).

All three nations were facing a shortage of foreign reserves when they began economic opening. To extract financial support from the IMF or Western nations, they needed to show their willingness to improve their capability to earn foreign exchange, and an economic opening policy was therefore necessary. But the degree of opening at the beginning was not the same. India and Russia liberalized not only trade but also foreign exchange for current account transactions in the first year of the economic opening, but China only made its currency convertible fifteen years after it had started its opening policy. China's economic opening proceeded very slowly compared to India's and Russia's. What caused this difference?

The depth of the crisis that led to the economic opening policy was different. Although China faced a short-term foreign exchange crisis, its capacity to earn foreign exchange was not weak at the time. China then was a rising petroleum producer and exporter. One of Japan's motives for providing ODA loans to China was to import petroleum and coal from China. The Japanese government did not impose any conditions on China when providing ODA because there seemed to be no problem for China to earn foreign exchange through petroleum and coal exports if the infrastructure for exports were in place. India and Russia, on the other hand, were having trouble paying their debts after receiving loans from foreign banks and international institutions. When those institutions provided relief loans it was natural for them to impose strict conditions to ensure that the borrowers could acquire the capability to pay their debts.

Dualism in the trade system

As discussed in the introduction, industries formed under a command economy will find it difficult to survive international competition. Therefore, transitional countries have a good reason to protect domestic industries and give them the time to improve their competitiveness by accumulating technology and human resources. However, if a country resorts to tariff and non-tariff measures to protect domestic industries, the price of intermediate goods which need to be imported will increase, and this will have an adverse effect on the competitiveness of the export industries that use those goods as inputs. To overcome this dilemma, some developing countries have adopted a dual trade system. Export processing zones (EPZs), which some Asian developing countries such as South Korea and Taiwan established during the 1960s, are typical examples of the dual trade system. A certain geographic area is designated an EPZ and made open to inward foreign direct investment. Enterprises which set up factories in EPZs will enjoy a reduction in import tariffs and income taxes but they need to export all the merchandise they process within it.

China's decision to establish special economic zones (SEZs) in 1979 was influenced by the experience of EPZs in South Korea and Taiwan. In SEZs, foreign enterprises can enjoy low income taxes, and materials and components are exempted from import tariffs. China's SEZs were, however, not simply a copy of the Korean and Taiwanese EPZs. They also served as a test bed for experimenting with the practices of a market economy. To limit the influence of SEZs on other parts of the economy, the Chinese government restricted not only the flow of goods between the SEZs and other areas of the

32 *Economic development*

country but also the migration of people, leading to a rise of wages in the SEZs. Consequently, the SEZs' export industries did not develop as quickly as expected.

To supplement the SEZs, a trade scheme called 'processing trade' was introduced to promote exports. Under this scheme, the foreign trader provides the components and materials to a Chinese factory, and the latter assembles and processes the components and materials according to the instructions of the foreign trader. The components and materials that are imported for this type of trade are exempted from import tariffs but all of the merchandise made from them must be exported. This scheme resembles the bonded factory scheme introduced in South Korea, but the difference is that 'processing trade' in Guangdong Province has developed into a form of inward foreign direct investment. The factories that engage in processing trade are nominally village-owned enterprises in rural Guangdong, but all of the equipment there is brought in by the foreign counterpart and the production and labor management are also conducted by the latter. The actual operation of the factories is almost the same as 100-percent foreign-owned enterprises.

In most cases, 'processing trade' ends up as simple assembling and does not entail the development of supporting industries. This is because the suppliers of inputs for processing trade cannot use the 'processing trade' scheme. When the suppliers import intermediate goods, they need to pay tariffs because they do not export their products. EPZs can avoid this problem because all of the transactions in them are exempted from tariffs, but EPZs need to be strictly segregated from the rest of the economy to minimize the risk of goods being smuggled from them to the outside. In Guangdong Province, however, the 'processing trade' scheme has been operated flexibly to exempt all inter-firm transactions from import tariffs, regardless of where the transaction takes place. This practice is called *zhuanchang* (inter-firm transaction), which means that all of the transactions from the import of materials to the export of final products are exempted from import tariffs. This practice raises the risk of smuggling. In fact, the *zhuanchang* scheme did lead to rampant smuggling during the 1990s. However, the open economy created by processing trade and *zhuanchang* schemes led to the growth of huge industrial agglomerations of electronics, apparel, toys, and other consumer goods industries in Guangdong. If the processing trade scheme had been operated as strictly as in the case of other developing countries, Guangdong might have ended up creating an enclave economy engaged in simple assembling of imported components. The share of exports using the processing trade scheme in China increased from 16 percent in 1989 to 46 percent in 1992, and during 1996–2005 its share was around 55 percent. Since 2006, its share has been slightly declining. Processing trade was one of the most important institutional arrangements that contributed to the growth of exports in China.

With the growth of processing trade, the Chinese economy during the latter half of the 1980s and the 1990s created a dual trade system: one part was the domestic industries which were protected from foreign competition by high tariffs and quantitative restrictions on imports, and the other was the export industries whose inputs were exempted from import tariffs (Naughton, 1996). The dual structure is reflected in the gap between the average import tariff rate and the rate of import tariff burden (i.e., customs duty income/import value). In 1991 the average import tariff rate was 43.1 percent while the rate of import tariff burden was only 5.5 percent because imports for processing trade were exempted from import tariffs (Figure 2.1).

Processing trade is not a specialty of Guangdong, but only in Guangdong did the trade scheme develop into a form of inward foreign direct investment and only here is *zhuanchang* trade allowed. Such lax operation of the system was possible because Guangdong was far away from the industrial center of the planned economy. Because the domestic market was not very integrated, the central authorities could allow imported goods to flow freely into the southern part without worrying about their influence on the domestic industries which had been protected from foreign competition.

India also tried to create a dual trade system after the establishment of the Kandla Free Trade Zone in 1965. In 1973, Santa Cruz was designated as an export processing zone, and in 1985, five more districts were added. But the impact of the free trade scheme was limited because only a few enterprises entered the zones. No foreign-invested enterprise has established a factory in Kandla as of 1978 (Onishi, 1978). India's Foreign Exchange Regulation Act (1974) restricted the share of foreign investors in Indo-foreign joint ventures to below 40 percent. This restriction was relaxed in 1980 to allow 100 percent foreign-owned enterprises if the enterprises exported all of the products they manufactured. But the effect of this relaxation was also limited: as of 1987, only 100 foreign-owned enterprises had been established using this scheme

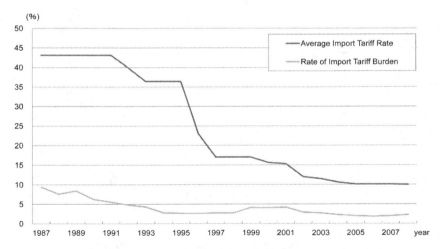

Figure 2.1 China's average import tariff rate and the rate of import tariff burden
Source: Ohashi (2003); *China Statistical Yearbook* (various years).

(Tateyama, 1988). India's dual trade system began to bear fruit after a new foreign trade policy was introduced in 1993. Enterprises which export most of their products can now import intermediate goods without paying import tariffs using EPZs and the scheme to promote export-oriented enterprises. If we compare India's average import tariff rate and the rate of import tariff burden, we find a gap between the two, indicating the existence of a dual structure, though the gap is narrower than in the case of China (Figure 2.2).

In marked contrast with China and India, Russia abandoned its protection after the beginning of its opening policy. The Russian Republic did establish eleven SEZs in 1990 (Shvidko, 2010), but these zones had little impact because in 1992 the whole country was opened drastically. In 1993, Russia's average import tariff rate was as low as 8.3 percent (Figure 2.3), which was close to the level of the United States (6.6 percent). Under this circumstance, SEZs were no longer 'special' in their openness. In 2005 Russia abolished all the SEZs except for the Kaliningrad and Magadan oblasts.

Russian SEZs started to function in a different way to those in China from the end of the 1990s. In 1995 the Russian government raised the tariff rate for most imported items. With the depreciation of the ruble after the economic crisis of 1998, domestic consumer industries revived (Uegaki, 2001). Against this backdrop, Kaliningrad SEZ became a base for manufacturing industries which targeted the domestic market. Considering its strategic importance as an enclave surrounded by Poland and Lithuania, the Russian government designated Kaliningrad Oblast as a whole an SEZ whose imports were exempted from tariffs and value-added taxes. Besides this, for goods exported from Kaliningrad to other parts of Russia, additional import tariffs and

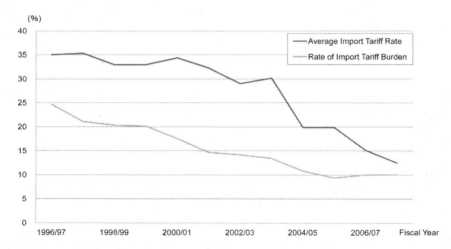

Figure 2.2 India's average import tariff rate and the rate of import tariff burden
Sources: Government of India, *Economic Survey* (various years); WTO, *Trade Policy Review* (various years).

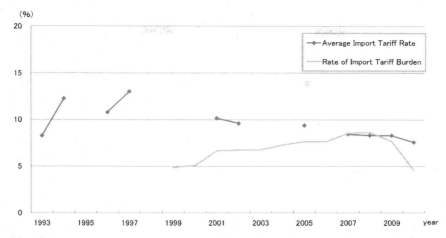

Figure 2.3 Russia's average import tariff rate and the rate of import tariff burden
Note: Average import tariff rate is the average of SITC 5 + 6 + 7 + 8 + 27 + 28 - 667.
Source: UNCTAD; Russian Federal Laws on the Federal budget executions (various years).

value-added taxes are not levied if more than 30 percent of their value is added in Kaliningrad. Therefore, importers of foreign merchandise can enjoy tax breaks if they import the components to Kaliningrad, assemble them, and sell the assembled product to other parts of Russia. Hence, assembly of television sets and passenger cars for the Russian market developed in Kaliningrad, and its gross regional product increased nine-fold during 2000–2008. In 2007, Kaliningrad accounted for 90 percent of television set production in Russia (Hasumi, 2011).

With the reduction in import tariffs in 2008, and the forthcoming abolishment of the privilege to export goods from Kaliningrad to other parts of Russia, which is scheduled to be implemented in 2016, the future of its manufacturing does not seem very bright. Russia's dual trade system did not contribute to the growth of its export industries, but added competitive pressure to domestic industries which were somewhat protected from foreign competition by import tariffs. By comparing Russia's average import tariff rate and its rate of import tariff burden (Figure 2.3), we find that the gap between the two was narrow and that the latter increased after 2000, even exceeding the former in 2007 and 2008. This shows that the dual trade system in Russia did not work like those in China and India.

A comparison of openness

As we have seen in the above section, Russia's average import tariff rate was as low as 8.3 percent in 1993 while that of China in 1993 was 36.4 percent and that of India in 1996/97 was 35 percent. But we cannot simply judge from

36 *Economic development*

these figures that Russia was more open to foreign trade than China and India. Since a large part of the foreign trade of China and India was exempted from import tariffs, we will underestimate the level of openness of China and India if we simply adopt the nominal tariff rate as a measure of trade openness. The rate of import tariff burden which we have shown in Figures 2.1–2.3 can also be a measure of openness, but it cannot capture the effect of quantitative import restrictions and quotas which do not entail customs duties. The coverage ratio of non-tariff barriers can also be a measure of openness, but it is difficult to quantify the severity of these barriers, and furthermore, it is unclear how the average tariff rate and non-tariff coverage ratios should be combined to create a comprehensive measure of openness.

Outcome-based openness index

An alternative measure of trade openness is the 'outcome-based' index. It assesses the deviation of the actual outcome from what the outcome would have been if there were no trade barriers. In this study, we have adopted Leamer's approach (Leamer, 1988, pp. 147–204) to evaluate the openness of China, India and Russia. Leamer estimated a modified Hecksher-Ohlin-Vanek (HOV) model which presupposes that there is a linear relationship between the net exports of each commodity group of each country and the country's resource endowments, and uses the estimated result as a measure to evaluate trade openness. Using the data of sixty-six countries (which do not include China, India and Russia) in 1982, he estimated the linear model, and predicted the net export value of each commodity group of each country by fitting the data on each country's resource endowments into the model. The deviation of the predicted value from the actual value of net export was taken as an indicator of trade barriers for each commodity group of a country. The openness measure of a country as a whole was computed by aggregating these deviations across all commodities. Following Leamer's practice, we estimated the following linear model by ordinary least-squares (OLS) regression analysis using the data of seventy-three countries including China, India and Russia in 2000:

$$Y_{ij} = \beta_0 + \beta_1 X_{i1} + \beta_2 X_{i2} + \dots + \beta_m X_{im} + \varepsilon_{ij,}$$

where Y_{ij} indicates the value of net exports of commodity j by country i. Commodities are aggregated into ten groups, namely, petroleum (PETRO), raw materials (MAT), forest products (FOR), tropical agriculture products (TROP), animal products (ANL), cereals (CER), labor-intensive manufactured goods (LAB), capital-intensive manufactured goods (CAP), machinery (MACH), and chemicals (CHEM).[2] Independent variables X_{im} indicate the supply of productive resources in each country. We have identified ten types of productive resources: three types of labor force, three types of land, three types of natural resource, and capital stock.[3]

A comparison of trade policy reform   37

The net exports of each commodity group predicted by the above model and the actual value were compared, and they were aggregated to create a comprehensive index, namely, the adjusted trade intensity ratio (TIR), to evaluate the openness of each country. As indicated by the following equation, the TIR of country is calculated by subtracting the aggregate of the absolute value of predicted net export from the aggregate of the absolute values of GDP: net exports for each commodity group, which is divided by the country's GDP:

$$\text{TIR} = (\Sigma|N_{ij}| - \Sigma|N^*_{ij}|) / GDP_i.$$

N_{ij} indicates the actual net exports of commodity j by country i, while N^*_{ij} indicates the predicted net exports calculated from the regression results above and factor supply in each country. The idea behind TIR is as follows: as trade barriers will reduce the amount of trade, if the actual trade value of a certain country exceeds the value predicted from its factor endowments, it indicates that the country's trade barriers are lower than the world average. If the actual trade value is smaller than the predicted value, it means that the country has higher trade barriers than the world average. Therefore, if the index takes a positive value, it means that the country is more open than the world average, and if the index is negative, the country is less open.

Trade openness of China, India, and Russia

The TIRs of the selected countries are reported in Table 2.1. According to our calculation, China reveals the highest openness among the three countries, ranking 25th among the seventy-three countries included in our calculation. China's TIRs for resources, agricultural goods and manufactured goods were all zero, and the composite TIR of China was hence also zero, indicating that the level of China's trade barriers in 2000 was the same as the world average. India ranks 32nd, showing a slightly lower level of openness in resources and manufactured goods than China. Russia has a high level of openness in resource trade but an extremely low level of openness in manufactured goods trade, which is the main reason for the low level of openness of the country as a whole.

Our calculations revealed that China in 2000 had a high level of openness close to some developed countries such as the United States and Japan, while Russia had a low level of openness close to other developing countries such as Brazil and Egypt. Our evaluation runs contrary to the widely held view which regards Russia as a radical reformer and China and India as gradual reformers.

Openness and trade policy

To understand the reason for the difference in trade openness of the three countries, let us examine the net export data for ten commodity groups. Table 2.2

Table 2.1 Trade openness index

Rank	Country	Resources	Agricultural Goods	Manufactured Goods	Total
1	Ireland	0.01	0.02	0.26	0.29
5	Finland	0.00	0.09	0.01	0.10
10	Sweden	0.00	0.04	0.01	0.05
17	Norway	0.07	0.01	-0.04	0.03
18	Germany	-0.01	-0.00	0.03	0.03
23	United States	0.00	0.00	0.01	0.01
24	Japan	-0.00	0.00	0.01	0.01
25	China	-0.00	-0.00	0.00	0.00
32	India	-0.01	-0.00	-0.02	-0.03
34	Turkey	-0.03	-0.01	-0.02	-0.06
37	Indonesia	-0.02	0.01	-0.10	-0.11
43	Brazil	-0.01	-0.00	-0.13	-0.15
45	Russian Federation	0.04	-0.02	-0.21	-0.19
47	Egypt	-0.05	-0.01	-0.18	-0.25
55	South Africa	-0.08	-0.07	-0.34	-0.49
58	Bulgaria	-0.21	-0.20	-0.45	-0.86
59	Georgia	-0.22	-0.52	-0.66	-1.40
64	Ethiopia	-0.52	-0.24	-2.25	-3.00
70	Moldova, Republic of	-1.07	-1.50	-3.56	-6.12
73	Dominica	-2.15	-5.14	-8.05	-15.34

Source: Konno (2012b, pp. 12–13).

reports the trade openness of each commodity group, its actual net export value, the predicted net export value calculated on the basis of the country's factor endowments, and the difference between the actual and predicted net export values. All of these figures are indicated as percentages of the country's GDP. The aggregation method of TIR presupposes that all trade policies are restrictive on trade, that the signs of actual and predicted net exports are always the same, that export restrictions will be introduced only when the net export value is positive, and that import restrictions will be introduced only when the net export value is negative. But, in reality, there may be cases when these presuppositions are not satisfied. In such cases, the difference in actual and predicted net export values (A-P) in Table 2.2 may indicate the depth of distortions which are not captured by the openness indices (|A|-|P|).

In the case of China, the difference in actual and predicted level of net export is fairly small in every commodity group, indicating that China's trade flows are basically guided by its factor endowments. The largest deviation is observed in labor-intensive manufactured goods, in which the actual net export value exceeds the predicted value, while in the cases of other manufactured goods the actual net export values are less than the predicted values. The deviation in labor-intensive manufactured goods can be explained by the dual trade system. Most of the commodities that are exported using the processing trade scheme are labor-intensive manufactured goods. The scheme has strongly promoted the export of such goods, while promoting imports of machinery. Both the deviations in labor-intensive goods and machinery contributed to enhancement of China's trade openness index.

In the case of India, the openness index of the machinery trade is extremely low, and the differences between actual and predicted net exports are all positive in the case of manufactured goods. These facts suggest the existence of high import barriers against imports of manufactured goods, and that the dual trade system was not effective enough to offset the distortions created by import barriers.[4] India's import tariff rate on manufactured goods in 2001/02 was as high as 33 percent, and the Indian government imposed various tariff and non-tariff barriers even on imports of textiles and apparel, which accounted for nearly 30 percent of India's exports. These restrictions on imports raised India's net exports of labor-intensive and capital-intensive goods, leading to high levels of trade openness indices in these commodities, while reducing the net imports in the machinery trade, resulting in its low level of trade openness.

In the case of Russia, trade openness indices are extremely low in the cases of machinery and labor-intensive manufactured goods, which are the main reason for the low openness of Russia as a whole. The actual and predicted net exports in labor-intensive and capital-intensive manufactured goods have different signs, suggesting that the actual degree of distortion is greater than that indicated by the openness indices. Our calculation suggests that Russia is implementing a strong policy to promote exports or to restrict imports. Though the nominal import tariff rates are low, there are two institutional

Table 2.2 Actual and Predicted net export of Russia, China and India (percent of GDP)

	China				India				Russia			
	Openness |A|-|P|	Actual (A)	Predicted (P)	A-P	Openness |A|-|P|	Actual (A)	Predicted (P)	A-P	Openness |A|-|P|	Actual (A)	Predicted (P)	A-P
PETRO	-0.08	-1.19	-1.28	0.08	-0.83	-3.40	-4.22	0.83	3.77	12.87	9.09	3.77
MAT	-0.03	-0.54	-0.57	0.03	-0.01	-0.54	-0.55	0.01	0.41	9.59	9.18	0.41
FOR	-0.04	-0.56	-0.60	0.04	0.10	-0.21	-0.11	-0.10	-1.93	1.07	3.00	-1.93
TROP	-0.02	0.20	0.22	-0.02	-0.08	0.22	0.29	-0.08	0.48	-1.41	-0.94	-0.48
ANL	-0.00	0.29	0.29	-0.00	-0.10	0.39	0.49	-0.10	-0.46	-0.58	1.05	-1.63
CER	-0.00	-0.34	-0.34	0.00	-0.14	-0.04	0.17	-0.21	-0.26	-1.14	1.40	-2.55
LAB	0.17	6.26	6.09	0.17	0.58	1.98	1.40	0.58	-4.00	1.55	-5.55	7.11
CAP	-0.02	0.50	0.52	-0.02	0.45	1.49	1.03	0.45	0.60	1.77	-1.17	2.94
MACH	0.04	-1.06	-1.02	-0.04	-2.87	-1.13	-3.99	2.87	-17.45	-2.06	-19.51	17.45
CHEM	0.03	-1.55	-1.52	-0.03	-0.46	-0.15	-0.61	0.46	-0.34	-0.10	-0.44	0.34
Total	0.02	2.01	1.80	0.21	-3.35	-1.39	-6.10	4.72	-19.18	21.54	-3.90	25.44

Source: Konno (2012b, p. 7).

factors that work as import restriction and export promotion policies. First, there is the red tape in customs procedures. The complications of trade procedures in Russia are considered to be among the worst in the world, and this may act as a serious non-tariff barrier to trade, especially to imports.[5] Second, special institutional arrangements with other CIS countries, such as bilateral free trade agreements (FTA) and the common standard certification system (GOST) with them, may work for Russia as policies promoting exports to these countries.[6]

Infant industry protection under trade liberalization: the localization of automobile production

In the previous section we evaluated the opening policies of China, India and Russia using the outcome of trade as a measure. However, whether or not the trade pattern should be commanded by the country's factor endowments is a topic that has been discussed by economists and policymakers for a long time. The effectiveness of protecting 'infant industries', which means that a country distorts its current trade structure to create comparative advantage for its infant industries in the future, is still advocated by many economists and policymakers (Chang, 2002). The fact that China, India and Russia impose high tariffs on the import of certain items is an indication that they are also influenced by the 'infant industry' argument. One of the focuses of their protectionist policies is the automobile industry. In 2011, the production volume of automobiles in China reached 18 million units, while that of India was 4 million and that of Russia was 2 million. Russia's production volume in 2011 was roughly equivalent to China's in 2000 and India's in 2006. In this section, we will compare the protectionist policies on automobiles of the three countries when their production volumes were around 2 million units a year.

Protection by import tariffs

Since automobile production enjoys economies of scale, it is difficult for latecomer nations to have their own automobile industry that can survive competition with foreign automobiles. But if there are tariff barriers against the import of automobiles, international and domestic automakers will be induced to make investments in the developing country to prepare for growth in the future. Based on such reasoning, many developing countries around the world are imposing high import tariffs on automobiles.

In 1996, China imposed 100-percent import tariff and import quotas on small and mid-sized passenger cars. China reduced the tariff rate to 70 percent in 2000, and to 51.9 percent when it became a member of the WTO in 2001. The tariff rate was gradually reduced to 25 percent in 2006 and quota restrictions were relaxed. India imposed quantitative restrictions on automobile imports even after it had started the opening policy in 1991. But, in 2001, India's automotive industrial policy was judged to breach the Trade-Related

42 Economic development

Investment Measures (TRIM) Agreement by the WTO. The government had to scrap quantitative restrictions on imports, but instead increased the tariff rate on automobile imports from 35 percent to 60 percent. With other additional taxes, the effective tariff rate may amount to 85–120 percent. In 2006, the Indian government reduced the tariff rate on imports of commercial vehicles and buses to 12.5–15 percent, but the tariff rate for passenger cars maintained a high level (60 percent). Russia's tariff rate on passenger car imports was 30 percent in 2011, and was reduced to 25 percent in 2012 when Russia joined the WTO (Sakaguchi, 2012).

The tariff rate on passenger car imports when the size of domestic automobile production was around 2 million was 70 percent (plus quantitative restrictions) in the case of China, 60 percent (plus other additional taxes) in the case of India, and 30 percent in the case of Russia. The volume of imports is related to the level of protection: the three-year average of automobile imports was 2 percent of annual domestic production during 1998–2000 in the case of China, 2 percent during 2005–07 in the case of India, and 88 percent during 2008–10 in the case of Russia.

Localization of components

High import tariffs on automobile imports may be effective in promoting the domestic production of automobiles, but such a policy often ends up in promoting knock-down assembly which imports most of its inputs. The government may also impose high import tariffs on automobile components to promote their production, but such a policy will make automobiles produced in the country very expensive. To avoid such a dilemma, developing countries often promote the localization of automobile components by requiring automakers to achieve a certain level of local content, or by linking the tariff rate of component imports with the level of local content achieved by each automaker. However, such practices will be judged as an infringement of the TRIM agreement by the WTO.

Before entering the WTO, China made full use of localization policies to promote the growth of its domestic automobile industry. Its 1994 automobile industry policy put a ban on knock-down assembly of automobiles and stipulated that only those which could achieve more than 40 percent local content from the start would be allowed to establish new car plants. If they increased the local content ratio to 60 percent and 80 percent, the import tariffs on the rest of the components would be further reduced. With China's entry to the WTO in 2001, however, the industrial policy lost its effectiveness. China tried to revive the localization requirement in its new automobile industrial policy promulgated in 2004, but it was made ineffective because the policy was judged to be incompatible with the TRIM agreement.

India also obliged automakers to gradually increase their local content using the licensing system introduced in the 1950s. Even after 1991, each automobile manufacturer had to supply a memorandum on the plan for

A comparison of trade policy reform   43

raising local content to the Indian government. But, as mentioned before, such a practice was found to be in conflict with the TRIM agreement. India's new automobile industrial policy in 2002 had no requirements on local content.

Russia introduced industry assembly measures in 2005 which promoted the localization of automobile components. This policy allowed automobile manufacturers to engage in knock-down assembly at the outset of their operation, but the range of components that were exempted from import duties would be narrowed. Since this policy was not very effective in promoting the localization of component production, Russia introduced stricter restrictions on knock-down assembly in the 2011 industrial policy, demanding that automakers achieve more than 30 percent local content in the fourth year of operation and more than 40 percent local content in the fifth year. However, these requirements were judged to conflict with the TRIM agreement during the negotiations for Russia's entry to the WTO, and Russia declared that these requirements would not be effective after 2018 (Sakaguchi, 2012; Konno, 2012a).

In sum, all three countries had localization policies for automobile components. Let us examine the results of such policies by comparing the local content ratios of foreign-invested automobile manufacturers when the automobile production of each country grew from 1 million to 2 million units a year.

The first passenger car that was assembled in China by a foreign-investing automaker was Volkswagen's Santana. Its localization rate reached 80.5 percent in 1993, the eighth year since its assembly started. Since the progress of Santana's localization entailed the growth of component suppliers, later models achieved high localization rates more rapidly. Volkswagen's Jetta and Suzuki's Alto achieved 84.0 percent and 85.3 percent respectively in their fourth year of production.

In India, Suzuki started assembling the Maruti 800 in 1983, and its localization rate reached 46 percent in 1986 and 95 percent in 1993, in conformity with the company's agreement with the Indian government. Suzuki launched a new model in 1993, which had an 85 percent localization rate from the beginning. Hyundai's Santro, which the company started assembling in 1998, had a 90 percent localization rate in 2003. As in the case of China, more recent models could increase their localization rates more rapidly than older models.

The progress in the localization of passenger cars assembled in Russia was slow. The assembly of Renault's Rogan started in 2005, but in 2011 its localization rate was still only 53 percent. Volkswagen started producing cars in Russia from 2007, but as of 2010, the highest localization rate among its models was only 30 percent.

All three countries had an indigenous automobile industry during the command economy era, so they had created basic industrial capabilities before the arrival of foreign automobile manufacturers. Therefore, the reason

44   *Economic development*

for the divergence in the speed of localization lies not in the initial conditions but in the difference in their localization policies. China and India had strict policies, while Russia's was lax. Besides this, China and India limited the number of manufacturers and models at the early stage of their automobile industry development. Therefore, component suppliers in China and India could concentrate on the localization of a limited number of automotive components. If the production of a certain model lasts long and its cumulative production volume increases, local component manufacturers will have the time to improve the quality of their products, and the possibility of recovering initial investments will increase. In Russia, by contrast, most of the major automakers around the world erected assembly plants there and started producing many models. Component manufacturers will hesitate to localize the production of components because the demand for a certain type of component will be limited under such circumstances. China and India's policy of limiting the number of models created favorable conditions for the localization of components, while Russia's policy of allowing many automakers to enter the market proved to be detrimental to localization. However, consumers had few choices of model in China and India while their governments were pursuing localization. The price of a passenger car was extraordinarily high in China during the 1990s, because competition was lacking and the government allowed car manufacturers to shift the cost of localization to consumers. Component localization in China and India was achieved by sacrificing consumer welfare during the development period.

Conclusion

This chapter compared the policies and outcomes of economic opening by China, India and Russia. Having created autarchic industrial structures under the command economy system, the first motive of the three countries in starting economic opening was to find a remedy for their economic crises. The depth of the crisis determined the degree of economic openness. India and Russia, which faced deep crises in the early 1990s, had to resort to drastic reforms in order to extract support from Western countries and international institutions, while China made only small steps towards opening because it was facing only a temporary crisis.

If we compare the trade regimes of the three countries, we find that China made full use of the dual trade system to relieve the shock of economic opening on the old industrial system while promoting exports. India also had a dual trade system but the impact on its economy was much smaller than in the case of China. Russia did not at first create a dual system but has been developing one since the late 1990s.

If we measure the openness of the three countries from the outcome of their trade, we find that, contrary to the conventional view, China was the most open economy, followed by India. Though Russia had the lowest average tariff rate among the three, we find that its trade structure was a severe distortion of the pattern predicted by its factor endowments. The reasons for these results lie in the fact that, first, the high import tariffs of China and India were largely offset by their dual trade system, and second, Russia had serious non-tariff barriers to its imports.

Even after the economic opening, the three countries protected their infant industries. While China and India strongly protected their automobile industries, Russia's protection was weaker, resulting in the difference in import penetration. The three countries also had very different results regarding the localization of automobile components, because China and India pursued localization at the expense of consumer welfare while Russia did not.

China started from a partial opening, made full use of the dual trade system to promote exports and protect infant industries at the same time, and finally achieved a high level of openness. Russia started from a radical opening, and it failed to promote exports except for petroleum and gas, and also failed to protect its infant industries. Russia ended up creating a rather closed economy because of the inefficiency of its customs procedures. In many respects, India stands in between the two extreme cases.

Notes

1 The figure is from the NASSCOM (National Association of Software and Services Companies) website (www.nasscom.org/).
2 We aggregated two-digit-level trade data (SITC rev. 1) reported by UN Comtrade into ten commodity groups following the method employed by Leamer (1984, pp. 67–68).
3 For details of the model and data, see Konno (2012b).
4 A WTO report points out that the impact of export processing zones on the promotion of exports was limited (WTO, 2002, p. 55).
5 According to a World Bank report, Russia ranked 155th out of 178 nations on the ease of 'Trading Across Borders', which was judged by the number of documents, time and cost that were required to engage in international trade, while China and India ranked 42nd and 79th respectively (World Bank, 2007).
6 Russia had comparative advantage in CIS markets in several manufactured goods such as machines, electrical equipment, ships and optical apparatus in 1994 and 2005 (Konno, 2008).

References

Aslund, Anders (1995) *How Russia Became a Market Economy*, Washington, DC: Brookings Institution, Ch. 2.
Chang, Ha-Joon (2002) *Kicking Away the Ladder: Development Strategy in Historical Perspective*, London: Anthem Press.
Hasumi, Yu (2011) 'Kikigo no Kariningurado shu keizai' [The Development of Kaliningrad Oblast's Economy after the crisis], *Russia & NIS Business Monthly*, vol. 56, no. 2, pp. 74–79. Japan Association for Trade with Russia and NIS (in Japanese).
Ito, Shoji and Hideki Esho (1995) *Tachiagaru Indo keizai: aratanaru keizai pawa no taito* [The Indian Economy Awakens: Rise of a New Economic Power], Tokyo: Nikkei Publishing Inc (in Japanese).

46 Economic development

Kojima, Sueo (2012) 'Puranto keiyaku mondai' [The Problem of Plant Contracts], in Kenji Hattori and Tomoo Marukawa, eds., *Nitchu kankeishi 1972–2012 II Keizai* [Forty Years of Japan-China Relations: Economy], Tokyo: University of Tokyo Press, pp. 73–80 (in Japanese).

Konno, Yugo (2008) 'Roshia no tai CIS boeki no kozo bunseki: Sono tokucho to keizai togo eno gan'i' [Analysis of Structural Changes in Russia's Trade with CIS Countries], *Suravu kenkyu* [Slavic Studies], no. 55, Sapporo: Slavic Research Center pp. 29–59, (in Japanese).

——(2012a) 'Roshia no jidosya sangyo seisaku ni henka' [The Change in Russia's Automobile Policy], *Mizuho Insights: Europe*, March (in Japanese).

——(2012b) 'Comparison of Trade Liberalizations in Russia, China, and India', in Takahiro Sato, ed., *The BRICs as Regional Economic Powers in the Global Economy*, Comparative Studies on Regional Powers, Sapporo: Slavic Research Center, pp. 1–13.

Leamer, Edward E. (1984) *Sources of International Comparative Advantage: Theory and Evidence*, Cambridge, MA: MIT Press.

——(1988) 'Measures of Openness', in Robert E. Baldwin, ed., *Trade Policy Issues and Empirical Analysis*, Chicago, IL: University of Chicago Press, pp. 147–204.

Naughton, Barry (1996) 'China's Emergence and Prospects as a Trading Nation', *Brookings Papers on Economic Activity* no. 2, pp. 273–344.

Ohashi, Hideo (2003) *Keizai no kokusaika* [Globalization of the Economy], Nagoya: Nagoya University Press (in Japanese).

Onishi, Katsukuni (1978) 'Indo no yushutsu kakoku' [India's Export Processing Zones], in Hideo Fujimori, ed., *Ajia shokoku no yushutsu kakoku* [Export Processing Zones of Asia], Tokyo: Institute of Developing Economies, pp. 263–92 (in Japanese).

Sakaguchi, Izumi (2012) 'WTO kamei de Roshia jidosya sangyo wa do ugokuka' [How will the Russian Automobile Industry Change after Russia's Entry to the WTO?], *Russia and NIS Business Monthly*, vol. 57, no. 2, pp. 10–25. Japan Association for Trade with Russia and NIS (in Japanese).

Shvidko, V. (2010) 'Roshia no keizai seisaku taikei ni okeru keizai tokku no ichizuke' [SEZs' Position in Russia's Economic Policy], *Russia and NIS Business Monthly*, vol. 55, no. 3, pp. 1–8. Japan Association for Trade with Russia and NIS (in Japanese).

Tabata, Shinichiro (2008) 'Keizai no sekiyu gasu eno izon' [Economic Dependence on Petroleum and Gas], in Shinichiro Tabata, ed., *Sekiyu gasu to Roshia keizai* [Petroleum, Gas and the Russian Economy], Sapporo: Hokkaido University Press (in Japanese).

Tateyama, Somahiko (1988) 'Gaikoku shihon' [Foreign Capital], in Shoji Ito, ed., *Indo no kogyoka: Kiro ni tatsu haikosuto keizai* [Industrialization of India: High-Cost-Economy at a Crossroads], Tokyo: Institute of Developing Economies, pp. 118–138 (in Japanese).

Uegaki, Akira (2001) 'Taigai keizai kankei' [Foreign economic relations], in Hiromasa Nakayama, Akira Uegaki, Manabu Suhara and Yoshimasa Tsuji, *Gendai Roshia keizai ron* [Contemporary Russian Economy], Tokyo: Iwanami Shoten, pp. 77–113 (in Japanese).

World Bank (2007) *Doing Business 2008*, Washington, DC: World Bank.

WTO (2002) *Trade Policy Review Report by the Secretariat: India*, WT/TPR/S/100, www.wto.org/.

3 Emergence of regional powers in the international financial system

Shinichiro Tabata

The purpose of this chapter is to analyze the emergence of regional powers in the international financial system in the 2000s and to consider their presence in the future world. For this purpose, I compare the mechanisms of foreign reserve accumulation in regional powers, i.e. China, Russia and India. They amassed substantial foreign reserves during the 2000s. China, Russia and India ranked first, third and sixth in their amount of foreign reserves accumulated at the end of 2007. Together, the three countries accounted for 33.3 percent of the world's total foreign currency reserves at that time, while the corresponding figure was 13.5 percent at the end of 2001. The three countries accounted for 42.7 percent of the increase in the world's official reserves from 2001 through 2007 (*IFS*, 2014).

I focus on foreign reserves, because by their accumulation regional powers began to play an important role in the international financial system. There occurred the so-called global imbalance in the 2000s, which was characterized by a growing current account deficit of the United States and a tremendous accumulation of foreign reserves in emerging countries, especially in regional powers. As shown below, three types of mechanism of foreign reserve accumulation in regional powers may represent the mechanisms observed in other emerging economies. This is sometimes called the new Bretton Woods system, where emerging economies have reestablished the United States as the center of the world monetary system by forming a new periphery, supplanting the original of the 1950s consisting of Europe and Japan, through their commitment to the maintenance of an undervalued exchange rate.

The global financial crisis in 2008–9, however, seemed to have changed the situation considerably. In this chapter I analyze these changes in order to obtain some hints for the prospects of the international financial system.

In the next section, I compare the mechanisms of foreign reserve accumulation before the global financial crisis in China, Russia and India. Discussion of the global imbalance follows. Then, I analyze the changes in the aforementioned mechanisms during and after the global financial crisis. The concluding section discusses future prospects.

48 *Economic development*

The mechanism for accumulating foreign reserves before the global financial crisis

Exchange rate arrangement

The exchange rate arrangements of China, Russia and India in the period from 2001 to 2007 were more or less de facto pegged, although they were sometimes called managed floating rates by the respective central banks. As a result, as shown in Figure 3.1, especially in the period from 2004 to 2006, fluctuations of their currencies were small. It should be noted that although in 2007 intervention in foreign exchange markets or the increase in foreign reserves recorded the largest amount ever in these three countries, their national currencies appreciated rather rapidly against the dollar in that year. As we see below, this was due to the largest inflow of foreign currencies into these countries in 2007.

As for China, in the period from 1997 to 2005, the renminbi (RMB) was pegged to the dollar. On July 21, 2005 the currency basket was introduced, and the International Monetary Fund (IMF, 2008, pp. 304–5) recognized China's exchange rate arrangement as a crawling peg.[1] For three years from July 2005, the RMB appreciated against the dollar by 20.4 percent. There was an assessment by some specialists in the Chinese economy, however, that this appreciation was attributable to appreciation of the euro against the dollar, and that the exchange rate regime could be better described as a basket peg (Tabata, 2011, p. 416).

Russia has allegedly adopted a managed floating exchange rate policy since 1998. However, the IMF (2008, pp. 1152–53) regarded it as a de facto pegged

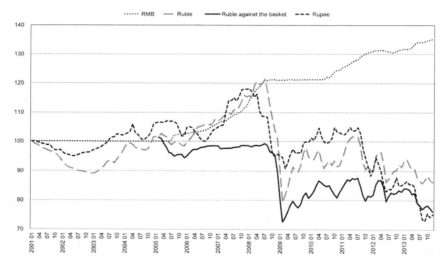

Figure 3.1 Nominal exchange rates of three currencies against the dollar, monthly average in percent (January 2001 = 100), 2001–2013
Sources: Compiled by the author from *IFS* (2014) and CBR's website (www.cbr.ru/statistics/?Prtid=svs) last accessed January 16, 2014.

arrangement against a currency basket during the period from March 2006 through August 2008, because fluctuations in exchange rates were very small. This currency basket was introduced in 2005 and its coefficients of the dollar and the euro used to calculate the ruble's exchange rate with the currency basket have been 55 percent and 45 percent, respectively, since February 2007. Accordingly, the ruble was almost pegged against the currency basket, while it appreciated against the dollar in 2006 and 2007 (Figure. 3.1).

India has adopted de jure a managed floating exchange rate policy since 1993. Many researchers on the Indian economy, however, agree that it was de facto a crawling peg to the dollar and that India's monetary authorities have pursued the stability of a real effective exchange rate of the rupee against the dollar (Tabata, 2011, p. 418). In fact, if we calculate coefficients of variation in the period from April 2000 through March 2007 by using monthly data, they were 2.69 and 1.87 for the rupee's exchange rates in nominal and real terms, respectively. If we calculate them in a shorter period from April 2000 through March 2005, the corresponding coefficients were 2.63 and 1.30, respectively.

Factors contributing to the increase in inflow of foreign currencies

The maintenance of more or less stabilized exchange rates in these countries and the considerable growth in foreign reserves in them imply that currency authorities of these countries have intervened strongly in foreign exchange markets. There was a discussion about whether the intervention in exchange markets deliberately aimed to keep the value of its currency low or whether it was necessitated by the inflow of foreign currencies. In either case, it should be noted that there was indeed a growing inflow of foreign currencies in the foreign exchange markets in these countries. This consisted of a surplus in current account as in China and Russia, and inflow of foreign investments as in all three countries.

With respect to China, the main factor contributing to the increase in inflow of foreign currencies was the extraordinary increase in current account surpluses. China's current account surplus in the period from 2004 to 2007 was almost seven times larger than the corresponding amount in the period from 2000 to 2003 (Table 3.1). In addition, foreign direct investment (FDI) was a significant contributor to the inflow of foreign currencies for China. Net inflow of FDI in China was the largest among the three countries both in terms of its absolute amounts and as a percentage of GDP (Table 3.1).

In Russia, the increase in inflow of foreign currencies was largely a result of a substantial current account surplus as well, but was caused largely by oil price increases. As a percentage of GDP, Russia's current account surplus exceeded that of China for the period 2000–2007 (Table 3.1). The contribution of 'other investment' from abroad, mostly loans provided to Russian firms and banks, increased, especially in 2007. It should be noted that although the contribution of net FDI appears to be insignificant in Table 3.1, this is due to a considerable increase in outward FDI. During the period

Table 3.1 Factors contributing to the increase in foreign reserves in China, Russia and India, 2000–2012

	In billion dollars				In percent of GDP			
	2000–03	*2004–07*	*2008–09*	*2010–12*	*2000–03*	*2004–07*	*2008–09*	*2010–12*
China								
Increase in foreign reserves	67.7	296.5	440.0	318.7	4.5	11.2	9.3	4.8
Current account surplus	29.8	196.5	331.9	189.0	2.1	7.0	7.1	2.7
FDI	42.2	95.7	101.0	202.8	3.0	3.6	2.1	2.9
Portfolio investment	-5.6	-9.2	31.0	30.5	-0.5	-0.3	0.7	0.4
Other investment	-6.2	-1.8	-16.2	-59.6	-0.5	0.2	-0.4	-0.6
Russia								
Increase in foreign reserves	15.5	90.8	-17.8	26.5	4.6	9.5	-1.0	1.5
Current account surplus	36.3	77.1	77.2	78.7	11.4	9.0	5.1	4.3
FDI	-0.5	4.5	6.2	-6.2	-0.1	0.4	0.3	-0.4
Portfolio investment	-3.9	2.6	-18.8	1.2	-1.4	0.2	-1.1	0.0
Other investment	-4.3	16.3	-69.1	-33.5	-1.9	1.1	-4.3	-1.7
India								
Increase in foreign reserves	14.9	38.7	21.2	-2.0	2.8	3.8	1.6	-0.1
Current account surplus	3.2	-6.7	-28.6	-69.5	0.5	-0.7	-2.2	-3.8
FDI	3.4	5.6	21.8	16.9	0.7	0.6	1.7	0.9
Portfolio investment	3.6	15.9	1.3	22.9	0.7	1.6	0.1	1.3
Other investment	4.7	23.4	15.5	32.1	0.9	2.3	1.2	1.7
Reference								
USA								
Current account surplus	-447.3	-720.0	-531.5	-449.2	-4.2	-5.6	-3.7	-3.0

Source: Compiled by the author from *IFS* (2014).

2004–2007, inward and outward FDI averaged, respectively, $28.3 billion (2.9 percent of GDP) and $23.9 billion (2.5 percent of GDP) annually. In comparison, outward FDI from China amounted to $12.8 billion (0.5 percent of GDP) on average for the same period.

Contrary to China and Russia, India has recorded a current account deficit in most of the recent years. In fact, its trade deficit (3.9 percent of GDP) was significantly larger than the current account deficit (0.7 percent of GDP) during the period from 2004 to 2007. The trade deficit was largely compensated for by a large current transfer surplus, mostly in the form of remittances from abroad, which on average amounted to $27.3 billion (2.9 percent of GDP) in this period.[2] Therefore, the growth in inflow of foreign currencies in India resulted totally from the inflow of foreign investments. Portfolio and other investments were larger in India than in China and Russia, both in terms of absolute amounts and as percentage of GDP during the period from 2004 to 2007 (Table 3.1).

Savings and investment balance

I have demonstrated that in China and Russia a continuing large current account surplus was the main source of inflow of foreign currencies that tremendously increased foreign reserves. In the framework of the macroeconomy, the fact that the current account surplus was large implies that savings greatly exceeded investments in the economy as a whole:

$$GDP = C + I + EX - IM$$

$$GDP = S + C$$

From these two equations (definitions), we obtain:

$$S - I = EX - IM = CA$$

where C = consumption; I = investments; EX = exports; IM = imports; S = savings; CA = current account surplus.

If we look at the savings and investment balance (S-I balance) by institutional sector during the period from 2004 to 2007, we find that there were significant differences among the three countries (Table 3.2). In China, large net lending (surplus of savings over investments) was due to large savings by households and firms. In fact, both the savings and investment rate of the Chinese economy has in recent years been the highest among the world's major economies. In particular, savings (22.1 percent of GDP) and net lending (11.9 percent of GDP) in households were very large in 2004–07. The high saving rate of Chinese households is explained by savings necessary for education, health care and retirement. At the same time, savings by firms (22.1

Table 3.2 Savings and investment balance by institutional sector in China, Russia and India, annual average, in percent of GDP

	2004–2007				2010–2011			
	Total	*Firms*	*Households*	*Government*	*Total*	*Firms*	*Households*	*Government*
China								
Savings	48.2	22.1	22.1	4.0	51.1	20.6	25.1	5.4
Investments	42.5	27.7	10.2	4.6	48.2	31.8	11.1	5.4
Net lending	7.0[a]	-5.6	11.9	-0.6	3.0[a]	-11.2	14.0	0.1
Russia								
Savings	30.7	11.4	6.9	12.4	28.0	12.4	6.6	9.0
Investments	21.6	13.7	4.2	3.6	24.0	17.2	2.0	4.9
Net lending	9.2[a]	-2.3	2.6	8.8	4.9[a]	-4.8	4.7	4.1
India[b]								
Savings	34.3	7.8	23.2	3.3	32.4	7.6	22.9	1.9
Investments	35.3[c]	13.9	11.9	8.1	35.9[c]	12.0	13.7	8.1
Net lending	-1.0	-6.1	11.2	-4.8	-3.5	-4.4	9.2	-6.2

Notes: [a] Excludes statistical discrepancies.
[b] April–March data.
[c] Includes net acquisitions of valuables and errors and omissions.
Sources: Compiled by the author from NBS, 2012, pp. 80–89; 2013, pp. 80–81; Rosstat, 2012, pp. 26–29; 2013, pp. 28–55; RBI, 2013.

percent of GDP) were large by international standards as well, although investments by firms surpassed their savings by 5.6 percentage points. The large net lending of the economy as a whole seemed to stem only from large net lending in households. Ferguson and Schularick (2007, pp. 230–34; 2009, pp. 12–13) and Keidel (2011, p. 370) argue, however, that if we compare savings at the beginning and the middle of the 2000s, savings by firms increased more rapidly than those by households. The increase in firms' savings was due to profits obtained by exports, implying that some growing current account surpluses increased firms' savings.

With respect to Russia, large net lending in the period from 2004 to 2007 was mainly a result of government-sector actions. The reason that savings and net lending in the government sector were so large is explained by the allocation since 2004 of a portion of the tax revenues on crude oil to the stabilization fund (Tabata, 2007). This means that some current account surpluses earned by oil exports were accumulated as government's savings. Here, we see some similarities with China. In Russia, however, neither the savings rate nor the investment rate was as high as in China and India. In particular, savings and net lending in households were quite small, namely 6.9 percent and 2.6 percent of GDP in 2004–07, respectively. This reflects the specificity of the Russian economic growth model, in which GDP growth has been driven by increases in household consumption (Tabata, 2009, p. 684). Because net borrowing (deficit of savings against investments) in firms was small, savings surpassed investments by 9.2 percent for the entire economy in 2004–07.

India's S-I balance was completely different from China's and Russia's. Although Indian households have high savings and net lending in the world as is the case in China, investments in India have slightly surpassed savings in the overall economy due to large net borrowing by the government, i.e. a budget deficit (Table 3.2). Although savings in India's firms (7.8 percent of GDP) were relatively low, investments by firms (13.9 percent of GDP) increased considerably compared with the previous period. The corresponding figure in 2000–2003 was 3.9 percent and 5.6 percent of GDP, respectively. As Uegaki (2010, p. 65) has observed, India is now showing the features of a typical capital-shortage, developing industrial country, in which investments are actively undertaken and public spending is growing to cover social needs in a rapidly changing society.

Costs of the increase in foreign reserves

As explained in preceding sections, in all three countries, currency authorities intervened strongly in foreign exchange markets and increased foreign reserves, especially during the period from 2004 to 2007, although there were considerable differences among these countries in the dynamics of balance of payments and S-I balance. These interventions in exchange markets led to the undervaluation of national currencies at least to a certain degree, which in turn contributed to the increase in exports, constraint on imports, and the increase in inflow of foreign investments. However, the costs of such interventions in exchange markets should be taken into account. In general, purchases of foreign currencies at exchange markets imply an increase in base money of national currencies. If some measures for sterilization are not adopted adequately, inflationary pressure increases.

With respect to China, in April 2003, the People's Bank of China (PBC), China's central bank, began to issue PBC bills to further support the sterilization effort. Since around 2007, however, the amount of PBC bills outstanding has not matched the increase in foreign reserves (Figure 3.2), implying that this sterilization process was incomplete (Tabata, 2011, pp. 420–21). Kajitani (2011, pp. 87–89), based on analysis of PBC's balance sheets, demonstrated that the main reason for the increase in base money in China in the 2000s, especially in 2004–07, was the increase in foreign reserves, though sterilization by PBC bills was substantial in this period. As Ferguson and Schularick (2009, p. 11) suggested, sterilization measures (even though partial or incomplete) were pursued under circumstances of the overwhelming presence of state-owned banks or the strong presence of the state in the banking sector.

As for Russia, the marked correspondence between the magnitude of growth in foreign reserves and in money supply (M2) from the mid-2000s to the middle of 2008, shown in Figure 3.3, suggests that the level of sterilization has not been adequate (Tabata, 2009, pp. 685–87). The stabilization fund, mentioned above, has been almost the sole tool for sterilization employed in Russia. However, although accumulation in the stabilization fund increased from year to year, base money increased rapidly due to the massive interventions in foreign exchange markets by the Central Bank of Russia (CBR).

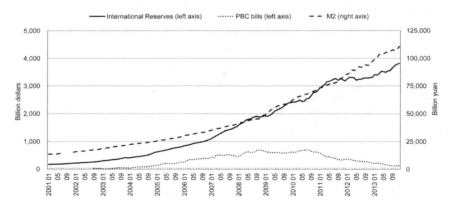

Figure 3.2 International reserves, PBC bills and money supply (M2) in China, 2001–2013
Notes: At end of month. PBC bills are converted from yuan to dollars by the author. International reserves exclude gold, SDRs and reserve position in the IMF.
Source: Compiled by the author from PBC's website [http://www.pbc.gov.cn/] last accessed on January13, 2014.

Regional powers in international finance 55

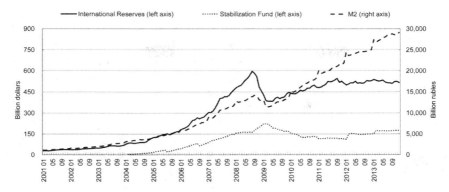

Figure 3.3 International reserves, stabilization fund and money supply (M2) in Russia, 2001–2013
Notes: At beginning of month. In February 2008, the Stabilization Fund was transformed into Reserve and National Welfare Funds. After 2008, the sum of these two funds is shown.
Sources: Compiled by the author from websites of CBR [http://www.cbr.ru/], Ministry of Finance, Russia [http://www.minfin.ru/ru/] last accessed on January 20, 2014, and Federal Treasury [http://www.roskazna.ru/] last accessed on January 20, 2014.

During the period from 2004 to 2007, the increase in the stabilization fund was equal to 39.0 percent of the increase in foreign reserves. One of the causes of rapid inflation (average annual increase in the consumer price index (CPI) of 13.7 percent from 2000 through 2007) was the increase in money supply. As high inflation continued, exchange rates of the ruble in real terms increased as well, because its nominal rates were kept stable. This appreciation

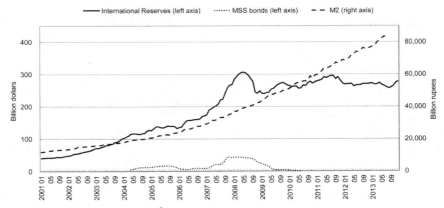

Figure 3.4 International reserves, MSS bonds and money supply (M2) in India, 2001–2013
Notes: At end of month (last Friday). MSS bonds are converted from rupees to dollars by the author.
Sources: Compiled by the author from *IFS* (2014) and RBI's website [http://www.rbi.org.in/] last accessed on October 31, 2012.

56 *Economic development*

of the ruble in real terms has contributed to the appearance of at least some symptoms of Dutch disease in Russia (Tabata, 2012, p. 233).

India in April 2004 introduced the Market Stabilization Scheme (MSS), under which the Reserve Bank of India (RBI), India's central bank, was empowered to issue government treasury bills for sterilization purposes. Figure 3.4 suggests that the volume of MSS bond issues increased only in 2007 and early 2008. The burden of sterilization for India has not been large, compared with China and Russia (Tabata, 2011, pp. 421–22).

Global imbalance

Revived Bretton Woods system

In the 2000s, foreign reserves increased in many emerging economies, including China, Russia and India. One of the reasons for this was the lesson learnt from the Asian and Russian currency and financial crises of 1997 and 1998. There appear to be at least three different mechanisms among such countries for accumulating foreign reserves. One mechanism applies to countries with a large current account surplus, derived from exports of manufacturing goods, another to oil and gas exporting countries, and a third to those receiving substantial foreign investments, while maintaining a small positive or negative current account balance. Prime examples or prototypes of each mechanism can be found in China, Russia and India, respectively. In this sense, these three countries have provided models for other emerging economies. According to cluster analysis (Tabata, 2011, pp. 411–12), among countries with large foreign reserves, Hong Kong, Malaysia and Singapore may be included in the Chinese type (manufacturing exports); Norway, Saudi Arabia and Libya belong to the Russian type (oil and gas exports); and Korea, Brazil and Mexico are candidates for the Indian type (inward FDI).

While a tremendous amount of foreign reserves was accumulated in these countries, the current account deficit of the United States continued to increase at an unprecedented rate (Table 3.1). Since in most of these countries, i.e. countries classified as the Chinese and Russian type, current account surplus was the main source for increasing foreign reserves, the deficit of the United States was counterbalanced by the surplus of these countries. Other countries except for the United States are not able to maintain a current account deficit, because it leads to a depreciation of their currency that makes them reduce the current account deficit. But, as we have seen in the case of China, Russia and India, the currency authorities of these countries intervened in foreign exchange markets in order to keep their currency low against the dollar. This was the revived Bretton Woods system, where the United States was able to keep the value of the dollar high in spite of the tremendous increase in current account deficits (Dooley *et al.*, 2003; Eichengreen, 2007; Obstfeld and Rogoff, 2010, pp. 157–58). It should be recalled that in the original Bretton Woods system (1944–73), the core was the United States and the periphery was Europe (especially West Germany) and Japan. The periphery was committed to export-led growth, based on maintenance of an undervalued exchange rate.

Causes of the global imbalance

Roughly speaking, there are two opinions regarding the causes of the global imbalance. Some scholars emphasize the undervaluation of national currencies in emerging economies as its major cause. They argue that emerging economies intervened in foreign exchange markets in order to undervalue their currency, which led to the accumulation of a current account surplus. The idea of the revived Bretton Woods system is based on this argument. Ferguson and Schularick (2007) further advanced this idea into a two-country model, called 'Chimerica', where all emerging economies are represented by China and where China and the United States form the world. They argued that before the global financial crisis, there were win-win relations: the export-led growth in China and the expansion of consumption in the United States. Keidel (2011, pp. 369–71) also contended that China's trade surplus caused high savings in the country, but he emphasized that the large trade deficit of the United States was not due to China's trade surplus, but due to malregulation of the financial sector in the United States.

Other scholars stress savings and investment imbalance as the main cause of the global imbalance. They argue that the currency authorities of emerging economies intervened in foreign exchange markets in the face of a growing inflow of foreign currencies, caused by savings and investment imbalance. For example, Caballero *et al.* (2008) insisted that large net lending in emerging economies due to the underdevelopment of capital markets in their countries prompted the inflow of investment resources, including foreign reserves, into the United States. Obstfeld and Rogoff (2010, pp. 137–38, 147) stressed savings and investment imbalance in China as the underlying causes of the global imbalance, but they advocated oversavings in emerging economies, since they may be necessary as a buffer against future financial crises.

Since a current account surplus equals the net lending of the economy as a whole, I cannot say which opinions regarding the cause of the global imbalance are right. But, I may point out the following. First, my argument in this chapter is in line to some extent with the first opinion. For example, I explained the cause of net lending in China's firm and Russia's government sectors by the current account surplus (trade surplus) earned by firms and the government, respectively. Second, nonetheless, I agree that oversavings in emerging economies led to low interest rates in the world, which in turn stimulated overinvestment in developed economies, including the United States. Low interest rates increased stock and commodity market prices, including oil prices, foreign investments to developing countries, and the notorious subprime loans.

58 *Economic development*

Changes during and after the global financial crisis

There seem to be considerable changes in the mechanisms for accumulating foreign reserves in China, Russia and India after the global financial crisis in 2008–9. In Russia and India, their currencies depreciated sharply and their foreign reserves greatly decreased in defense of their currencies during the crisis. Even after 2010, their foreign reserves have not increased as rapidly as before due to the decrease in inflow of foreign currencies into exchange markets. In China, the increase in foreign reserves continued even in the crisis period. Their rate of increase, however, has fallen since 2011 due to some changes in inflow of foreign currencies and S-I balance. On the part of the United States, there were substantial changes in its current account and net lending of the economy.

China

China returned to the dollar peg in July 2008 just before the outbreak of the global financial crisis (Figure 3.1). In 2008 and 2009, while almost all other emerging economies suffered from significant depreciation of their national currencies, the RMB significantly appreciated in tandem with the dollar. The peg to the dollar in this difficult period may have been made possible by the existence of enormous amounts of international reserves. In June 2010, China announced a return to the managed float. IMF (2011, pp. 601–2) has classified China's exchange rate arrangement as a 'crawl-like arrangement' since then.[3] The RMB has gradually appreciated since 2010, reflecting some loosening in exchange rate management.

In contrast to Russia and India, China's foreign reserves continued to increase during the crisis in 2008–10 by more than $400 billion every year (Figure 3.2). This means that there was pressure towards appreciation, not depreciation, of the RMB during this period. In this situation, the policy of keeping the nominal rate of the RMB stable has not much changed. However, as a percentage of GDP, both the increase in foreign reserves and current account surpluses have significantly decreased since 2009 (Table 3.1).[4] Net inflow of FDI remains large in terms of absolute amounts and as a percentage of GDP after 2010. It should be noted that in terms of outbound FDI, China has outstripped Russia since 2008 and outflow of FDI reached $116.8 billion in 2012 (1.4 percent of GDP).

In accordance with the decrease in current account surpluses as a percentage of GDP after 2010, net lending of the economy decreased substantially. This was mainly due to the increase in net borrowing in firms, which increased from 5.6 percent of GDP in 2004–07 to 11.2 percent of GDP in 2010–11 (Table 3.2). This in turn was caused by the increase in the investment rate of firms: from 27.7 percent to 31.8 percent of GDP in the same period. As a result, China's investment rate for the whole economy increased from 42.5 percent in 2004–07 to 48.2 percent in 2010–11. This may reflect the change in the orientation of China's economy from exports to a domestic economy.

Regional powers in international finance   59

While foreign reserves are still increasing, the increase in money supply has continued and issuing of PBC bills has decreased considerably, which means that sterilization has become increasingly insufficient (Figure 3.2).[5]

Russia

In Russia, the ruble fell against the currency basket by 29 percent from August 2008 to February 2009 (Figure 3.1). During this period, the CBR strongly intervened in foreign exchange markets to defend the ruble, but was unable to maintain the de facto pegged arrangement against the basket. From November 2008, the CBR explicitly adopted a policy of gradual depreciation, which, unfortunately, stimulated further depreciation. Russia's foreign reserves decreased by $210 billion (35.1 percent) from August 2008 to February 2009 (Figure 3.3). On January 23, 2009, the CBR abandoned the policy of gradual depreciation of the ruble and declared a new lower limit of the ruble rate against the basket. Since then, the exchange rate of the ruble has more or less stabilized, while the magnitude of intervention of the CBR into exchange markets has decreased considerably. The IMF (2009, pp. 1967–68) has classified Russia's exchange rate arrangement as 'other managed arrangement' since November 2008, admitting more flexibility in exchange rate policies.

The adoption of a more flexible exchange regime than before was a result of a change in monetary policy as a whole. Since 2009, the CBR has paid more attention to restricting inflation than to the stability of the exchange rate of the ruble. The monetary authorities had also to take into consideration that in 2009 and 2010 the federal budget recorded a deficit, which made sterilization more difficult to pursue. In this period, budget deficits became one of the main causes of the increase in money supply in Russia. This made a strong contrast with the period from 2004 to 2008, when a great amount of budget surplus was accumulated in the stabilization fund.

Accordingly, the annual increase in foreign reserves fell from $90.8 billion (9.5 percent of GDP) in 2004–07 to $26.5 billion (1.5 percent of GDP) in 2010–12 (Table 3.1). Both the current account surplus and inflow of foreign investments as a percentage of GDP have decreased considerably. In accordance with this change, net lending of the economy fell to 4.9 percent of GDP in 2010–11, mainly due to its decrease in the government sector, which declined from 8.8 percent of GDP in 2004–07 to 4.1 percent of GDP in the same period (Table 3.2).

India

As was the case in Russia, the national currency of India during the global financial crisis depreciated and foreign reserves fell remarkably. The rupee's value fell by 23 percent from January 2008 to March 2009 (Figure 3.1). The monetary authorities tried in vain to defend the rupee, and as a result India's foreign reserves fell by $66 billion (21.6 percent) in this period (Figure 3.4).

60 *Economic development*

The amount and percentage of this decline, however, were smaller than in Russia. One of the underlying factors in the depreciation of the rupee was the increase in current account deficits.

The exchange rate of the rupee recovered from April 2009, and there seems to be no change in the exchange rate policy that aimed for stability of the exchange rate in real terms. As a result, foreign reserves gradually increased in 2009 and 2010.

From August 2011, however, the rupee considerably depreciated until the end of 2011 and its recovery afterwards was not remarkable. In the period from August to December 2011, India's foreign reserves fell by $23.1 billion. The depreciation of the rupee in 2011 was due to the instability of the European financial markets as was the case in many emerging economies. The specificity of India lies in the fact that the current account deficit in 2010–12 ($69.5 billion) was larger than that in 2008–09 ($28.6 billion) (Table 3.1). Especially in 2012, it amounted to $91.5 billion (4.9 percent of GDP). This was the largest ever in the history of India both in terms of its amount and its ratio to GDP. The increase in current account deficits corresponded to the increase in net borrowing of the economy, mainly due to the increase in net lending in the government sector from 4.8 percent of GDP in 2004–07 to 6.2 percent of GDP in 2010–11 (Table 3.2).

USA

The current account deficit of the USA has significantly declined since 2007 after peaking at $798.5 billion in 2006. Its average for 2010–12 ($449.2 billion) was somewhat larger than the average for 2000–2003 ($447.3 billion) (Table 3.1). Its ratio to GDP peaked at 6.0 percent in 2006 as well and fell to 3.0 percent in 2010–12. Accordingly, net borrowing of the economy decreased significantly. There was a change from net borrowing (0.7 percent of GDP in 2001–07) to net lending (7.8 percent of GDP in 2010–12) in the private sector (domestic business and households), while net borrowing in the government sector increased from 4.1 percent to 10.7 percent of GDP in the same period due to the increase in expenditure for counter-measures against the global financial crisis.[6]

Prospects of the international financial system

Although their underlying mechanisms significantly differed, China, Russia and India accumulated foreign reserves and contributed to the global imbalance to a great degree. Under the global financial crisis, however, the mechanism for accumulating foreign reserves seems to have come to a halt in these countries. In fact, in Russia and India, foreign reserves have not increased, and in China, their rate of increase has significantly slowed since 2011. On the part of the United States, there were some substantial changes in economic policy, and there is little possibility that the continued increase in current account deficits through the expansion in imports for household consumption will resume in the near future.

If we consider the role of these regional powers in the world economy in the future, we should take into account the following two points. The first is the fact that they hold a huge amount of foreign reserves in dollars. Since they will suffer a considerable loss due to possible depreciation of the dollar, these assets should be regarded as hostage. As of the end of 2012, while developed countries accounted for 35.3 percent of foreign reserves (Japan's share was 10.7 percent), 64.7 percent was owned by emerging and developing economies. Among them, Asia accounted for 36.6 percent (China 29.1 percent and India 2.4 percent), the Middle East and North Africa accounted for 11.3 percent (Saudi Arabia 5.7 percent), and Russia accounted for 4.3 percent.[7] In the absence of a key currency other than the US dollar, most of these reserves are held in dollar-denominated assets like US Treasury securities.[8] Thus, in the 2000s, regional powers not only became responsible for the international financial system, but also found themselves in a position of inevitably having to cooperate so as to maintain the value of the dollar. This situation may not change in the foreseeable future.

Second, we have to take account of the costs of increasing foreign reserves. In particular, when sterilization is insufficient, the inflation risk becomes large in any country, and if foreign reserves increase too fast, in other words, the monetary authorities buy too many dollars in foreign exchange markets, sterilization apparently becomes insufficient. In addition, in countries like Russia and China, where a factor contributing to the increase in foreign reserves is current account surplus, large net lending of the economy continues due to either an extraordinary high savings rate as in China or an extraordinary low investment rate as in Russia.

Concerning the future development scenario of the world economy, we may forecast that worldwide stagnation and financial turmoil will continue for a while. This forecast is based on the conventional way of thinking that the growth of the world economy depends on the economic situation in developed countries after all. It follows from this that if the European and US economies recover, then the mechanism of foreign reserve accumulation will resume, not only in China, but also in other emerging economies, including India and Russia.

But we may argue the possibility that in no distant future the growth of the world economy will be driven not by developed countries, but by regional powers. We had better doubt whether developed countries will be able to continuously boost demand for goods and services supplied by regional powers. Instead, increases in demand in regional powers with large domestic markets may become the driving force for economic growth in the rest of the world. In this scenario, current account surplus and deficit in the world would be completely differently distributed, compared with the period of global imbalance. In fact, there are visible signs of this trend. For example, demand for exports to China has great significance for the economies of developed countries; the Russian

62   *Economic development*

market for passenger cars is becoming important for Japanese, European and US automobile makers; and some foreign investors have begun to regard India as a promising location for manufacturing industries.

It is true that developed countries dominate the international financial market in terms of gross assets or liabilities. But we cannot ignore the presence of regional powers in global business fluctuations and in the movement of capital, including foreign reserves. In this way, the period of global imbalance may have been only the first stage at which the role of regional powers in the world economy started to grow.

Notes

1 Crawling peg is one of the exchange rate arrangements in which the currency is adjusted in small amounts at a fixed rate or in response to changes in selected quantitative indicators (IMF, 2012, p. 61).
2 China's current transfer surplus was large as well, amounting to $29.0 billion (1.1 percent of GDP) in 2004–07. Russia during this period registered a small current transfer deficit ($1.7 billion and 0.2 percent of GDP).
3 A crawl-like arrangement is an exchange rate arrangement in which the exchange rate must remain within a narrow margin of 2 percent of a statistically identified trend. The minimum rate of change is greater than that allowed under a stabilized (peg-like) arrangement (IMF, 2012, p. 61).
4 In 2012, the increase in China's foreign reserves was 'only' $96.6 billion, while it was $387.8 billion in 2011. In contrast, 'other investment' fell from $8.7 billion in 2011 to minus $260.0 billion in 2012 (*IFS*, 2014). Hanemann and Rosen (2013) argued that this was due to the temporary change in the behavior of firms and households: they preferred to maintain foreign currency deposits in expectation of future depreciation of the RMB.
5 The analysis by Kajitani (2011, pp. 87–89) based on PBC's balance sheets demonstrated the decline in significance of sterilization by PBC bills after 2008. Kwan (2011) argues that, since 2007, the monetary authorities have switched to hiking the statutory reserve requirement ratio in order to reduce the increase in money supply.
6 Calculated from the website of the Bureau of Economic Analysis, US Department of Commerce (www.bea.gov/iTable/iTable.cfm?ReqID=9&step=1) last accessed on January 13, 2014.
7 Russia and India lowered their ranking from third to fourth and from sixth to tenth, respectively, in the period from 2007 to 2012.
8 It is well known that there is a long-term trend of official reserve diversification away from US dollars among emerging economies (Obstfeld and Rogoff, 2010, pp. 160–61).

References

Caballero, Ricardo J., Emmanuel Farhi and Pierre-Olivier Gourinchas (2008) 'An Equilibrium Model of "Global Imbalances" and Low Interest Rates', *American Economic Review*, vol. 98, no. 1, pp. 358–93.

Dooley, Michael, David Folkerts-Landau, and Peter Garber (2003) *An Essay on the Revived Bretton Woods System* Cambridge, MA: NBER Working Paper Series, no. 9971.

Regional powers in international finance 63

Eichengreen, Barry (2007) *Global Imbalances and the Lessons of Bretton Woods*, Cambridge, MA: MIT Press.

Ferguson, Niall and Moritz Schularick (2007) 'Chimerica and the Global Asset Market Boom', *International Finance*, vol. 10, no. 3, pp. 215–39.

——(2009) *The End of Chimerica*, Harvard Business School, Working Paper, 10–037.

Hanemann, Thilo and Daniel Rosen (2013) *China's International Investment Position: An Update*, April 23 (http://rhg.com/notes/chinas-international-investment-position-an-update) last accessed on January 8, 2014.

International Financial Statistics (IFS) (2014) (on CD-ROM), Washington, DC: IMF, last accessed January 15, 2014.

International Monetary Fund (IMF) (various years) *Annual Report on Exchange Arrangements and Exchange Restrictions*, Washington, DC: IMF.

Kajitani, Kai (2011) *Gendai chugoku no zaisei kinyu sisutemu* [Financial System of Contemporary China]. Nagoya: University of Nagoya Press (in Japanese).

Keidel, Albert (2011) 'China's Exchange Rate Controversy: A Balanced Analysis', *Eurasian Geography and Economics*, vol. 52, no. 3, pp. 347–74.

Kwan, Chi Hung (2011) 'Growth in Money Supply Slowing Down Sharply on the Back of Credit Tightening', *China in Transition*, July 28 (www.rieti.go.jp/en/china/11072801.html) last accessed on January 31, 2014.

National Bureau of Statistics (NBS) (various years) *China Statistical Yearbook*, Beijing: China Statistics Press.

Obstfeld, Maurice and Kenneth Rogoff (2010) 'Global Imbalances and the Financial Crisis: Products of Common Causes', in Reuven Glick and Mark M. Spiegel, eds, *Asia and the Global Financial Crisis*, San Francisco, CA: Federal Reserve Bank of San Francisco, pp. 131–72.

Reserve Bank of India (RBI) (2013) *Handbook of Statistics on Indian Economy 2012–13* (www.rbi.org.in/scripts/AnnualPublications.aspx?head=Handbook%20of%20Statistics%20on%20Indian%20Economy) last accessed January 12, 2014.

Rosstat (Federal State Statistics Service of Russia) *Natsional'nye scheta Rossii* [*National Accounts of Russia*], Moscow: Rosstat, various years (in Russian).

Tabata, Shinichiro (2007) 'The Russian Stabilization Fund and Its Successor: Implications for Inflation', *Eurasian Geography and Economics*, vol. 48, no. 6, pp. 699–712.

——(2009) 'The Impact of Global Financial Crisis on the Mechanism of Economic Growth in Russia', *Eurasian Geography and Economics*, vol. 50, no. 6, pp. 682–98.

——(2011) 'Growth in the International Reserves of Russia, China, and India: A Comparison of Underlying Mechanisms', *Eurasian Geography and Economics*, vol. 52, no. 3, pp. 409–27.

——(2012) 'Observations on Russian Exposure to the Dutch Disease', *Eurasian Geography and Economics*, vol. 53, no. 2, pp. 231–43.

Uegaki, Akira (2010) 'Balance of Payments in Comparative Perspective: China, India and Russia under Globalization', in Akira Uegaki and Shinichiro Tabata, eds, *The Elusive Balance: Regional Powers and the Search for Sustainable Development*, Comparative Studies on Regional Powers, no. 2, Sapporo: Slavic Research Center, Hokkaido University, pp. 59–82.

Part II
Political systems and diplomacy

4 Power and limitations of dominant party control

United Russia, the Indian National Congress and the Chinese Communist Party compared

Atsushi Ogushi and Yuko Adachi

Introduction

There is no doubt that the rise of regional powers in Eurasia (China, India and Russia) is having a significant impact on the world order. These countries are to become new centers in the international economic system, a revived Bretton Woods system (Tabata and Uegaki, 2011; Tabata, 2011). In terms of international politics, some argue that if the world community fails to incorporate these rising powers, we may face a new 'twenty years' crisis' (Sakwa, 2008).

Still, the impact of the regional powers may not be limited to international relations. They can remind us of several important factors in establishing a political order in a huge country with a rapidly developing economy, diversifying social strata, and various ethnic and linguistic groups. Such difficulties make regional powers particularly interesting to comparative political scientists, because the regional power countries we analyze have been more or less successful in solving the difficulties of making a political order (had they failed, they would have been just failing states, and not regional powers, by definition). We argue that one of the keys to establishing a stable political order is the role of the dominant party, which works as an integrating mechanism in such huge, developing and changing countries. As all dominant parties are not similar, we advance two different ideal types of dominant party: the regime-building and the regime-adapting types. Within this framework, we locate three dominant parties in Eurasia: the Chinese Communist Party, the Indian National Congress, and United Russia. We discuss the functions and limitations of dominant party control in these countries.

Why dominant parties in regional powers?

Conventional wisdom states that a political party is essential for stable political order in any changing society (Huntington, 1968). Moreover, the presence of dominant parties is certainly not limited to growing regional powers.[1] Still, there seem to be several reasons why a dominant party is a useful

68 *Political systems and diplomacy*

mechanism for sustaining the political order in regional powers. First, a dominant party is useful for containing regionalism. It can channel various interests into the central authority. This function is of particular importance in Eurasian regional powers, because they have diverse ethnic and linguistic groups in their huge territories. In other words, Eurasian regional powers need elaborate mechanisms for integrating centrifugal forces. A dominant party seems to be one such mechanism. It co-opts almost all important elites into a single political organization, which makes it difficult for them to defect from the party line.

Second, a dominant party, by definition, dominates parliament. Therefore, the law-making process is much smoother under dominant party rule, which, in turn, makes it easier for the political leadership to adapt to a changing environment. This problem is also more acute in regional powers; they are rapidly growing in terms of their economy; their social change is more rapid; and the international community tends to put strong pressure on them. For example, joining the WTO required China and Russia to make a lot of legal adjustments. Without dominant parties, their law-making would have necessitated greater efforts.

Third, the dominant party can play a redistributing function under the growing economy of a regional power. As typically exemplified by the Liberal Democratic Party of Japan (LDPJ), a dominant party frequently undertakes so-called pork-barrel politics (benefiting the electorate in return for electoral support). Although this practice has been criticized in terms of unfair competition, it also means redistribution from the wealthy capital city to the regions. For such pork-barrel legislation, the merger of political and executive forces, which usually takes place under a dominant party regime, seems a necessary condition.

Fourth, a dominant party secures the continuity of a general policy line despite changes of leadership. In an authoritarian regime, as Geddes (1999) argues, the succession problem can be solved more easily under a dominant party. If this issue fails to be solved, it may lead to regime breakdown. Because regime breakdown entails a fall from regional power status, the stability that a dominant party can provide is of importance in regional powers.

Typology of dominant parties

Even if, as we discussed, the dominant party plays an important role in establishing political order in regional powers, dominant parties are not identical. Rather, the dominant parties that we analyze are very different. We should at least distinguish two ideal types of dominant party. First, some dominant parties can build the essential characteristics of the political regime. Parties of this kind have very strong discipline, systemic ideology, and centralized control. They usually become dominant through revolution, civil war, and/or harsh struggles (Smith, 2005; Levitsky and Way, 2012). We call this type a 'regime-building dominant party', a typical example of which is the Communist Party of the Soviet Union (CPSU). In our case, the Chinese Communist Party is included in this type. We can also include religious fundamentalist parties in this category.

Second, other dominant parties do not shape a political regime but adapt themselves to the existing political regime. They are based more upon patronage. Political elites may ally with a dominant party because of the benefits or 'pork' that the party in government can supply. A party of this kind can be called a 'regime-adapting dominant party'. The LDPJ was, we believe, such a regime-adapting dominant party. The LDPJ was formed as a result of conservative politicians' adaptation to post-World War II democracy in Japan, but we cannot contend that the politicians of the LDPJ constructed the Japanese democratic regime. As we will see, the Indian National Congress in its dominant party period can be regarded as a regime-adapting one.

It should be noted that our typology of dominant parties is an ideal: one real party can have both features or can change its nature as its domination becomes stable. Although, for example, the Soviet Communist Party was much closer to the regime-building type in its early period, it was compromised by regime-adapting or patronal elements in the Brezhnev era. On the other hand, a regime-adapting party may transform itself into an ideological one to strengthen its identity.

The regime-building dominant party is frequently identified in a rather strict authoritarian regime. A party of this kind does not allow fair competition in national elections and seeks to sustain its dominance through monopoly of the political space. Organized opposition, for example, was strictly prohibited in the Soviet Union. Neither would religious fundamentalist parties allow oppositions. On the other hand, regime-adapting dominant parties more often than not emerge in more competitive political regimes. In order for the dominant party to be continuously dominant in a competitive environment, it necessarily becomes prone to resorting to the pork-barrel, which, in turn, defines the nature of the party.

This is also connected with party–state (executive) relations. Party control over the executive body is often a striking feature of the political regime under a regime-building dominant party. In communist countries, the communist parties claimed (or, in the case of the CCP, is still claiming) the 'leading role'. In the case of a regime-adapting dominant party, it depends on the executive body to a significant degree. For the party, its ties with the executive body are the key to distributing the 'pork' that the executive body can supply. If it loses connection with the executive body, it cannot sustain itself. The Japanese case clearly demonstrates this. When the LDPJ lost its governmental position in 1993, many LDP deputies switched their party affiliation to the governmental coalition because it was essential for the switched deputies to keep their ties with the executive body in order to attract investments, and invite development programs, etc. to their electoral districts. Thus, we can recognize a continuum from a leading party type to an executive-dependent one.

The contrast between a regime-building dominant party and a regime-adapting one is also obvious in their internal structures. A regime-building dominant party usually has strong discipline. Therefore, its structure is centralized. Party leadership claims greater control over cadre policy. It is well known

70 *Political systems and diplomacy*

that the communist parties had/have the *nomenklatura* system, through which the party leadership managed/manages cadres of the party and the entire country as well. The decision-making process is also a top-down one. The leader's decision, however difficult, must be implemented. The communist parties' 'democratic centralism' is a well-known example of this. A regime-adapting dominant party is, on the other hand, frequently loosely organized. A party of this kind tends to become a coalition of regional notables who have a mobilizing capacity in elections. Strict control over them may damage their capacity. The decision-making process is, rather, a bottom-up one. Final approval of a decision by the party leadership is obtained through long negotiations among various deputies, interest groups, and civil servants. Table 4.1 summarizes the discussion of two ideal types of dominant party.[2]

Functions of dominant parties in Eurasian regional powers: an overview

Let us locate the three dominant parties in our case: the Chinese Communist Party (CCP), United Russia and the Indian National Congress (INC), in the scheme above. Table 4.2 shows a basic outline of each party. We locate the CCP in the regime-building dominant category; the INC is situated in the regime-adapting one; and United Russia is somewhere between the two types.

Table 4.1 Typology of dominant parties

	Regime-Building Dominant Party	Regime-Adapting Dominant Party
Political Regime	Authoritarian	Competitive or democratic
Party-State Relations	Party-led	Dependence upon the executive body
Internal Structure	Centralized	Loose

Table 4.2 Characteristics of dominant parties in Eurasian regional powers

Name of Party	Chinese Communist Party	United Russia	Indian National Congress
Type of Party	Regime-building dominant party	Regime-adapting dominant party	Regime-adapting dominant party
Political Regime	Authoritarian	Competitive authoritarian/ hybrid regime	Democratic
Party-State Relations	Party-led	Executive-led	Merger of the party and state
Internal Structure	Highly centralized	Moderately centralized	Flexible (at the early time)

The Chinese Communist Party

The CCP can be considered to be a regime-building dominant party.[3] Just like other communist regimes, the CCP has framed the basic characteristics of the political regime in China. Some may question the ideological element of the CCP. Although the ideology certainly plays a much less significant role at the present time than in the Mao period, some lip service to communist ideology is still paid by the party leaders; it is instructive that, when the party leadership decided to accept rising economically rich social groups as party members at the 16th Party Congress, there were some debates over the ideological correctness of the policy. Besides ideology, the CCP is an essential part of the regime; the CCP has not only strong coercive power, but also a systemic cadre allocation mechanism, as we shall see. Its democratic centralism and ban on factions are still important factors in sustaining the cohesion. These mechanisms derive, at least in part, from the communist ideology and the preceding example of the Soviet Communist Party (we can add the experience of the war against Japan and the civil war, of course). At any rate, the CCP is one of the most typical examples of a regime-building dominant party.

The present political regime that the CCP has built is ordinarily authoritarian or post-totalitarian. It has neither its previous mobilizing capacity nor a charismatic dictator, that is, it is no longer totalitarian. But it never permits competitive elections at the national level, and organized opposition is strictly prohibited, which means that it is not a competitive authoritarian regime or a hybrid regime.

Party–state relations are one of the keys to understanding the communist party regime. The constitutional 'leading role' is an essential part of the CCP. The CCP, like the Soviet Communist Party, has developed mechanisms for controlling the state bodies. For instance, the party groups are organized into executive bodies, which monitor the executive bodies' work; the party apparatus is structured in parallel to the state branches. This leads to the 'substitution' of executive work by the party. Moreover, in the *nomenklatura* system, the party allocates personnel to the state bodies. Several attempts to reform them in the late 1980s notwithstanding, these mechanisms are basically intact or restored after the Tiananmen Square incident (Tang, 1997, Chs 1–3; Chan, 2004). The Soviet demise, it seems, further strengthened the CCP leaders' determination not to change party–state relations. This highly centralized nature of the CCP is also clear in its center–regional relations (as we will see in the next section).

In addition, the elite recruitment system of the party has worked reasonably well. Among party ranks, the proportion of peasants and workers is decreasing constantly. In the late 1990s, it became less than half. At its expense, the ratio of intellectuals, professionals, state and party officials, managers and others is increasing. The 16th CCP congress in 2002 officially decided to broaden its social base. Despite some criticisms, it is attempting to change itself from a class party to a national one (Mouri, 2004, pp. 137–42).

72   *Political systems and diplomacy*

The Indian National Congress

The Indian National Congress (INC) is situated at the opposite pole to the CCP. That is, it is a regime-adapting dominant party. However, the INC had more regime-building elements than the LDPJ that we mentioned as a typical example of a regime-adapting dominant party. The INC originated in the anti-colonial independence movement, which gave the INC an all-embracing character. In its early period, the INC was a party of the whole nation. As it was more movement than party, its organizational principle was flexible. It allowed active internal discussion and regional autonomy; it was proud of its secularism and charismatic leaders like Mahatma Gandhi and Nehru; and, remarkably, the INC for long time sustained its dominance under democratic conditions. India maintains more or less fair competitive elections and the INC won the majority until 1989 (except for a short rupture in 1977–80 due to the emergency declaration in 1975). Kothari (1999), a well-known Indian political scientist, called the INC's early dominance a 'congress system' based on national consensus and flexible organization.[4] Some may argue that the INC was a regime-builder.

Nevertheless, taking into account the reasons for its long-term dominance, the INC can be included in the regime-adapting category. In addition to the reasons mentioned above (the INC's authority deriving from the independence movement, its developed organizational basis, charismatic leaders and its secular character), the weakness of opposition parties was a factor as well (Hirose, 1994, pp. 97–100; 1991, pp. 79–80). Still another important factor seems to be the patronage function that the INC played. Chandra (2004, pp. 115–42) argues that the Indian political system is a 'patronage-democracy', in which the state provides people with security (policing), jobs, such materials essential for livelihood as land and water through regulation procedures, credit of nationalized banks, paved roads, anti-poverty programs, state-run hospitals, and so forth. Under harsh living conditions, ordinary, and especially poor people have no choice but to rely on the state services. Politicians in a ruling party can, in turn, convert their control over the governmental bodies into votes. This was one of the reasons for the INC's strength. Hirose, a Japanese scholar, demonstrates the activities of the INC party workers to redress ordinary people's grievances. People go to party workers to ask for help in resolving many personal (not political at all) issues. For example, a party leader met someone who had a problem with his eyesight. The party worker wrote a letter to governmental officials asking to have his applicant treated at a state hospital. Such onerous work by party leaders provided the INC with sufficient power (Hirose, 1994, pp. 94–95; 1991, pp. 76–78; see also Hankla, 2008).

This mechanism could not be sustained without the close interpenetration or merger of the state and the INC. There seem to have existed trianglar relations among the party, executive bodies, and voters. The party could press the executive bodies to serve the ordinary people's demands; the executive bodies exercised a variety of regulating powers over ordinary people (voters); and, then, the ultimate basis of INC dominance was voters' support. This necessitated flexible organization within the INC. If the lower party organizations were not responsive to regional demands, these triangular relations would no longer be sustainable. Contrary to the CCP's organizational principle, the INC had a less disciplined or very flexible organization that was necessary for collecting votes under democratic conditions.

Similarly, the INC's elite-recruitment system used to be open. Competitive rules in the party were established in 1920, that is, well before independence. The INC could recruit rural elites into the party, many of whom at that time were landlords and high-ranking castes (Chandra, 2004, pp. 249–51). In this sense, Congress dominance reflects the social hierarchy in rural areas. Based on his observation of Bihar State, Nakamizo (2010, p. 202), a Japanese specialist in Indian politics, states that Congress dominance was rule of the landlord class. For a long time, the landlord class's rule worked well for successful independence, and sustained the social hierarchy of Indian society.

United Russia

United Russia is located somewhere between the highly centralized and disciplined CCP and the very flexible and less centralized INC. Still, United Russia is reasonably closer to a regime-adapting dominant party than to a regime-building one. Let us briefly discuss the origin and functions of United Russia.[5] In the 1990s, one characteristic of the Russian party system was that there was no strong national party (with the partial exception of the Russian Communist Party). Regional governors monopolized the so-called 'administrative resource', including such social infrastructure as heating, housing, and so forth. This turned into governors' mobilizing power in an electoral period. When the regional administration made clear its favored candidate and brought informal pressure to bear on the electorate (e.g. spreading rumors of the possibility of a heating problem during winter time in the case of failure of the administration's candidate), the electorate would be vulnerable to such pressure. In addition, the lower elites in a region tried to mobilize voters to demonstrate their loyalty to their boss, the regional governor. There was, therefore, a variety of regional parties existing in the 1990s. Regional bosses were, as Hale (2006) argues, 'party substitutes' and no well-institutionalized national party emerged (see also Golosov, 2004).

Putin changed this picture to a certain degree. In addition to several legal measures, including the law on parties, electoral reform, and so forth, he centralized the executive power. Reform of the Federation Council was attempted; power to dismiss regional governors and to dissolve the regional parliaments was attained by the president; and regional governors were to be appointed by the president (with the approval of the regional parliament). Finally President Putin made clear his commitment to United Russia. When these three effects (pressure to create a national party, centralization, and the president's clear commitment to United Russia) combined, regional governors rapidly allied with United Russia, which made United Russia the first dominant party in

74 *Political systems and diplomacy*

post-communist Russia (Hale, 2004; Aburamoto, 2008; Reuter and Remington, 2009; Reuter, 2010). This party is an organization in which regional governors participated under the direction of the central executive leadership.

The political regime in Russia is regarded as competitive authoritarianism in which competitive elections take place but where competition is not fair (Levitsky and Way, 2010). This regime characteristic defines the nature of United Russia. Under competitive authoritarianism, elections are one of the most important mechanisms for regime legitimacy and it is necessary for the dominant party to continue to win elections. In order to win elections, regional bosses keep some autonomy under the guise of the centralized party. When the central leadership presses regional governors to mobilize the electorate for United Russia, the mobilization in practice depends on the 'administrative resource' that the regional governor has, which gives them some kind of regional autonomy. Thus, the appointing power of the president notwithstanding, Putin reappointed most governors (more than 65 percent). As Aburamoto (2010), a Japanese scholar, argues, many influential regional governors were untouchable even for the Kremlin. This is considered to exemplify reciprocal relations between patron (center) and clients (regional governors). Based on such a patronage network from the central, through the regional, to the local level, United Russia has so far sustained its dominance. Its character of a partially centralized and partially regional-autonomous organization is a reflection of Russian competitive authoritarianism. Therefore, we can regard United Russia as more of a regime-adapting dominant party.

Now, we can recognize one of the reasons that dominant parties are/were strong in each country. Under non-competitive conditions, the disciplined CCP leads the state and works rather effectively. The CCP framed the nature of the political regime in China. On the other hand, the flexible organization of the INC was necessary for sustaining its dominance under competitive or democratic conditions. Under partially competitive or competitive authoritarian conditions, the moderately centralized United Russia party functions as a dominant party. In these two countries, the nature of the political regimes define(d) the characters of the dominant parties. There then arises this question: what happens to the party when centralization is attempted? We discuss this in the next section.

Centralization by dominant parties in Eurasian regional powers

As will be shown, there have been centralization attempts in these countries. Centralization has worked well so far in China, but it had a destructive effect in India. In Russia, some mixed process seems to be taking place.

China

In China, some de facto decentralization occurred after the economic reforms. When Deng Xiaoping tried to change the economic system immediately after Mao's death, he needed some supporters among provincial politicians, as his political base was not consolidated at that time (Wu, 2000, pp. 40–42). Economic reform afterwards unleashed economic decentralization and even led to some conflicts between the center and the provinces, and among provinces. So-called 'dukedom economies' flourished (Zhao, 1998). The central leadership criticized 'localism', but could not do more than that.

The Chinese centralization efforts took place in response to this de facto decentralization. In addition, it is important to note that the decentralization mentioned above mostly concerned the economic rather than the political sphere. The center, therefore, always had the potential to recover the initiative. First, the center reshuffled the provincial cadres. On July 7, 1990, the CCP Central Committee decided to transfer party and state cadres between the central and provincial levels and among provinces (and even the lower levels).[6] This prevented a provincial politician (a party secretary, for example) from establishing a base in the province. According to a recent report, some 633,000 party and state officials were transferred in the whole country after the 17th Party Congress of October 2007 to 2008. At the central level, some 307 cadres were shuffled from the 17th Party Congress until December 2009. Among them, some 107 were transferred within the central party and state level; some 40 moved down to the provinces; within the provincial level, some 53 officials were relocated; and from the provincial to central level, 66 were moved.[7] Such massive reshuffling of provincial cadres is unimaginable even in the Soviet Union, in which some sort of 'affirmative action' regarding ethnic groups was applied and when, in the Brezhnev period, a policy of 'trust in cadres' was implemented, which led to the situation whereby a regional party secretary was born, educated, and promoted in the region itself. Arbitrary reshuffling like China's would have provoked strong resistance in the CPSU. In this sense, the CCP is more centralized than the CPSU.

Second, the party introduced the mandatory retirement system in 1987. Provincial party secretaries, for example, have to retire at the age of 65 as a rule, which encouraged cadre turnover (Tang, 2000, p. 263). Again, this is a stricter policy than in Brezhnev's CPSU, in which gerontocracy was a constant problem. A mandatory retirement system was attempted under Gorbachev (and the CPSU dissolved itself a few years later).

Still more remarkably, such large reshuffling of party-state cadres has so far coexisted with rapid economic growth in China. One report states that the better the economic performance of a province is, the more likely is the promotion of provincial cadres (Li and Zhou, 2005). Although we cannot decide whether or not this policy is a main factor in Chinese economic growth, it is clear that cadre reshuffling has not damaged the economy and political stability so far. One reason for such relative stability seems to be the highly centralized nature of the CCP and its strong control over the state under *noncompetitive* conditions. The crisis in the CCP took place just before the Tiananmen Square incident, when the separation of party and state was discussed. The key to the CCP's dominance seems to be how long it can monopolize the political space. In a competitive environment, centralized dominant party control is detrimental, as we will see in the Indian and Russian cases.

India

In India, the INC was gradually centralized in the process of factional struggles. Especially after Indira Gandhi assumed power in 1966, centralization was accelerated. Faced with some defeats in the state elections of 1967, she had to orient the party's policy toward a leftist direction, to which the so-called 'syndicate' group was opposed. She ousted the 'syndicate' group; party elections at the lower levels were suspended in 1972; and the competence of lower party organizations was reduced. Instead, Indira appealed directly to the people with a populist slogan and a war against Pakistan. At first this appeared to be successful. The INC won state elections. Even the declaration of a state of emergency in 1975 pleased many people. Although the following national election was disastrous, the INC could return to power with 67 percent of the parliamentary seats in 1980 (Rudolph and Rudolph, 2008, pp. 28–31).

However, it became increasingly clear that centralization was damaging the INC in the long term. First, the suspension of party elections caused the failure of elite recruitment. Although Indira stopped holding party elections due to struggles with 'bossism', their suspension created defections of the regional elites from the party (Chandra, 2004, pp. 254–55). It is of particular importance that this took place against a background of the gradual politicization of the lower castes (Nakamizo, 2010). Even when these people wanted to participate in politics, the INC did not provide any channel for them because there were no party elections. It continued to be a party of landlords. Dissatisfied lower-caste people began to ally with opposition parties, including regional, ethnic and religious ones, which led to the multi-party system in India. Now, only two national parties play a more or less national role in the Indian party system, but a variety of regional parties are emerging and competing with each other. We wonder whether or not such a situation can continue without unleashing centrifugal forces, because a national party usually plays an integrating role in a large, highly fragmented country (Ordeshook, 1996). Many specialists whom we met in India were optimistic, or they said that there were so many cleavages (social, ethnic, linguistic, religious and so forth) even in a single Indian state that a regional party could not advance separatist demands, because it could not rally popular support (see Miwa, 2008 for another example of an optimistic view). This may be the case, but we still have some suspicions about an 'optimistic' view in the long term. It might become a serious problem when economic growth slows and the economy cannot provide a substitute for political legitimacy.

Russia

In China, the Communist Party kept its centralized organization under non-competitive conditions, while the Indian National Congress lost its dominance due to centralization in a competitive political system. The United Russia party is a mixed case. There were some centralizing attempts, which created a crisis.

First, under former president Medvedev, there was a large turnover of regional governors. From the time he assumed the presidency until December 2011 when a parliamentary election was held, some sixty-five governors were appointed, among whom only twenty-six (some 40 percent) were reappointed. That is, thirty-nine (about 60 percent) regional governors were newcomers.[8] These 'replaced' governors included very strong ones like Moscow mayor Yurii Luzhkov, Tatarstan president Mentimir Shaimiev, and Bashkortostan president Murtaza Rakhimov among others.

Second, among the thirty-nine newcomers, there were fourteen 'outsiders' who had never lived in the region before. These people were usually appointed by the pressure of the Kremlin despite the resistance of the regional elites. In such a case the 'outsider' governor frequently failed to manage regional problems.

Third, Medvedev changed the way of appointing regional governors. According to the new method, the central leadership of the majority party in the regional parliament can recommend several candidates for the governorship. Then the president chooses one for a governor.[9] Because now United Russia has a majority in all regional parliaments, this is a method that United Russia recommends de facto. After this method was enacted in November 2009, Medvedev continued to replace old governors with new ones, though there were fewer appointments of outsiders. From November 2009 to December 2012, some forty-eight governors were appointed of which twenty-five were newcomers.

However, such huge turnover seems to have damaged the authority of the governors and lowered the mobilizing capacity. Figure 4.1 shows the trend of

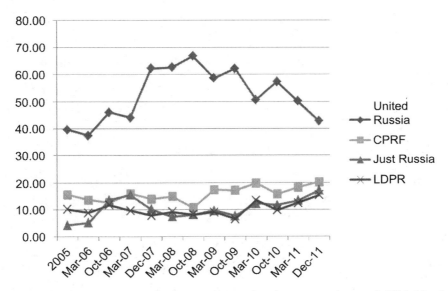

Figure 4.1 Results of regional elections (proportional representation part) 2005–March 2011

78 Political systems and diplomacy

regional elections. Although United Russia has won the majority in all elections since Medvedev's presidency, their percentage of the vote is declining. Moreover the result of the parliamentary election in December 2011 was disastrous, and mass demonstrations alleging electoral fraud followed. Thus, strict control over governors is a double-edged sword for the Kremlin. Let us discuss the two cases in further detail.

The case of Murmansk is a typical for our argument. The former governor Yurii Evdokimov worked as Murmansk Communist Party secretary in the Soviet period. He showed competence in the construction industry and was elected as governor in 1996. Evdokimov was re-elected in 2000 and 2004 by a large majority. He joined United Russia in 2006 and was appointed by President Putin as governor again in 2007 (Zen'kovich, 2007, pp. 133–36). This career indicates that he had a strong base in Murmansk.

The Kremlin later wanted to remove Evdokimov. The precise reason for this is uncertain. Still, first there was a rumor that Evdokimov had a problem with Gazprom, which may have asked the Kremlin to remove him (Petrov and Titkov, 2010, p. 156).[10] In general, development of gas fields is problematic because the central capital wants to cut the cost of constructing the infrastructure, while a governor usually hopes to benefit regional construction companies to the extent possible. Second, there was a conflict between Evdokimov and Mikhail Savchenko, mayor of the regional capital. Savchenko had also worked in the Murmansk City Communist Party organization and in the city administration for long time.

Against a background of conflict between governor and mayor, a mayoral election was to take place in March 2009. Although the Murmansk United Russia organization decided to support Savchenko, Evdokimov refused to support him, and instead supported Sergei Subbotin, deputy regional governor at that time. This split among influential regional elites resulted in a very competitive election. In the first round, Savchenko garnered 31.22 percent of the votes and Subbotin, 24.28 percent. In the final round, Subbotin won. United Russia faced a humiliating defeat.[11] Swiftly, the United Russia party responded by dismissing Evdokimov,[12] but the new governor was 'outsider' Dmitrii Dmitrienko, deputy head of the Federal Fisheries Agency at that time.[13] He failed to create a stable situation in the region. Subbotin resigned his mayoral post a few years later. After that, the city had two mayoral changes. Moreover, as Table 4.3 shows, the number of party members declined in Murmansk, despite the general growth trend in the whole country. In the parliamentary election of December 2011, United Russia gained only

Table 4.3 Number of United Russia members in Murmansk

Date	2009.1.1	2010.1.1	2011.1.1	2012.1.1
Number of members	7,987	8,098	7,947	7,828

Source: Website of the Russian Judicial Ministry (http://www.miniust.ru/ru/activity/nko/partii/ER/). The link is lost.

32.02 percent in Murmansk – the fourth worst result of all regions for the party. Faced with this result, Dmitrienko resigned in April 2012. This Murmansk case demonstrates, first, that United Russia effectively worked as a tool for the Kremlin for removing a strong governor, but, second, that such a strong centralizing measure can create confusion in a region, which may lead to reducing the mobilizing capacity of the United Russia party.

Our argument is supported by the case of Primorskii Krai in the Russian Far East, where the APEC summit of 2012 was held in Vladivostok. Sergei Dar'kin was governor from 2001 to 2012. He joined United Russia in 2004 and became the very first appointed governor since the system of gubernatorial appointments was introduced by Putin in February 2005. Dar'kin voluntarily submitted his resignation and asked Putin to confirm his presidential confidence in him in January 2005.[14]

In May 2008, the mayoral election of Vladivostok took place. The candidacy of Igor' Pushkarev was backed by United Russia, as the Kremlin sought to entrust Pushkarev with preparations for APEC.[15] Dar'kin opposed him, and instead supported a different candidate who eventually withdrew from the race due in part to pressure from the Kremlin. Just three days prior to the Vladivostok mayoral election, law enforcement officers searched Dar'kin's home and office in a corruption probe, although he escaped arrest.[16] Although Dar'kin's removal from office had been speculated, he was able to maintain his position. Pushkarev won the election and became mayor, but failed to show sufficient competence. The Kremlin had to acknowledge that Dar'kin was necessary to make things work in Primorskii Krai, particularly with a view to Russia's hosting of APEC.[17] Eventually he was reappointed by Medvedev in 2010. That is, after United Russia as a majority party in the regional legislature put forward Dar'kin and three other gubernatorial candidates, Medvedev nominated Dar'kin, who was then approved by the regional legislature.[18] However, United Russia in Primorskii Krai suffered a humiliating result in the 2011 parliamentary election, which led to Dar'kin's resignation in February 2012.

Centralization through the United Russia party indicates a mixed picture. It works effectively as a tool of centralization just like the Chinese Communist Party, but centralization itself created confusion and crises in the party, as with the Indian National Congress. As a regime-adapting dominant party under a competitive authoritarian regime, United Russia's capacity to integrate various regional interests has certain limitations. This is, in our view, one of the reasons for United Russia's failure to assume a predominant majority in the 2011 parliamentary election. Medvedev's gubernatorial appointment policy damaged United Russia's mobilizing capacity by lowering governors' authority in the regions.

Conclusion

In this chapter we have compared three dominant parties among Eurasia's regional powers. For the comparison, we advanced two different types of dominant

80 *Political systems and diplomacy*

party: the regime-building and the regime-adapting type. The Chinese Communist Party is a regime-building one and the Indian National Congress a regime-adapting one. United Russia is located somewhere between them. While a regime-building dominant party forms a centralized authoritarian regime, the nature of the regime-adapting dominant party is defined by a competitive political regime, and it cannot coexist with strong centralization. Centralization was a sign of decline of the INC and created some critical problems for United Russia.

We argued that a dominant party is a particularly useful mechanism for regional powers with a huge territory, various ethnic, regional, linguistic and regional groups, a changing social structure, and a growing economy. At the same time, it has some limitations. In the case of a regime-adapting dominant party, as mentioned above, over-centralization is detrimental to the party. While recent literature on comparative politics pays much attention to dominant parties, our argument that focuses on center–regional relations will shed new light on the dominant party regime. In the case of a regime-building party, on the other hand, the problem seems to be whether or not it can continue to monopolize the political space and resist pressure from the international community. We should take into account the fact that the rise of competitive authoritarian regimes around the world was the product of a US hegemony that argued for competitive elections as an international norm. It is still to be seen whether the decline of US hegemony today will contribute to sustaining the CCP's dominance.

Notes

1　We follow Duverger's definition of a dominant party: 'a party is dominant when it holds the majority over a long period of political development' (Duverger, 1954, p. 308). The merit of his definition for us is in that it crosses the conventional boundaries of political regimes. Under this concept, we can treat three very distinct dominant parties. Some may question if United Russia is a dominant party (Roberts, 2012). Certainly it seems to be more a tool of the executive body than a 'ruling' party. Nonetheless it has been a majority party since 2001 and a very useful tool for the Kremlin. We believe it deserves to be called a dominant party. Some other scholars have called United Russia a dominant party (Reuter and Remington, 2009; Reuter, 2010).
2　Our typology is certainly close to that of Sartori (1976): ideological hegemonic party and pragmatic hegemonic party. Still, his narrowly divided categorization makes it difficult for us to deal with the similarities among predominant, hegemonic and single parties. The Chinese Communist Party, according to his typology, should be classified as an authoritarian single party; United Russia is probably regarded as a pragmatic hegemonic party; and the Indian Congress was a predominant party. This is correct from his perspective, but not appropriate for our purpose, which is to consider the three parties within a single scheme. On the other hand, the term 'dominant party' denotes 'whatever major party outdistances the other parties in whichever type of party system', which is more useful for our purposes. See Sartori (1976, p. 230).
3　As a general discussion of the CCP, we are heavily indebted to the following literature: Tang (1997); Mouri (2004); Tang (2008); Nishimura and Kokubun (2009).
4　For a general discussion of Indian politics and the INC, we drew upon the following literature: Gowda and Sridharan (2007); Rudolph and Rudolph (2008); Hirose (1994).

5 We have conducted original research on the United Russia party, which includes Ogushi (2007; 2008; 2009; 2012; 2013). We freely draw upon these.
6 *News of the Communist Party of China* (http://cpc.people.com.cn/GB/64162/71380/71387/71591/4855056.html) (in Chinese), accessed on February 6, 2014.
7 The Central People's Government of the People's Republic of China (www.gov.cn/jrzg/2010-03/16/content_1556993.htm) (in Chinese), accessed on February 6, 2014.
8 The data on the regional governors is constructed by ourselves from several internet sites, including an independent institute of election studies (www.vibory.ru/index.htm), gubernatory.ru (www.governors.ru), and sites of regional administrations among others. See also Blakkisrud (2011).
9 Federal Law no. 41-F3, April 5, 2009.
10 *Gazeta Ru*, February15, 2007; *Nezavisimaya gazeta*, February 16, 2009;
11 *Kommersant*, March 21, 2009. For the election results, see the Central Electoral Commission's website (www.cikrf.ru/).
12 *Kommersant*, March 17, 2009.
13 Website of the Russian president (http://news.kremlin.ru/news/3505); Ukaz Prezidenta RF, March 21, 2009, N 302.
14 *RIA Novosti*, May 15, 2008.
15 *Polit.ru*, June 5, 2008.
16 *Vedomosti*, May 16, 2008.
17 *Novaya gazeta*, January 15, 2010.
18 *Rossiiskaya gazeta*, February 4, 2010.

References

Aburamoto, Mari (2008) 'Posutokyosanshugi Roshia ni okeru "yoto" no kigen: 'kenryokuto' no gainen wo tegakari toshite' [The Origin of the 'Ruling Party' in Postcommunist Russia: In the light of the 'Party of Power'], *Kokkagakkai zasshi* [The Journal of the Association of Political and Social Sciences], vol. 121, no. 11–12, pp. 197–263 (in Japanese).

——(2010) 'Who Takes Care of the Residents? United Russia and the Regions Facing the Monetization of *L'got*', *Acta Slavica Iaponica*, no. 28, pp. 101–15.

Blakkisrud, Helge (2011) 'Medvedev's New Governors', *Europe-Asia Studies*, vol. 63, no. 3, pp. 367–95.

Chan, Hon S. (2004) 'Cadre Personnel Management in China: the *Nomenklatura* System, 1990–98', *The China Quarterly*, vol. 179, pp. 703–34.

Chandra, Kanchan (2004) *Why Ethnic Parties Succeed: Patronage and Ethnic Head Counts in India*, New York: Cambridge University Press.

Duverger, Maurice (1954) *Political Parties: Their Organization and Activity in the Modern State*, London: Methuen & Co.

Geddes, Barbara (1999) 'What Do We Know about Democratization after Twenty Years?' *Annual Review of Political Science*, vol. 2, pp. 115–44.

Golosov, Grigorii V. (2004) *Political Parties in the Regions of Russia: Democracy Unclaimed*, Boulder, CO: Lynne Rienner.

Gowda, M. V. Rajeev and E. Sridharan (2007) 'Parties and the Party System, 1947–2006', in Sumit Ganguly, Larry Diamond and Marc F. Plattner, eds, *The State of India's Democracy*, Baltimore, MD: Johns Hopkins University Press, pp. 3–25.

Hale, Henry E. (2004) 'The Origin of United Russia and the Putin Presidency: The Role of Contingency in Party-System Development', *Demokratizatsiya*, vol. 12, no. 2, pp. 169–94.

82 *Political systems and diplomacy*

——(2006) *Why Not Parties in Russia? Democracy, Federalism, and the State*, New York: Cambridge University Press.

Hankla, Charles R. (2008) 'Parties and Patronage: An Analysis of Trade and Industrial Policy in India', *Comparative Politics*, vol. 41, no. 1, pp. 41–60.

Hirose, Takako (1991) 'Indo kokumin kaigiha no soshiki to kino: itto yuitaisei no hokai' [The Organization and Functions of the Indian National Congress: A Decay of the Single Predominant Party System], *Ajia kenkyu* [Asian Studies], vol. 37, no. 3, pp. 61–87 (in Japanese).

——(1994) *Two Asian Democracies: A Comparative Study of the Single Predominant Party Systems in India and Japan*, Delhi: Konark Publishers.

Huntington, Samuel P. (1968) *Political Order in Changing Societies*, New Haven, CT: Yale University Press.

Kothari, Rajini (1999) *Indo minshu seiji no tenkan: itto yuisei no hokai* [Democracy in India: Changing Perspectives], Tokyo: Keiso Shobo (in Japanese).

Levitsky, Steven and Lucan A. Way (2010) *Competitive Authoritarianism: Hybrid Regimes After the Cold War*, New York: Cambridge University Press.

——(2012) 'Beyond Patronage: Violent Struggle, Ruling Party Cohesion, and Authoritarian Durability', *Perspectives on Politics*, vol. 10, no. 4, pp. 869–89.

Li, Hongbin, and Li-An Zhou (2005) 'Political Turnover and Economic Performance: The Incentive Role of Personnel Control in China', *Journal of Public Economics*, vol. 89, no. 9–10, pp. 1743–62.

Miwa, Hiroaki (2008) 'Indo ni okeru seiji shisutemu no anteisei ni kansuru kosatsu' [Some Considerations on the Stability of the Indian Political System], in Norio Kondo, ed., *Indo minshusei no yukue: tatoka to keizai seicho no jidai ni okeru anteisei to Gendai* [Indian Democracy in Perspective: Stability and Limitation in the Age of Multiparty and Economic Growth], Tokyo: Institute of Developing Economies, pp. 57–88 (in Japanese).

Mouri, Kazuko (2004) *Gendai Chugoku seiji* [Politics in Contemporary China], Nagoya: Nagoya University Press (in Japansese).

Nakamizo, Kazuya (2010) 'Jinushi to gyakusatsu: Indo Biharushu ni okeru shihei shudan no kessei to seiji hendo' [Landlord and Massacre: The Formation of Ranvir Sena and Political Change in Bihar, India], *Ajia Afurika kenkyu* [Asian and African Studies] vol. 9, no. 2, pp. 180–222 (in Japanese).

Nishimura, Shigeo and Ryosei Kokubun (2009) *To to kokka: seiji taisei no kiseki* [Party and State: Evolution of the Political Regime], Tokyo: Iwanami Shoten (in Japanese).

Ogushi, Atsushi (2007) 'Toward a Government-Party Regime? United Russia in Perspective', paper presented to the annual Convention of the American Association for the Advancement of Slavic Studies (AAASS), New Orleans.

——(2008) 'Seifu to taisei no seidoka: Toitsu Roshia to no hatten' [Institutionalizing a Government-Party Regime: The Development of United Russia], in Toshihiko Ueno and Shinji Yokote, eds, *Roshia no seiji ishiki to seiji* [Political Attitudes and Politics in Russia], Tokyo: Keio University Press, pp. 63–87 (in Japanese).

——(2009) 'From the CC CPSU to Russian Presidency: The Development of Semi-Presidentialism in Russia', in Tadayuki Hayashi and Atsushi Ogushi, eds, *Post-Communist Transformations: the Countries of Central and Eastern Europe and Russia in Comparative Perspective*, Sapporo: Slavic Research Center, Hokkaido University, pp. 3–25.

——(2012) 'Zhipeixing zhengdang de tongzhi jiexian?: Tongyi Eluosidang yu defang lingdaoren' [The Limitation of Dominant Party Control? United Russian and Regional Governors], *Eluosi yanjiu*, [Russian Studies], no. 174, pp. 101–21 (in Chinese).

——(2013) 'Shihai seito no kochiku no genkai to shippai: Roshia to Ukuraina' [The Limitations on Building a Dominant Party: Russia and Ukraine from a Comparative Perspective], *Ajia keizai* [Asian Economy], vol. 54, no. 4, pp. 146–67 (in Japanese).

Ordeshook, Peter C. (1996) 'Russia's Party System: Is Russian Federalism Viable?', *Post-Soviet Affairs*, vol. 12, no. 3, pp. 195–217.

Petrov, N. and A. Titkov (2010) *Vlast', biznes, obshchestvo v regionakh: nepravil'nyi treugol'nik* [Power, Business, Society in Districts: Incorrect Triangle], Moscow: Carnegie Center (in Russian).

Rudolph, Suzanne Hoeber and Lloyd I. Rudolph (2008) 'Congress Learns to Lose: From a One-party Dominant to Multiparty System in India', in Edward Friedman and Joseph Wong, eds, *Political Transitions in Dominant Party Systems: Learning to Lose*, Abingdon: Routledge, pp. 15–41.

Reuter, Ora John (2010) 'The Politics of Dominant Party Formation: United Russia and Russia's Governors', *Europe-Asia Studies*, vol. 62, no. 2, pp. 293–327.

Reuter, Ora John and Thomas F. Remington (2009) 'Dominant Party Regimes and the Commitment Problem: The Case of United Russia', *Comparative Political Studies*, vol. 42, no. 4, pp. 501–26.

Roberts, Sean (2012) *Putin's United Russia Party*, Abingdon: Routledge.

Sakwa, Richard (2008) '"New Cold War" or Twenty Years' Crisis? Russia and International Politics', *International Affairs*, vol. 84, no. 2, pp. 241–67.

Sartori, Giovanni (1976) *Parties and Party Systems: A Framework for Analysis*, New York: Cambridge University Press.

Smith, Benjamin (2005) 'Life of the Party: The Origin of Regime Breakdown and Persistence under Single-Party Rule', *World Politics*, vol. 57, no. 3, pp. 421–51.

Tabata, Shinichiro (2011) 'Growth in the International Reserves of Russia, China and India: A Comparison of Underlying Mechanisms', *Eurasian Geography and Economics*, vol. 52, no. 3, pp. 409–27.

Tabata, Shinichiro and Uegaki Akira, (2011) 'Gendai no kokusai kin'yu kozo ni okeru Roshia, Chugoku, Indo' [Russian, China, and India in the Contemporary International Financial System], *Hikaku keizai kenkyu* [Japanese Journal of Comparative Economics], vol. 48, no. 1, pp. 15–26 (in Japanese).

Tang, Liang (1997) *Gendai Chugoku no tosei kankei* [Party–State Relations in Contemporary China], Tokyo: Keio University Press (in Japanese).

——(2000) 'Shoshido taisei to jinji ni yoru chuo tosei' [Provincial Leadership System and Central Control through Staffing], in Satoshi Amako, ed., *Gendai Chugoku no kozo hendo* [Structural Changes in Contemporary China], vol. 4, Politics, Tokyo: University of Tokyo Press, pp. 249–74 (in Japanese).

——(2008) 'Gendai Chugoku no seiji taisei to seiji hen'yo' [The Political Regime and Political Change in Contemporary China], in Satoshi Amako and Ryo Asano, eds, *Chugoku, Taiwan* [China, Taiwan], Kyoto: Minerva Shobo, pp. 29–55 (in Japanese).

Wu, Guoguang (2000) 'Chihoshugi no hatten to seiji tosei, seido taiko' [The Development of Localism, Political Control, and Institutional Decay], in Satoshi Amako, ed., *Gendai Chugoku no kozo hendo* [Structural Changes in Contemporary China], vol. 4, Politics, Tokyo: University of Tokyo Press, pp. 39–59 (in Japanese).

84 *Political systems and diplomacy*

Zen'kovich, N. A. (2007) *Gubernatory novoi Rossii: Entsiklopediya kar'er* [Governors of New Russia: Encyclopedia of Careers], Moscow: OLMA Media Grupp (in Russian).

Zhao, Hangwei (1998) *Chugoku no juso shuken taisei to keizai hatten* [Multilayered Centralized Political Regime and Economic Development in China], Tokyo: University of Tokyo Press (in Japanese).

5 Client, agent or bystander?

Patronage and village leadership in India, Russia and China

Fumiki Tahara

Introduction

This essay focuses on the patronage networks of village leaders in three regional power states in Eurasia. Employing two indices, the inclination toward electoral patronage and selectivity of patrons, I will argue that the characteristics of today's village leaders can be conceptualized as the 'competitive client' in India, the 'faithful agent' in Russia, and as either the 'principal' or the 'bystander' in China (Figure 5.1). These four village-level leadership characterizations are byproducts of different forms of patronage networks that reflect specific political features in each of the three countries.

In these three rapidly growing regional powers, local residents have become more affluent and their lifestyles more complex, and subsequently the need for and requirements of local governance and public service have extended beyond the scope of the relatively simple rural governance of the preceding era. For example, as local people began consuming foods that packaged in plastic, garbage disposal has become an important task for local administration. Similarly, as more local people buy cars, the need for better paved roads to connect local residents with places beyond the village is expected to grow.

With this shifting socio-political environment in common, India, Russia and China have taken a dissimilar approach from many Western countries

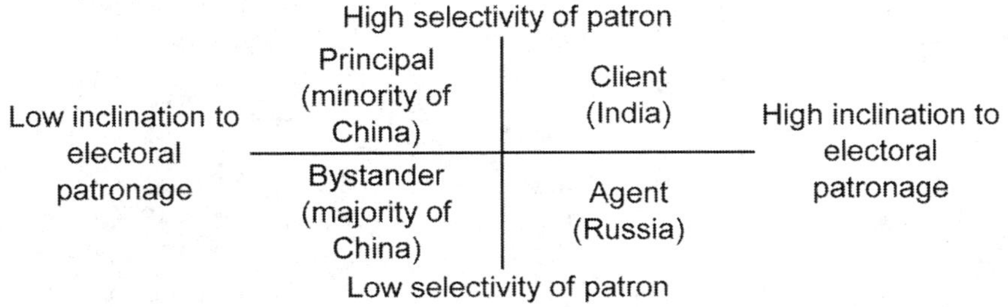

	High selectivity of patron		
Low inclination to electoral patronage	Principal (minority of China)	Client (India)	High inclination to electoral patronage
	Bystander (majority of China)	Agent (Russia)	
	Low selectivity of patron		

Figure 5.1 Typology of village leadership
Source: Author.

86 *Political systems and diplomacy*

and Japan which eradicated administrative villages, merging them into larger local self-governing bodies in the process of modernization. India, Russia and China are unique for having preserved the village unit as an important level of local government. The reasons for this preservation are not the focus of this chapter, but it is easy to imagine that since all three countries are characterized by vast territory and large population, it was reasonable from the viewpoint of administrative cost for the state, to utilize the autonomous functioning of the village community (Matsuzato and Tahara, 2014).

At the same time, village organizations in these countries frequently confront the dilemma of choosing between 'what should be done' and 'what actually can be done' because of financial shortages. In interviews in Russia, a government official dealing with local self-governance issues commented that it was almost unimaginable that the local municipality be provided with 'enough' financial resources.[1] This is the very condition that motivates village leaders, in an effort to mobilize resources, to create a broad patronage network outside of formal financial arrangements. 'Patronage' here means the system by which important persons give support, especially financial, to local communities in return for their allegiance to those patrons. Under common structural conditions, village leaders in the three countries have developed unique patronage networks. This is the starting point for our comparative analysis.

Nonetheless, despite such distinctiveness, relatively little scholarship has paid attention to the relationship between the village and outside resources. Village studies by anthropologists and rural sociologists tend to spotlight social relations and organizations, as well as the power structure *within* villages, rather than focusing on the interaction between the village and the larger political and economic environment.[2]

In this sense, there is much to learn from Indian village studies. In the Indian context, which has showcased the combination of competitive electoral politics in a huge agrarian population, election studies and political science have not treated the political behaviors of rural residents as a mere exception.[3] At the same time, many works in village studies have attempted to trace national- or state-level politics at various stages from the village perspective (Opler *et al.*, 1959; Mitra, 1979; Krishna, 2007). Combined, these studies show Indian villages in the process of becoming more involved in national- and state-level politics.

Based on preexisting studies including those in India,[4] the goal of this chapter is to clarify the diverse development patterns of modern rural communities by employing a comparative perspective. More broadly, the comparison will contribute to deepening our understanding of a multi-polar structure of the modern political world.[5] Of the three countries, little has been presented about the patronage politics evolving in Russian villages under the rule of the United Russia party (hereafter UR). Similarly, while much research has focused on village-level balloting in China, little has been written about the patronage networks between village leaders and outside actors, perhaps because they are essentially 'invisible'. Comparative study will help to overcome the shortcomings in our tacit understanding of the politics of the three countries.

Patronage and village leadership 87

Aside from secondary written materials on village life in the three countries, the village information on which this paper is primarily based was collected during my fieldwork in four villages in China, two in Russia, and two in India.[6] Although data collected in these villages cannot perfectly represent the social reality of each country and should be complemented by written sources, I can confirm that none of them are extreme cases in terms of geographical or economic conditions, and that they are representative of important aspects of the local politics of each region.

National electoral arrangements

In order to illustrate the political background in which patronage networks develop, this section will offer a brief overview of the electoral arrangements employed in the three countries. Descriptions from my research sites will be used to provide a concrete picture.

In India, as clarified by Table 5.1, all administrative levels including the village, block, district, and state, up to the federation have representative bodies. Viewed by rural residents, there are as many as five levels of patrons: ward members of Gram Panchayat (GP hereafter),[7] members of Panchayat Samiti (block level), members of Zilla Parishad (district level), MLA (Member of Legislative Assembly at the state level), and MP (Member of Parliament at the country level) act as representatives and increase the

Table 5.1 People's representatives of Indian research sites

Level	Category	Term (years)	AP	Orissa
Country	MP (Raja Sabha)	6	233 seats, 18 of which are from AP	233 seats, 10 of which are from Orissa
	MP (Lok Sabha)	5	543 seats, 42 of which are from AP, 1 from Nizamabad	543 seats, 21 of which are from Orissa, 1 from Cuttack
State	MLA (Members of Legislative Assembly)	5	AP has 294 seats, 9 of which are from Nizamabad, 1 from Kamareddy constituency	Orissa has 147 seats, 9 of which are from Cuttack, 1 from Badamba block
District	Members of Zilla Parishad	5	Nizamabad has 36 seats, 1 of which is from Bhiknoor block	Cuttack has 46 seats, 5 of which are from Badamba block
Block	Panchayat samiti	5	Bhiknoor block has 14 seats from 18 GPs, 2 of which are from Peddamallareddy GP	Badamba block has 36 seats from 36 GPs, 1 of which is from Desarathipur GP
Village	Ward members	5	Peddamallareddy GP has 14 seats from 14 wards	Desarathipur GP has 11 seats from 11 wards

Sources: Author's interviews and the website of Election Commission of India (http://eci.nic.in/eci_main1/index.aspx), accessed 11 January 2013.

88 *Political systems and diplomacy*

opportunities for mobilizing government resources. All of the electoral constituencies, including the GP election, are single-member constituencies.

One factor that affects the motivation of elected representatives is clear correspondence with their electoral constituencies. For example, Pedda-mallareddy Village in Andhra Pradesh (hereafter AP) has fourteen wards, roughly equivalent to electoral districts. Each ward in the village has a clear-cut membership of between 50–200 households and encompassing a particular territory. Since the ward simultaneously functions as an electoral constituency, the village level representatives are called 'ward members' and are supposed to represent interests of the residents of the ward in which they are elected.

At the block level, representatives are called 'Panchayat Samiti' and are supposed to represent the interests of their GP. The same kinds of correspondences are found at the district level, state level, and in the Lower House of the Indian Federation (Lok Sabha). The distinct relationship between the representative of the people and their constituency can enhance a representative's motivation to bring 'pork' to their own constituency, as well raising the expectations for it.

The scope of 'village leaders' in this chapter includes leaders who hold formal positions in GP organizations including sarpanch (village chief) and other elected ward members, namely Paddamallaredy in AP, which has fifteen leaders, and Desarathipur in Orissa, which has twelve.

Now, looking at Russia, the electoral system is comprised of a four-layer representative body: the federation, *oblast'* or republic, county (*raion*) and the village (Table 5.2), among which the latter two are regarded as local self-government municipalities. The *oblast'*-level election employs a combination of proportional representation and a single mandate system, but there is momentum recently to move toward a system based exclusively on proportional representation (Ross, 2011, p. 642). In the Tambov regional election in 2011, twenty-five out of fifty seats were for the single-member constituency, while the remaining twenty-five were for proportional representation. In general, the single-member constituencies are composed of two *raion*s (e.g. Znamenka *raion* and Petrovskoe *raion* hold one elected deputy in common).

At the *raion* level, a deputy normally represents one village or central town. However, there seems to be great regional variation; in the Tambov case, we found that twelve of the twenty-one deputies resided in the central town of Znamenka, while the remaining nine came from villages; some big villages like Poklovo-Marfino had more than one deputy.[8] In the Tatarstan case, all forty deputies of Kamskoe Ust'e *raion* come from twenty villages in the territory and uniformly each village has two deputies. Interestingly enough, one of these two deputies is simultaneously the village chief while the other is a member of the village soviet.[9]

At the village level, council members seem largely to represent streets or hamlets in the territory. For example, Poklovo-Marfino has eleven council members, seven of whom are residents of the central hamlet while the remaining four are from small surrounding hamlets. Ten'ki Village in Tatarstan has ten

Patronage and village leadership 89

Table 5.2 People's representatives of Russian research sites

Level	Category	Term (years)	Poklovo-Marfino (Tambov)	Ten'ki (Tatartan)
Federation	Senators of Federal Council	none	166 seats, 2 senators are appointed from each of the 83 federal subjects	
	Deputies of State Duma	4	450 seats, proportional representation	
Oblast, republic	Deputies of *Oblast'* Duma	5	50 seats, 25 of which are single-member constituency and 1 from Znamenka-Petrovskoe constituency	100 seats, 50 of which are single-member constituency and 1 from Kamskoe Ust'e-Apastobo-Kaibitsy-Tetyushi (partly) constituency
Raion	Deputies of *Raion* Duma	5	Znamenka *raion* has 21 seats, 2 of which are from Poklovo-Marfino Village	Kamskoe Ust'e *raion* has 40 seats, 2 of which are from Ten'ki Village
Village	Deputies of Village Soviet	5	Poklovo-Marfino Village has 11 seats from the whole village	Ten'ki Village has 10 seats from 10 constituencies, each of which is composed by 1–5 streets

Source: Author's interview.

council members who represent each constituency, each of which is composed of between one and five streets (the village has forty streets in total[10]). Formal village leaders include village chief and deputies, totaling twelve in Poklovo-Marfino, Tambov and eleven in Ten'ki, Tatarstan.

Now turning to China, first we will look at two particular aspects of the Chinese electoral system; one being the weakness of the council system and the comparative strength in the party and administrative system. At the village level, the person regarded as most powerful is the secretary of the Chinese Communities Party (CCP, hereafter) branch while the second most powerful is the village chief. The secretary is not popularly elected but directly appointed by the town or township's CCP organization, while members of the villagers' committee are elected every three years by popular vote. Elections for the village representative assembly (*cunmin daibiao dahui*) are much less systematized than those for the villagers' committee, and these representatives, if they exist, are not normally regarded as 'village leaders'.[11]

The second conspicuous feature of the Chinese electoral arrangement is that the village, as a 'self-government' body, is the only stratum in which a substantially competitive election can take place. In fact, representatives to the town/

90 *Political systems and diplomacy*

township and county level People's Congress have also been directly elected by popular vote since 1979. Representatives higher than the county level (city, province and center) are to be elected through indirect voting by lower-level representatives. However, these congresses are normally considered rubber-stamping organizations that are controlled and manipulated by the CCP and the government. Due to the limited power of these representatives, few people take the congresses or their elections seriously (Zhong, 2003, pp. 62–67). Obviously, it is quite difficult to regard these congresses as equivalent to those in India and Russia

Patronage and village leadership

India: from the agent of the Congress Party to the competitive client

The patronage networks of Indian village leaders are formed exclusively through elections and party politics. Although the patron–village leader relationships inevitably hinge on personal elements, in most cases they are only byproducts of party-based relationships.[12] Under such competitive party politics, the village leader can switch patrons in an attempt to bring resources to his or her constituency. Thus, a combination of a high inclination to electoral patronage and the high selectivity of patrons encourages leaders to become what I have named the 'client' type of village leader. In the current Indian system, clients proactively choose their patrons rather than passively waiting for the patrons to find them.

Village politics and party competition

A remarkable facet of India's electoral arrangement is that this competitive electoral system, particularly at the federal and state assembly level, has a relatively long history, dating back to the enactment of the Indian Constitution in 1950. Moreover, competitiveness among political parties has grown harsher over time. In the 'Congress system' (1947–67) of post-independence India, efforts at ballot mobilization at the village level overall were undertaken in every village by the landlord caste, upon whom the Congress Party depended. Under this system, the mobilization pattern was 'vertical': villagers were mobilized top-down to vote in favor of an economically powerful landlord-Congress candidate. During this period, village leaders in India with a lower selectivity of patronage played the 'agent' role in the Congress Party. Therefore, the village leaders' role as the 'competitive client', each leader representing different segments of a village population, grew conspicuous only after the political climate became increasingly competitive during the multi-party rivalry after 1989.

Figure 5.2 illustrates that a diversion from the 'Congress System' in AP and Orissa began as early as the end of 1970s or early 1980s. The following thirty years revealed a more competitive trend in state politics. Both in AP and Orissa, two or three major parties are in cut-throat competition.[13] In recent years the ruling parties of the AP and Orissa state governments have changed frequently.

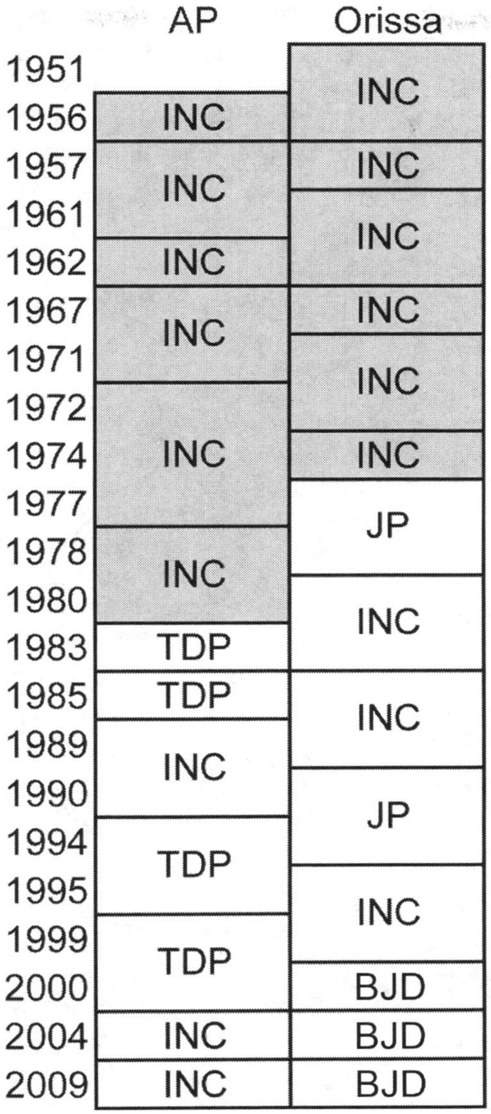

	AP	Orissa
1951		INC
1956	INC	
1957	INC	INC
1961		INC
1962	INC	
1967	INC	INC
1971		INC
1972		
1974	INC	INC
1977		JP
1978	INC	
1980		INC
1983	TDP	
1985	TDP	INC
1989	INC	
1990		JP
1994	TDP	
1995		INC
1999	TDP	
2000		BJD
2004	INC	BJD
2009	INC	BJD

Figure 5.2 Winning party in AP, Orissa MLA elections
Notes:* INC = Indian National Congress, TDP = Telugu Desam Party, JP = Janata
Party, BJD = Biju Janata Dal.
** Gray parts indicate the period of 'Congress system' in two states.
Source: Website of Election Commission of India (http://eci.nic.in/eci_main1/index.
aspx), accessed January 11, 2013.

92 *Political systems and diplomacy*

Nakamizo (2012, pp. 58–66, 296–306) conceptualized the transformation of village-level politics as a change from a 'landlord mobilization strategy' to a 'caste mobilization strategy'. In the 'caste mobilization strategy', two or three different political parties in search of potential clients try to find and connect themselves to different segments of village society, namely caste groups.

Parties in the eyes of village leaders

In the present competitive political arrangement, the party that village leaders have supported and will support in the future becomes a vital issue because the party they support directly affects their access to resources. In this sense, patron–client relations in India are created in a 'bottom-up' manner instead of 'top-down'.

The council members, excepting ward members and sarpanch at the village level, are entitled to discretionary funds that they can use for any purpose. At the lowest level, Panchayat Samitis in AP, locally called MPTC, are entitled to two types of fund; one is a general fund amounting to 15,000 rupees per member, per year, and the others is BRGF fund that is 90,000 rupees per member, per year.[14] Among others, MLAs in the state government control large amounts of resources and actually facilitate many rural development projects (Wilkinson, 2007, pp. 114–31). One such important fund is called LAD (Local Area Development) funds. An important project carried out with MLA funds in both of my research sites (AP and Orissa) was the construction of drinking water facilities.

Unlike upper-level council members, the village leaders, sarpanch and other elected ward members are not entitled to use discretionary funds. Since the independent panchayat income is very limited,[15] they are expected to extract funds from their patrons or decide how to allocate government project funds within the village.[16] It is difficult to imagine the representative (ward members) at the very bottom level mobilizing funds from higher up. A ward member in Peddamallareddy village told me that he was an activist in the Congress Party and had a good relationship with Shabir Ali, the ex-MLA from his constituency. Through Congress relationships, he mobilized 200,000 rupees to construct two cement roads in his ward, which is a SC (Scheduled Caste) area. Both of the roads were constructed with MLA funds.[17] Again, the husband of a sarpanch in Peddamallareddy village told me that it was difficult to raise funds for public construction. In order to obtain information about funds, he went to meet with Mr. Govardan, the current MLA for this constituency. He is from Baswarpur village (within the same block) and an old friend. They have also strengthened their connections through activities of the TDP (Telugu Desam Party).[18]

What is remarkable about the Indian version of patron–client relationships is that they are party-based and created through competitive elections. Naturally, individual village leaders have different patrons at different levels, for example, one is a Congress MLA and another a Zilla Parishad member from

TDP. In fact, at least eleven out of fourteen ward members in Peddamallar-eddy reported that they had parties they supported at the moment; six supported TDP, three supported Congress and two supported TRS (Telangana Rashtra Samithi).

While the patron–client relationships are party-based, and not genuinely personal, one can also strategically switch one's supported party in favor of another patron. A ward member in the village told me that before the election she switched from TRS to the Congress Party. She chose to do so because she could get funds more easily, because the MP from this constituency was in Congress. During her term she obtained funding from the MP for several projects, including 150,000 rupees to build a cement road, 30,000 rupees for a bridge, and 50,000 rupees for a drinking water borehole.[19]

These traits are particularly interesting when considered in comparison to China, where patron–client relationships are overwhelmingly personal and the village is much less likely to be affected by upper-level politics.

Russia: convergence into the faithful agent

When the patronage system has a relatively high inclination to electoral patronage, and at the same time the selectivity for patrons by village leaders is fairly low, we can assume leaders fall into the 'agent' category. Current Russian village leadership roughly represents this type. More specifically, these leaders, firmly and vertically integrated into a cascade-like patronage system, are acting as the 'faithful agents' of the UR, the dominant party of twenty-first-century Russia.

From fragmentation to 'unity'

Taking the questionable sustainability of electoral arrangements into account, Russia should be the most unstable of the three countries. After the collapse of the Soviet Union, the era of party politics in mid-1990s Russia was one of 'hyper-fragmentation', where forty-three parties competed for popular votes during the 1995 parliamentary election (Gel'man, 2008, p. 914). It was only after President Putin took power in this century that a relatively stable regime began to emerge. As some scholars have suggested, 'the organizational power in Russia increased from medium low in the early 1990s to medium high in the 2000s' (Levitsky and Way, 2010, p. 190).

At the moment, Russian politics is still categorized as a multi-party system. Nevertheless, many observers have already come to the consensus that under the Putin regime the ruling UR party has established a 'competitive authoritarianism' that does not allow the outward competition with opposition parties.[20] As a result, in the Tambov Duma election in March 2011, forty-three seats out of fifty (86 percent) were won by UR candidates. At the *raion*-level council, in Znamenka, seventeen out of twenty-one deputies belong to UR, of whom fifteen have formal membership.[21] One notable current

94 *Political systems and diplomacy*

situation is that the party is deeply interlocked in administrative power that obliges administrative chiefs at the *oblast'*, *raion*, as well as village level to play a part in the UR. Among others, after the abolition of gubernatorial elections in early 2005, 'the appointment and further survival of regional chief executives largely depended on their loyalty to UR' (Gel'man, 2008, p. 919). In the Znamenka *raion* in Tambov, four out of seven village chiefs had membership in United Russia in 2009, while the remaining three were sympathisers.[22] In Kamskoe Ust'e County in Tatarstan, all twenty village chiefs in the county territory were members of UR.[23] Among the ten deputies of the village council of Ten'ki Village, Kamskoe Ust'e County, at least seven and possibly eight are UR members.[24]

Village leaders in the eyes of the party

Under the present overwhelming dominance of UR, government resources are allocated to local leaders in exchange for the 'loyalty' or 'faithfulness' proven in elections. During electoral campaigns, local administrative leaders are supposed to work ardently as 'ballot collecting machines' and those locals who fail to mobilize ballots are seen as 'unfaithful' and are not to be awarded advantages. The former county chief of Znamenka, V. F. G., resigned in May 2011, just after the Tambov Duma election noted above. The reason for his sudden resignation is said to be that he was not passionate enough in the campaign and could not satisfy officials at the UR headquarters in Tambov.[25]

How does the UR party procure loyalty from local leaders and local residents? There are some unique ways in Russia. First, unlike in India where material benefits are the main motivators for winning votes, face to face contact between party members and residents is more important in Russia.[26] Members of the regional council often visit their constituency to communicate with local residents. In Tambov, one of the ongoing projects is called 'Don't Forget Even One', in which county leaders make courtesy visits to every veteran of World War II. In Znamenka County, there are 150 veterans on the list. According to the chief of the county council, while the living conditions of the veterans is fair, it is important to pay respect by actually visiting them at home. One of the veterans is an elderly woman who worked as a spy during World War II. The chief of her village forgot to visit her on her birthday and was reprimanded by the leader of the county council for carelessness. On Women's Day on March 8th, local leaders sent some gifts to assuage her anger.[27] As shown here, through daily, face to face contact, village leaders are expected to grasp residents' hearts.

Another UR method of exacting loyalty from residents is an emotional mobilization, calling on patriotic feelings. For example, the Tambov regional government is now promoting a project to erect war memorials. UR headquarters in Tambov is very supportive of this project. The plan is to build fifty monuments across the whole region, two of which are in Znamenka County. The county chief of Znamenka, speaking on behalf of the UP party, told us

Patronage and village leadership   95

that the erection of monuments is a substitute for history education. He stressed that 'without a proper history education, another government will emerge within two years'.[28]

China: fluctuation between the principal and the bystander

In China, where the national electoral arrangements follow a different logic, patronage networks surrounding village leaders differ from those in India and Russia. First, since China does not have competitive elections above the village level, village leaders are unable to seek patrons among electoral representatives outside the village. It is not the electoral patronage as observed in Indian and Russian cases but personal patronage, if any, that they can rely on. As noted before, since these networks are essentially intangible and it is not so easy to study them in a systematic way, relatively little scholarship has paid attention to their functioning. Even when mentioned, these networks tend to be treated as specific cases and are not investigated for the structural arrangements in which the networks have developed.

Second, the selectivity of personal patronage varies greatly across regions, which has led Chinese village leaders to fall into two broad categories, 'principal' and 'bystander' (Tahara, 2013). While keeping in mind that reality is much more complex than a twofold typology, in this section I will offer some typical forms of village patronage networks from my own research sites.

Case 1: the village level 'diplomacy' to create connections

As is often the case with 'model villages' in China, Xiaofengying Village in suburban Beijing is located advantageously. It is only five kilometers from the county seat and well connected to the city center and its outdoor market. Ha Yunchao was a prominent leader who held the position of secretary of the village CCP branch from 1983 through 2000. After the late 1990s, he and other village leaders sought the development of the village through vegetable production (such as lettuce and broccoli). In order to raise funds for the village, Ha and other leaders made every endeavor to create personal connections with county (*xian*) and town (*zhen*) government cadres. As a result, they were quite successful in securing government project funds to construct a vegetable wholesale market and purchase refrigerators in which to store vegetables. They also built an intimate relationship with private traders from Guangdong province who came to purchase the produce. In this sense, the village leaders played the role of 'diplomat' by managing village development with politicians from elsewhere.[29]

Case 2: 'the third force' as a local patron

Simen Village, in southern Henan (central China), displays another intriguing development style regarding patronage networks. One of the hamlets in Simen

96 *Political systems and diplomacy*

Village (administrative village) is Qiaoying Hamlet. It has two good paved cement roads that connect the hamlet to the highway beyond. One is 2.5 kilometers long and was completed in 2010 with an investment of 350,000 yuan (about US$58,000). An officer in the public security bureau of the central government who was a native of the village brought in this funding. The other road is 1.5 kilometers long and was completed in 2012 with an investment of 250,000 yuan (about US$41,000). Funds were also raised by a native of the hamlet presently working as a vice magistrate of the People's Government in a neighboring county. An informant commented that this style of fundraising has been only possible because their hamlet has an exceptional number of villagers in influential positions in the government or other party organs. Had that not been the case, they would have had to build hamlet roads by themselves, as did some of the surrounding hamlets in the area.[30] In previous Chinese rural studies, people working outside the village but eager to assist in the village's public matters are known as 'the third force' (*disanzhong liliang*).[31]

Case 3: 'entrepreneur turns village secretary'

Another research site of mine in Gansu province (western China), Linji Village, is also economically typical in the sense that it is a rural village with no collective economy. Yet in 2009, a private mine developer living elsewhere was appointed as party branch secretary by the local CCP organization in his native place, Linji. He had been working outside the village for a long time and was wealthy in comparison to other villagers. What local CCP leaders, as well as villagers, expected was that he could mobilize his own economic resources and personal networks in the local business and political circles in order to contribute to village public construction projects. From 2010 to 2011, he successfully applied for government funds for road building. Additionally, he utilized his own heavy mining machinery to launch the construction of village roads.[32]

Case 4: helpless 'bystander'

The situation of village leaders in Huadun Village in Jiangxi Province (central China) is quite dissimilar from the above three cases but is representative of the 'bystander' type of leader found in most Chinese villages. With no financial base in their own territory and no useful networks to connect them with high-level officials, village officials are quite inactive and unable to implement public construction works, including road building which is regarded as the most important step toward overcoming geographical remoteness. As formal village leaders became 'bystanders', responsibilities for development were handed down to more informal, hamlet-based leaders. Consequently, whereas some hamlets managed to introduce 'New Rural Construction' (*xin nongcun jianshe*) funds through personal connections with the township government, as well as raising funds by themselves to pave the local road, some other hamlets in the village have been rather unsuccessful in mobilizing resources (Tianyuan, 2012, pp. 121–43).

We should not assume the above cases are static village typologies because (1) diverse patronage patterns can develop simultaneously in one locality, and (2) specific types of patronage can weaken or even vanish as time goes by and under different circumstances. Although constantly fluctuating between principal and bystander, it seems that in this case, the 'bystander' role better reflects the normative state of the majority of today's Chinese village leaders.[33] The mainstream literature on today's Chinese rural society (e.g. Kennedy, 2007; He, 2012) attributes this growing 'bystander' type of leadership to the financial difficulties following the abolition of agricultural taxes in 2006. However, as shown at the end of this chapter, our comparative perspective draws out another interpretation.

Patronage type and selectivity

I will now reconsider two indices by which to categorize local political patronages: (1) inclination to electoral patronage, and (2) actual selectivity of patrons.

Patronage types: electoral or personal

In general, it seems to be the case that the harsher the competition becomes in a political campaign, the more likely it is that electoral patronage prospers, leading to less need for personal patronage-seeking by village leaders. India is characterized by a full-fledged, multi-layered electoral patronage and negligible personal patronage, while Chinese village leaders can mobilize extra resources only through personal patronage and face-to-face connections with upper-level government personnel (if they exist).

In Russia and China, village leaders seem to have more alternatives for considering potential patrons in non-political spheres, typically industrial entrepreneurs. Russian village leaders extract resources mainly from upper-level electoral patrons. At the same time, local agro-firms make unique contributions in providing employment opportunities, snow removal services, food for schools, etc.[34] A similar trend was observed in China, especially in coastal eastern China where industrial entrepreneurs are thriving. Cases 1 through 3 show us that in current Chinese marketization contexts, building good relationships with industrial entrepreneurs as potential patrons is becoming more critical.

Through comparison between Indian and Chinese cases, another major finding of this study is that the electoral patronage has much higher penetrating power than personal patronage. 'Penetrating power' here refers to the power to facilitate the even redistribution of government resources and circulation to the entirety of the local population, including every electoral territory. The ruling and opposition parties bring about this distribution power as both are

98 *Political systems and diplomacy*

vying to win the popular support of the vast rural population, of whom a good proportion belong to underprivileged groups including SCs, STs[35] and peripheral hamlets.[36]

China lacks such a mechanism. Personal patronage networks develop only unevenly across vast rural areas. Communities with abundant personal connections can access outside resources without difficulty, but this is not the case with the majority of ordinary inland villages. Fan (2008, pp. 135–36) also shows that in allocating poverty alleviation project funds, remote and consequently comparatively deprived communities that are most needy but lack the connections with county authorities, and are easily ignored.

Of course, one might argue conversely, that the CCP and the Chinese government, in an effort to lessen the rural–urban economic gap, have recently been investing a large proportion of their budget in rural and agricultural development. Surely this would give village leaders more access to government resources than before. However, the increase in government funds does not instantly substitute for the lack of electoral patronage networks because without an electoral constituency, distributive channels cannot cover all of the rural territory and inevitably misses links to government resources for residents of remote villages.[37]

On the part of the ruling CCP, there is little motivation to build extensive and tight networks with village leaders and local residents because there is no need to collect ballots from village leaders as their Indian and Russian counterparts do. Of course, this lack of motivation does not signal a lack of intention to maintain social order and control over the local population. More important here is that the legitimacy of the CCP is not being tested by popular elections but rather, by the party's ability to achieve economic development and foster improvements in local living conditions. That is the very reason why the top CCP leaders are extremely wary of the expanding regional inequality and the rural–urban gap, as these phenomena might stir up discontent among the deprived populations and in the end possibly undermine the ruling party's legitimacy.[38]

High/low selectivity

The selectivity of patrons mainly affects the autonomy of village leaders; the higher the selectivity, the more autonomous they become. As shown in Chinese cases, without competitive elections and electoral patronage, village leaders' chances to obtain personal patrons is rather adventitious, often determined by the socio-geographical position of the village. For many of the common rural areas, the number of patrons is so limited that there is little room for choice.

In comparing Russia and India, Russian village leaders have much less opportunity to choose their political patrons. Here, two conditions are crucial. First, in the Russian version of patronage politics, the loyalty of lower-level officials to higher-level ones forms a cascade-like structure, where regional leaders

Patronage and village leadership   99

require county leaders to pledge their allegiance and county leaders require the same of village leaders.[39] Among others, village leaders are under rigid surveillance by county (*raion*) leaders. For example, all village chiefs are called to weekly meetings at the county soviet office with the county chief. The county chief chairs a semi-annual residents' meeting in all the villages in his or her territory. According to a county chief in Tatarstan, the purpose of the residents' meeting is to give the village chief a chance to learn 'how to work for residents' (Tahara, 2013, pp. 95–96). The rigidity of vertical control, in one part, is a side-effect of the structural proximity of state (*oblast'*) county and village, which has enabled more frequent and intimate contact across different levels of administrative leaders. In Indian patronage politics, we have confirmed that lower-level leaders can simply bypass the next tier or tiers in the administrative strata allowing access to leaders higher up.

Second, from the view of chronological change, India and Russia are headed in opposite directions, leading them to dissimilar political values. Post-independence politics in India initially experienced 'unity' under Congress rule and then 'diversification' from the 1980s on. In today's Indian social context, 'competition' itself is highly praised as an embodiment of modern democratic values. Post-communist Russia first experienced a period of economic disorder and political fragmentation in the 1990s. It is only with the advent of the Putin regime in this century that it began to recover social order and, among other things, 'unity'. In the Russian context, competition as an embodiment of democracy *can* exist but should take place in a more subtle way. Mobilization of ballots is done in a less materialistic and more emotional way. Outward competition and material interests are sugarcoated in the rhetoric of national unity, harmony, patriotism, the mourning of war dead, and the subsequent stabilization of the whole society. No doubt the party is attempting to associate these sentiments with its own legitimacy. Since village leaders are at the frontlines of the realization of these intentions, their freedom to choose political patrons should be sacrificed.

Conclusion

Obviously, in the midst of rapid economic growth in recent years, vast rural populations in the three focus countries still need the 'village' administrative level. However, village leaders in the three countries are not guaranteed resources within the boundaries of formal financial arrangements, necessitating the cultivation of patronage networks outside the village. In an attempt to categorize patronage types, two indices have been employed: the inclination to electoral patronage and the selectivity of patrons. Accordingly, the three regional powers in Eurasia studied here have displayed different patronage types. Indian village leaders are competitive 'clients' with a high degree of electoral patronage and high selectivity of patrons, (2) Russian village leaders can be characterized as faithful 'agents' with mostly electoral patronage and low selectivity, and (3) Chinese village leaders have only personal patronage

100 *Political systems and diplomacy*

networks, with varied selectivity for patrons among communities, making only a few village leaders 'principals' while the majority are 'bystanders' who can provide few resources to improve local public life.

What factors, then, have ultimately brought about the above characteristics? The structure of party politics and competitiveness in national and local elections have determined village leadership. As summarized in Table 5.3, the three countries have clearly exemplified three different types of party politics.

To conclude this comparative study, it is crucial to emphasize a twofold set of implications of leadership types in China. First, a recent, growing tendency toward the 'bystander' type leadership in rural China should not be attributed only to the financial difficulty following the abolition of agricultural taxes in 2006. The 'bystander' phenomenon has a more profound institutional basis stemming from the fact that the CCP has not placed itself within the logic of competitive elections and does not need to create broad relationships with potential grassroots clients as in India and Russia. In this sense, the abolition of agricultural taxes has revealed the structural position of Chinese village leaders.

A second implication of this leadership type arises from the political structure; one cannot attribute the thriving 'connectionism' (*guanxi zhuyi*) in mainland China only to socio-cultural factors (e.g. Liu, 2000, pp. 161–64; Wong and Leung, 2001; Gold *et al.*, 2002). The lack of competitive elections above the village level can better explain the reason why village leaders need to pursue personal patronage through back door connections (often in vain). It also suggests that if competitive elections should take place in the distant future, the channels though which Chinese people obtain goods and resources will have changed drastically. Taiwan, which shares a socio-cultural background with mainland China, provides a good example because it has developed clientilistic networks through competitive elections (Wakabayashi, 1992, pp. 117–42). Accordingly, 'connectionism' can only explain a relatively small part of social life in Taiwan.

Table 5.3 Correlation between party politics and village leadership

Competitiveness in Elections	Inclination to Electoral Patronage	Selectivity of Patron	Type of Village Leadership	Example
high	high	high	client	India after the Congress system
middle	high to middle	low	agent	Russia under the UR, India under the Congress system
low	low	low/high	bystander/ principal	China

Source: Author.

In sum, the micro-level analysis done in this chapter has demonstrated that the development of the modern political world has been much more diverse than many have previously assumed. To deepen our understanding of this diversity, more effort should be made to elucidate the value systems hidden below the surface of political events in these three core nations.

Notes

1 Interview with head of Bureau of Mutual Relations with Local Municipality of Tambov Government, 2 September 2009, Tambov.
2 On this point, Migdal (1974, p. 23) holds a similar view to the author.
3 As review articles for this sphere, see Graham (1975), Brass (1978) etc.
4 In addition to the Indian case, some other studies on the developing world have posed similar questions; Wolters (1984) for the Filipino case, Thiele (1986) for the Tanzanian case, Antlöv (2004) for an Indonesian case, Kasuga (1988) and Ookama (1994) for cases in modern Japan. Few of these have dealt with problems in a broad comparative perspective.
5 The major regional powers in Eurasia in our project are regarded as challengers to the uni-polar order of the United States and an EU-dominated international order. Some of the commonalities among these countries are political independence, late growth, economic, military and cultural power that influences neighboring countries, and a semi-peripheral status which leads them to distance themselves from the norms of freedom, democracy and prevention of nuclear proliferation in international society based on the logic of strength. For detailed information, see the project website: (http://src-h.slav.hokudai.ac.jp/rp/english/outline/index.html).
6 The fieldwork in China was carried out intermittently from 2001 until now, while field research in Russia and India started in 2009. Specific names and the regions in which main sites are located are; (1) Xiaofengying, Beijing, China, (2) Simen and Zhaizhuang, Henan, China, (3) Huadun, Jiangxi, China, (4) Linji, Gansu, China, (5) Poklovo-Marfino, Tambov, Russia, (6) Te'nki, Tatarstan, Russia, (7) Peddamallareddy, Andhra Pradesh, India, (8) Desarathipur, Orissa, India. I am very grateful to Professor Kimitaka Matsuzato of Hokkaido University for accompanying my field trip to Russia in September 2009, March 2012 and August 2013. The Russian excursion would have been impossible without his kind assistance.
7 GP normally composes several administrative villages, which are locally called 'revenue villages'. Peddamallareddy GP is formed by two revenue villages (Peddamallareddy and Mallupally). Another research site, Desarathipur GP in Orissa, is also composed by two revenue villages (Desarathipur and Kharod).
8 Tambov cases in this section are based on the name list of *raion* deputies provided by Znamenka *raion*, obtained via Professor Dmitry G. Seltser of Tambov State University named after G. R. Derzhavin on 7 July 2012. Since the data do not provide information about the actual situation of electoral manipulations, I can only roughly associate the village with the constituency, judging by the home addresses of deputies.
9 Interview with Zufar Galimullovich Garafiev, chief of Kamskoe Ust'e *Raion*, 12 September 2009, Kamskoe Ust'e *Raion*, Tatarstan.
10 Data provided by Te'nki Village soviet, 11 September 2009.
11 See Zhong (2003, pp. 159–69) for general organizational structure in Chinese villages.
12 Dealing with a case in the Philippines, Wolters (1984, pp. 198–99) distinguishes political patronage from the 'patron–client relationship' in a traditional sense

102   *Political systems and diplomacy*

because 'in general the relationships between politicians and the electorate were short term, impersonal, instrumental and based on a specific transaction'.

13 Yadav and Palshikar (2006, pp. 112–13) note that there is a trend towards opening the competitive format and that single party dominance by the Congress Party is now an exception rather than the rule; they point out that a large number of states have shifted to a two party or two-plus party competition, and there are many more multi-polar systems than before.

14 Interview with a Panchayat Samiti from Peddamallareddy Village, 23 December 2011, Peddamallareddy Village, Nizamabad District, AP.

15 In 2009, the independent income of Peddamallareddy included; house tax, personal income tax, documentation tax, auction income of village markets, housing permission, shop license tax, water tap bills, etc., which amount to approximately Rs.560,000.

16 In regard to this role, Joshi and Narwani (2002, p. 189) note that after the introduction of the Community Development Program in 1952, Panchayat Raj institutions at the village, block and district level are recommended and expected to properly utilize the development funds by the government.

17 Interview with Eeshwar Reddy, a ward member in Peddamallareddy Village, 19 December 2011, Peddamallareddy Village, Nizamabad District, AP.

18 Interview with husband of sarpanch in Peddamallareddy Village, 22 December 2010, Peddamallareddy Village, Nizamabad District, AP.

19 Interview with Patluri Kondal Reddy, son of P. Vimalamma, a ward member in Peddamallareddy Village, 18 December 2011, Peddamallareddy Village, Nizamabad District, AP.

20 Levitsky and Way (2010, pp. 186–201) argues that, as authoritarian consolidation progressed under the Putin regime from 2000 to 2008, elections became less competitive. For more on this point, see also Gel'man (2008, pp. 913–15).

21 Among the four non-UR deputies, two are Communist and the rest are independent. Interview with Anatolii Ivanovich Bushuev, chief of Znamenka council, 13 March 2012, Znamenka *Raion*, Tambov.

22 Interviews in Znamenka *Raion*, 3–8 September 2009, Tambov.

23 Interview with Khalim Khamidullovich Ibatov, chief of Bol'shie Saltyki Village, 12 September 2009, Bol'shie Saltyki Village, Kamskoe Ust'e *Raion*, Tatarstan.

24 Interview with Aleksandr Egorovich Khamkin, 22 August 2013, Ten'ki Village, Kamskoe Ust'e *Raion*, Tatarstan. He added that the high membership rate was not because they are village deputies but because most of them occupied important posts in various spheres.

25 Interview with Vladimir Penikov, deputy chief of social institute in Tambov state, 9 March 2012.

26 The more 'emotional', and thus less materialistic way of ballot mobilization in Russia might have something to do with its developmental stage. With this respect, Kitschelt and Wilkinson (2007, p. 19) point out that 'in many systems characterized by relatively high levels of poverty – such as Thailand, India, Pakistan, or Zambia – patrons directly purchase clients' votes in exchange for money, liquor, clothes, food, or other immediately consumable goods'.

27 Interview with Anatolii Ivanovich Bushuev, chief of Znamenka council, 12 March 2012, Znamenka *Raion*, Tambov.

28 Interview with the chief of Znamenka *Raion*, 12 March 2012, Znamenka *Raion*, Tambov.

29 See Tianyuan (2012, pp. 45–73). Earlier research (Liu, 1998) has also disclosed that village cadres, except for regular administrative contacts, have attempted to create good relationships with potential political patrons by means of holding banquets and gifting at ceremonial occasions.

Patronage and village leadership 103

30 Interview with Qiao Haijun, a villager of Simen Village, 9 August 2012, Nanyang, Henan.
31 See Luo (2002), Luo (2006, pp. 134–38), Shen (2006), Luo (2009, pp. 165–71). What they mean by 'third' is that it comes after the power of the state (first) and the village community itself (second).
32 From my field notes of Linji Village in August 2010 and August 2011. Largely focusing on rich coastal areas, recent scholarship has studied the 'entrepreneur turned village secretary' (*laoban shuji*) or 'entrepreneur turned village chief' (*laoban cunzhang*). See, for example, Lu (2010), He (2012, pp. 290–307).
33 Such villages are often labeled as *kongkecun* (empty village) or *tanhuancun* (paralyzed village).
34 On these points, see Tahara (2013, pp. 89–92), Matsuzato and Tahara (2014).
35 SC (scheduled caste) and ST (scheduled tribes) dwellings are often concentrated in a corner of a residential area in every village.
36 With regard to this penetrating power, Krishna (2003, pp. 1182) points out a recent trend where 'the budget for rural development has not only expanded many times, but it has also been fragmented into a large number of tiny parcels that can cover a larger number of villages than before'.
37 As a typical case, see Case 4 in the previous section.
38 On this point, Kou (2013) has come to a similar conclusion through a comparison of land acquisition cases in India and China.
39 This is equivalent to what Cameron Ross (2009, pp. 184–98) calls 'Putin's electoral vertical'.

References

Antlöv, H. (2004) 'National Elections, Local Issues: The 1997 and 1999 National Elections in a Village on Java', in H. Antlöv, and S. Cederroth, eds, *Elections in Indonesia: The New Order and Beyond*, London: RoutledgeCurzon, pp. 111–37.

Brass, P. R. (1978) 'Indian Election Studies', *South Asia*, vol. 1, no. 2, pp. 91–108.

Fan, H. (2008) *Xianyu Zhengzhi: Quanli Shijian yu Richang Zhixu*, Beijing: China Social Science Press.

Gel'man, V. (2008) 'Party Politics in Russia: From Competition to Hierarchy', *Europe-Asia Studies*, vol. 60, no. 6, pp. 913–30.

Gold, T., D. Guthrie and D. Wank, eds (2002) *Social Connections in China: Institutions, Culture, and the Changing Nature of Guanxi*, Cambridge: Cambridge University Press.

Graham, B. D. (1975) 'Studies on Indian Elections: A Review Article', *The Journal of Commonwealth and Comparative Politics*, vol. 13, no. 2, pp. 193–205.

He, X. (2012) *Zuzhi Qilai: Quxiao Nongyeshui hou Nongcun Jiceng Zuzhi Jianshe Yanjiu*, Jinan: Shandong People's Press.

Joshi, R. P. and G. S. Narwani (2002) *Panchayat Raj in India: Emerging Trends Across the States*, Jaipur: Rawat Publications.

Kasuga, M. (1988) 'Buraku suisen no rekishiteki hensen ni tsuite: Tottori-ken Yazu-gun Saji-son no Baai' [On Historical Change of Village Nomination: The Case of Saji Village, Yazu District, Tottori Prefecture], *Soshioroji*, vol. 33, no. 2, pp. 39–60 (in Japanese).

Kennedy, J. J. (2007) 'From Tax-for-Fee Reform to the Abolition of Agricultural Taxes: The Impact on Township Governments in North-west China', *The China Quarterly*, no. 189, pp. 43–59.

104 *Political systems and diplomacy*

Kitschelt, H. and S. I. Wilkinson (2007) 'Citizen–Politician Linkages: An Introduction', in H. Kitschelt and S. I. Wilkinson, eds, *Patrons, Clients, and Policies: Patterns of Democratic Accountability and Political Competition*, New York: Cambridge University Press, pp. 1–49.

Kou, Rai (Guang, L.) (2013) 'Tochi funso no mekanizumu to chiho seifu no taio' [Mechanism of Governmental Conflict and the Rise of Local Government], in R. Tou and K. Matsuzato, eds, *Yurashia chiiki taikoku no tochi moderu* [Models of Government for Eurasia Regional Powers], Kyoto: Mineruva Shobo, pp. 180–212 (in Japanese).

Krishna, A. (2003) 'What Is Happening to Caste? A View from Some North Indian Villages', *Journal of Asian Studies*, vol. 62, no. 4, pp. 1171–93.

——(2007) 'Politics in the Middle: Mediating Relationship Between the Citizens and the State in Rural North India', in H. Kitschelt and S. I. Wilkinson, eds, *Patrons, Clients, and Policies: Patterns of Democratic Accountability and Political Competition*, New York: Cambridge University Press, pp. 141–58.

Levitsky, S. and L. A. Way (2010) *Competitive Authoritarianism: Hybrid Regimes After the Cold War*, Cambridge and New York: Cambridge University Press.

Liu, J. (1998) 'Xiangcun Ganbu Jiaowang Jiegou Fenxi', *Zhongguo Nongcun Guancha*, no. 2, pp. 48–54.

Liu, X. (2000) *In One's own Shadow: An Ethnographic Account of the Condition of Post-reform Rural China*, Berkeley and Los Angeles: University of California Press.

Lu, F. (2010) *Nengren Zhengzhi: Siying Qiyezhu Zhicun Xianxiang Yanjiu*, Beijing: China Social Science Press.

Luo, J. (2009) *Shizi Lukou de Xiaohecun: Subei Cunzhi Moshi Chutan*, Jinan: Shandong People's Press.

Luo, X. (2002) 'Disanzhong Liliang', *Zhejiang Xuekan*, no. 1, pp. 24–25.

——(2006) *Zhishui: Guojia Jieru yu Nongmin Hezuo*, Wuhan: Hubei People's Press.

Matsuzato, K. and F. Tahara (2014) 'Russia's Local Reform of 2003 from a Historical Perspective: A Comparison with China', *Acta Slavica Iaponica*, vol. 34, pp. 115–39.

Migdal, J. S. (1974) *Peasants, Politics, and Revolution: Pressures toward Political and Social Change in the Third World*, Princeton, NJ: Princeton University Press.

Mitra, S. K. (1979) 'Ballot Box and Local Power: Elections in an Indian village', *The Journal of Commonwealth and Comparative Politics*, vol. 17, no. 3, pp. 283–99.

Nakamizo, K. (2012) *Indo: Boryoku to Minshushugi* [India: Violence and Democracy], Tokyo: Tokyo University Press (in Japanese).

Ookama, K. (1994) *Gyoseison no shikko taisei to shuraku: Akita-ken Yuri-gun Nishime-mura no 'keisei' katei* [Executive Structure of Administrative Village: The Process of 'Formation' of Nishime Village, Yuri District, Akita Prefecture], Tokyo: Nogyo Sogo Kenkyusho (in Japanese).

Opler, M. E., W. L. Rowe and M. L. Stroop (1959) 'Indian National and State Elections in a Village Context', *Human Organization*, vol. 18, no. 1, pp. 30–34.

Ross, C. (2009) *Local Politics and Democratization in Russia*, London: Routledge.

——(2011) 'Regional Elections and Electoral Authoritarianism in Russia', *Europe-Asia Studies*, vol. 63, no. 4, pp. 641–61.

Shen, D. (2006) 'Disanzhong Liliang: Jiangxi Ji'an Nongcun Diaocha Biji (1)', *Wenshi Bolan*, no. 1, pp. 58–59.

Tahara, F. (2013) 'Principal, Agent or Bystander? Governance and Leadership in Chinese and Russian Villages', *Europe-Asia Studies*, vol. 65, no. 1, pp. 75–101.

Thiele, G. (1986) 'The State and Rural Development in Tanzania: The Village Administration as a Political Field', *The Journal of Development Studies*, vol. 22, no. 3, pp. 540–57.

Tianyuan, S. (Tahara, F.) (2012) *Riben Shiye zhong de Zhongguo Nongcun Jingying: Guanxi, Tuanjie, Sannong Zhengzhi*, Jinan: Shandong People's Press.

Wakabayashi, M. (1992) *Taiwan: bunretsu kokka to minshuka* [Taiwan: Divided Nation and Democratization], Tokyo: Tokyo University Press (in Japanese).

Wilkinson, S. I. (2007) 'Explaining Changing Patterns of Party-Voter Linkages in India', in H. Kitschelt and S. I. Wilkinson, eds, *Patrons, Clients, and Policies: Patterns of Democratic Accountability and Political Competition*, New York and Cambridge: Cambridge University Press, pp. 110–40.

Wolters, Willem (1984) *Politics, Patronage, and Class Conflict in Central Luzon*, Quezon City: New Day Publishers.

Wong, Y. H. and T. Leung (2001) *Guanxi: Relationship Marketing in a Chinese Context*, New York: Haworth.

Yadav, Y. and S. Palshikar (2006) 'Party System and Electoral Politics in the Indian States, 1952–2002: From Hegemony to Convergence', in P. R. deSouza and E. Sridharan, eds., *India's Political Parties*, New Delhi: Sage Publications, pp. 73–115.

Zhong, Y. (2003) *Local Government and Politics in China: Challenges from Below*, Armonk, NY: M. E. Sharpe.

6 Loss of political leadership and passive 'triple transformation' in the former Soviet Union

A comparison with China's reform strategy

Liang Tang

Introduction

China's reform in the late 1970s and the reforms in the Soviet Union in the mid-1980s were both moderate in nature. Their initial motivations were to carry out within-system reforms to save the socialist system. Yet, the evolution and outcome of the two reforms turned out to be quite different. In China, with all its ups and downs over the decades, the political line of reform within the system still holds. Although China's market economy system is not yet completely established, and achievement in the development of democratic politics is not up to the expectations of the people, China has made tremendous achievements in economic and social development, and has made substantial progress in terms of broadening political freedoms and rights. In contrast, the Soviet Union underwent and completed a major societal transformation within a short period of five to six years – from a within-system reform to radical Western-style democracy and marketization of the economy – at the cost of the dissolution of the former Soviet Union and long-term political and economic disorder.

Of all the empirical works applying transition theory to the study of the Soviet/Russian transformation, *Russia's Unfinished Revolution* by Michael McFaul (2001) stands out as an excellent book. The author takes the scope of the reform and political dynamics as independent variables, and explains the outcome and tumultuous process of transition through analysis of a large amount of data as well as interviews with people involved in the reform process. McFaul points out that in their attempt to expand political influence, the opposition parties put forward new reform goals one after another, which led to serious conflicts between different forces both within and outside the system. As a result, the Russian transition turned out to be extremely difficult. Generally speaking, different political forces have different demands and assertions with regard to the goal of reform. They necessarily proceed with political maneuvers to shape the reform agenda. Therefore, the balance of forces among the political parties, that is, who has the upper hand and how to form a reform alliance, affect the government's capacity in setting its reform goals and in carrying out its reform strategies. By virtue of its focus on the political dynamics and reform objective, McFaul's analytical approach is also applicable to the analysis of China's political reform process. But McFaul's research is very much influenced by existing system transition theory and is also centered on explaining conflicts in the transition, and is less focused on stable and sustained reform or transformation. Therefore, it is necessary to make some major modifications in the framework before we can adapt it to a comparative analysis of the transitions in China and Russia.

First, in McFaul's study, there are three major goals of reform in Soviet Union: democratization, marketization, and the restructuring of the sovereign state. McFaul measures the scope of reform by whether it is systematically carried out separately or simultaneously, that is, the scope of the reform is considered to be small if all the reform goals are pursued separately while it is considered big if they are pursued all at the same time. However, my study argues that if a socialist country adopts a gradual course of reform, then it would be well justified to further divide the goal of political reform into three sub-goals of different dimensions or stages, namely administrative or government reform, moderate liberalization,[1] and democratization. We may regard government reform and moderate liberalization as the 'infrastructural development phase of democratization', defined as the first stage of political transition. Such a framework will not only enable us to make an analysis of China's political reform within the framework of transition theory, but it will also enable a comparative analysis between Soviet/Russia and China. That is to say, we can compare how the Russian reform has rapidly developed from the infrastructural phase to democratic transition and consolidation, and why China's political reform remains at the stage of infrastructural development.

Second, in his study, McFaul sets the political dynamics and the scope of reform as independent variables, yet he fails to give a sufficient theoretical explanation of why these two variables would keep changing in the Soviet/Russian reform. My study sets an intermediate variable based on achievement after implementation of reform strategies, and the standpoints of the elites both in and out of the system and that of the general population, so that we can analyze the mechanism of the interaction between political dynamics and reform strategies. Specifically speaking, at the initial stage of reform in a socialist country, the government has absolute political dominance and is relatively autonomous in making its reform strategy without much interference from the outside. However, once the reform is in progress, whether the reform strategy will fit the social environment, how the elites and population will understand and critique the reform, and to what extent the liberalization target can be materialized will all influence the change of the support base for the within-system reformists, the change of alliances in the reform, and the change in the government's controlling power. In other words, the reform strategy will act upon the dominant power of reform.

Third, in McFaul's study, both the political dynamics and scope of the reform are set as independent variables. In the present paper, it is argued, the scope of reform is, to a great extent, decided by the relative strength of political power

108   *Political systems and diplomacy*

and in particular by the government's political power or the strength of political control capacity; and, therefore, the scope of reform is not an independent variable but an intermediate variable that is influenced by the political dynamics of the transitional course and its results. At the initial stage of reform, as both Chinese and Soviet governments were in control of political initiatives, they were able to effectively resist demands and assertions from the opposition. Thereafter, the government in China was able to maintain strong political dominance by maintaining the system of one-party leadership. In contrast, in the course of radical liberalization in the Soviet Union/Russia, the opposition gained a relatively larger political space and rapidly extended its political influence, so that the government was forced to accept more radical demands in the reform, that is, Western-style democracy, marketization, and restructuring of the sovereign state.

Using the intermediate variable based on the result of system reform, that is, the achievement of economic development and liberal political space, this paper examines the dynamics of the ongoing interaction between the dominant political power and the political reform strategy. While comparing it with China's reform strategy, I explain why the Soviet/Russian reform, which started with a moderate inner-system reform strategy, soon turned to radical liberalization and finally embraced in a passive manner the 'triple transformation' of democratization, marketization and the restructuring of the sovereign state, all of which went far beyond Gorbachev's initial intentions.

Change from moderate reform to radical liberalization

In the early days after Mikhail Gorbachev took office as general secretary of the Communist Party of the Soviet Union in 1985, he expressed the idea of breaking the deadlock of economic stagnancy through the so-called New Thinking (Oshima and Ogawa, 2000, p. 80). In April 1985, the CPSU Central Committee adopted the 'strategy of speeding up development', whose major goal was to promote the Soviet economy through scientific progress and to speed up the socio-economic development of the Soviet Union (Wu, 2000). It is remarkable that Gorbachev attempted to develop the economy by strengthening the state administrative institutions within the framework of the central-planning economic system. In order to invigorate the economy, the Soviet government introduced the 'contract system' (1986) in the state farms and collective farms, and, on the other hand, promulgated the Individual Business Law (1986), the State Business Law (1987), and the Trade Association Law (1988). The new system featured some market mechanisms and increased autonomy in management on the part of businesses and workers.

Thus the early stage of Soviet reform was, by its nature, a reform within the socialist system (Shiokawa, 1994, p. 99) and had a lot in common with the early stage of China's reform. Nevertheless, at this stage the Soviet Union lagged far behind China in improving conditions for economic production and promoting economic reform. First, compared with China, the Soviet

Union had a much longer history of a planned economy, and its impact had already penetrated all aspects of economic activity, and thus created many more difficulties for marketization reform. Second, the Soviet Union had a much higher level of industrialization and urbanization than China in the late 1970s, and thus there was relatively less room for economic growth. And there was not as much enthusiasm as in China in terms of entrepreneurship among entrepreneurs or eagerness to get rich and free from poverty among the ordinary people. And third, the Soviet Union, as one of the two leading actors in the Cold War, had been competing with the US for world hegemony, which thus greatly limited its economic exchanges with Euro-American countries. And finally, due to a larger supply of crude oil on the international market, the oil price dropped sharply from US$30 a barrel in May 1985 to US$12 in April 1986, which caused tremendous loss for the Soviet Union, which depended heavily on crude oil exports for foreign currency. Besides this, the 'anti-alcohol campaign' also reduced revenues.

Under such disadvantageous conditions, the Soviet economy between 1985 and 1990 barely maintained its previous rate of growth and failed to achieve the expected goal of the 'strategy of acceleration' (Brown, 1997, p. 139). In addition, there was widespread shortage of commodities (Kotz and Weir, 1997, pp. 80–83). The pro-reform leaders headed by Gorbachev, believing that resistance to the reform by the conservatives and the massive bureaucracy with embedded interests in the existent system had caused the economic reform to stagnate, made the decision to take bold moves in political reform so as to win support from the masses and in particular the intellectuals, in order to overcome resistance from the conservatives and the huge bureaucracy. Entering the year of 1988, the Soviet Union further expanded glasnost, introduced more mechanisms of competition in elections at all levels, and, as a matter of fact, exercised tolerance toward non-official associations and their activities. In other words, the Soviet Union had not only shifted the focus of reform from the economy to political aspects but also drastically transformed the goal of political reform from government reform and moderate liberalization to radical liberalization and democratization.

The expansion of glasnost was an important turning point for the Soviet Union in moving from political reform to radical liberalization. In terms of its goals and contents, glasnost may cover two dimensions – information disclosure and liberalization – and to a great extent these two dimensions were associated with and differentiated from each other. Information disclosure aimed to improve administrative efficiency, enhance the managerial capability of the government, and promote socio-economic development. The information disclosed concerned regulations and policies related to people's lives, and the activities and management of enterprises and other social organizations. This can be taken as administrative reform. On the other hand, liberalization aimed mainly to loosen up restriction of speech and the press, which was more associated with the political rights and freedom. To what extent the government allows the people to expose or criticize political or social reality

110   *Political systems and diplomacy*

and to put forward propositions different from or even opposite to those of the government is an important indicator of the progress of liberalization. Measurement of the range of liberalization within a set time can be used to discern the speed of liberalization, that is, it is a major tool for distinguishing radical liberalization from moderate liberalization. If the openness of administrative affairs that China has so far promoted and the glasnost that the Soviet Union promoted at the early stage of the reform can be mainly considered to be measures for administrative reform, the expansion of glasnost after 1988 may then considered as radical liberalization.

In his report to the 27th Congress of the CPSU in February 1986, Gorbachev explicitly pointed out that 'the expansion of glasnost is to tell the people all things happening in the country and society, so that the work conducted by the Party and the Soviet Union is placed under the surveillance of the people'. That is to say, the main purpose of promoting glasnost was to increase political transparency and to enhance the vitality of social development (Kimura *et al.*, 2010, p. 80). When the Chernobyl nuclear plant disaster happened in April 1986, the Soviet government did not at first get accurate information and failed to manage the crisis in a timely manner. Retrospection over management of the crisis brought about an important opportunity to promote glasnost. In June 1986, when Yakovlev, the most radical leader of the reformists within the CPSU, took office as the Central Committee's secretary in charge of the realm of ideology, officials with a strong liberal tendency were assigned to positions in charge of some important magazines.

The expanded glasnost as a movement of radical liberalization was reflected in the media with high expectations and heated discussions. The ideas of radical reform were widely disseminated. Compared with China, where the reform very soon achieved economic development, the Soviet Union failed to achieve much in the economy in its first stage of reform and this induced discussions on how to promote economic reform. With the increase of freedom or openness of the media, ideas of radical reform occupied an increasingly larger market share both within and outside the system (Kotz and Weir, 1997). Such ideas of radical reform towards Western-style marketization and democratization, by their nature, signified a denouncement of the existing system, which dealt a heavy blow to the authority of the government and also stirred up serious inner-Party conflicts as the conservatives within the Party reacted vehemently to this shift in the status quo. Obviously, the polemics over system reform in the expansion of glasnost in the Soviet Union differed sharply from what happened in China – in its promotion of economic reform, China explored unknown waters with great courage and focused on the effects of its actions while trying hard to avoid any serious arguments over ideology.

In its long years in power, the CPSU had periods of coercion politics, particularly during Stalin's Great Purge, which turned tens of millions into innocent victims. With the expanded glasnost, on the demand of the people both within and outside the system to re-examine history and rehabilitate the victims, the CPSU set up ad hoc organizations to repudiate false and unjust cases.[2] Accompanied by large-scale rehabilitation and repudiation of such injustices, and with the further expansion of openness in the media and speech, there appeared in Soviet society a trend from denying Stalin to denying the Stalin model, and to denying Lenin and the Soviet political system, which severely damaged the image and authority of the CPSU.

The method by which the Soviet Union dealt with such historical wrongs was quite different from that in China. In June 1981, the 6th Plenary of the 11th Central Committee of the CPC passed the 'Resolution on Certain Historical Issues since the Founding of the People's Republic of China'. On the one hand, this resolution thoroughly rebuked the political line of the Cultural Revolution and criticized the mistakes committed by the Anti-Right Movement, the Big Leap Forward Movement, etc.; on the other hand, this resolution made a clear distinction between the rights and wrongs of the Party's basic political line and major policies since the founding of the New China, and evaluated Mao Zedong as a historic figure whose merits outweighed his errors. This official stance is still the principle by which all media and publications must abide in China today.

Another major move in the expanded glasnost was to enhance the transparency of political operations. Pre-Gorbachev politics in the Soviet Union was mainly operated in a black box, with a rigid and inflexible model of propaganda featuring a strong authoritarian style. Gorbachev pioneered the personal style of the top Soviet leader of communicating directly with the ordinary people in everyday language. The Soviet television station held a live telecast of the 19th National Party Conference held in the spring of 1988 and the National People's Congress in 1989. Different opinions and arguments at the meetings, including those of top-level leaders, drew much attention from the whole of society and raised the people's consciousness of political participation. The personal style of Gorbachev's leadership and the enhanced transparency of politics not only brought people a feeling of freshness, but also greatly reduced the feeling of distance between the people and politics. Glasnost had become a political tool to gain widespread social support to overcome the conservative forces. However, neither the economic reform nor the political reform promoted by Gorbachev achieved the success expected by the people and, as a result, he would very soon lose general support and suffer from criticisms and attacks from the conservatives and radicals both within and outside the system.

Whether the common people have the legal right of association, assembly, parade, demonstration, and strike is an essential measure of a country's political freedom. In the Soviet Union, the rapid expansion of these rights became a major symbol of radical liberalization. Starting in 1986, there emerged in the Soviet Union some 'unofficial organizations' such as forums, clubs, intellectual groups, etc. As Gorbachev advocated dialogue and with the revision of criminal law, these 'unofficial organizations' increased to more than 30,000 by the end of 1987 and reached over 90,000 in 1989. In China, by contrast, in the 1980s and especially since 1990, there also emerged increasingly more civil organizations. However, under the guidance and management of the government,

112 *Political systems and diplomacy*

these civil organizations were mainly active in the realm of public goods or public service rather than that of politics.

In the Soviet Union, in the course of promoting liberalization with boldness, there started to appear some protest demonstrations and strikes. The Democratic Alliance organized its first large-scale demonstration in August 1988. Though the demonstration was harshly cracked down on by the authorities, it was followed by more anti-government demonstrations on different occasions – on the Memorial Day of the Red Terror in September 1988, on International Human Rights Day in October 1988, and in the name of opposition to the suppression of Georgians in April 1989. After May 21, 1989, there would be almost daily assemblies in Moscow organized by elected Congress members and constituents. Although these were mainly political protests organized by opposition groups, as the economy worsened the Soviet Union would see strikes for economic reasons. In the summer of 1989, the coal miners of Kuznetsk in Siberia held a large-scale strike with 110,000 participants, demanding higher wages and improved living conditions. Later, the strike movement developed in other places such as the Donetskiy coal mine in Ukraine. Gorbachev's authorities had to negotiate with the miners and agree to raise their wages and provide more everyday-life necessities. In March 1990, the coal miners went on strike again. This time, they not only demanded higher wages but also openly supported Yeltsin while criticizing Gorbachev.

Democratization and changes in the contrast of political power

A major indicator that democratization is being promoted is the practice of competitive direct elections. At the 19th National Conference of the CPSU held in June 1988, Gorbachev put forward for the first time the concept of 'humanist democratic socialism'. The Conference brought up the old slogan of 'All rights belong to the Soviet' and passed a resolution to establish a 'Soviet system of people's congresses', in which one third of the representatives would be chosen by the CPSU and the National Federation of Trade Unions, and the other two thirds would be selected through competitive direct elections. Guided by this resolution, the Soviet Union carried out the first competitive direct election of people's representatives on March 26, 1989. Although most representatives elected were members of the CPSU, of the 160 first secretaries of the CPSU committees, 32 failed to be elected. On the other hand, Boris Yeltsin, a radical reformist within the Communist Party, Andre Sakharov, a famous anti-system social activist, and some others were elected as people's representatives. In the three Baltic republics many pro-independence candidates were elected. As a result, the balance of political power began to move clearly towards the opposition.

The implementation of competitive direct elections would also change the institutions of political power in the Soviet Union. As pointed out by Brown, a Soviet studies expert, up until mid-1988 the Central Committee of the CPSU had been making the most authoritative decisions on various public policies. But after 1990, as the CPSU no longer dominated the political scene, the decisions made at the Communist Party's Congress were no longer as important to the Soviet people. Outside observers were no longer as concerned about such decisions as before (Brown, 1997). Of course, since there were no developed and well-established operational systems, the Supreme Soviet was far less effective than the former Politburo in assuming power and fulfilling responsibilities as the institution of supreme power.

After the establishment of the Soviet People's Congress through competitive direct elections, anti-system activists, in order to coordinate their operations and at the suggestion of Gavriil Popov, held the first conference of the Inter-Regional Group of People's Deputies in July 1989. The conference elected the chairman of the Inter-Regional Group and set up a coordination committee. Since then, the Inter-Regional Group of People's Deputies played the de facto role of the opposition at the People's Congress. Meanwhile, in order to prepare for the 1990 elections to the Russian parliament, some anti-system scholars, civil movement activists, human rights activists, and others organized a 'voters' association' (MOI). In January 1990, the MOI reorganized itself into Democratic Russia, with its network expanding throughout the whole of Russia. Though members of Democratic Russia differed in their political views, they shared the same political stance against the CPSU.

After the election of the Congress of People's Deputies of the Soviet Union, each republic elected its own congress of people's deputies and president by means of direct elections but with even more openness and competitiveness. Acting according to the Law of Election of People's Deputies adopted by the Supreme Soviet of the Soviet Union in October 1989, Russia elected 1,068 deputies for the First Congress of People's Deputies of Russia in May 1990 and Democratic Russia, as an opposition party, garnered one third of the seats in the Congress. Then, the Congress of People's Deputies of Russia created through elections the Supreme Soviet of Russia, which would hold the powers of legislature, administration and supervision, and Yeltsin was elected as chairman of the Supreme Soviet of the Russian Federation. Soon after, Russia decided to adopt the presidential system. In June 1991, Yeltsin was elected as president of Russia in a landslide victory against the former prime minister Ryzhkov and other candidates.

Although the Soviet Union had adopted federalism, the Central Committee of the CPSU remained in strong control of local political power through its major personnel appointments and its strict organizational discipline. However, in the course of radical liberalization, there emerged nationalist movements that demanded more power of autonomy or even independence. Meanwhile, as competitive direct elections had changed the rules of power, this greatly increased the power of the local structure to stand against the central government with the justification of the people's will. As a result, the democratic movement and nationalist movement intertwined and thus greatly decreased the power and authority of the central government and Gorbachev as its top leader.

114   *Political systems and diplomacy*

In contrast to the rapid rise of anti-system parties, there appeared within the CPSU serious opposition and splits over the issues of radical liberalization and democratization. As mentioned above, at the early stage of the reform there was fairly good agreement within the Communist Party on the political line of inner-system reform. But when Gorbachev considered the conservatives to be obstructing further reform and tried to reduce their influence by utilizing the power of the media or through frequent high-level personnel changes, he met with fierce resistance and opposition. In 1989, the inner-Party conservatives set up the Workers' United Front of Russia and, in June 1990, reorganized it into the Communist Party of Russia, which gained about 40 percent of the total seats at the First Congress of People's Deputies of Russia.

Within the CPSU there were also some radical reformists with an even stronger stance than Gorbachev in favor of Western-style democratization and marketization. At the first stage of the reform, however, they were strictly restrained by Party discipline. However, as a result of democratization, the radical reformists, represented by Yeltsin, could legally gain political power with the support of the will of the people, even if they had acted against the will of the CPSU Central Committee or that of the CPSU's general secretary. This led to the situation where radical reformists within the Party who were no longer satisfied with Gorbachev's reform process left the CPSU without hesitation and joined the political opposition. In January 1990, Yeltsin, Popov and others took part in the founding conference of the Democratic Platform, and the conference called for a multiparty system and demanded that the CPSU recognize the historical crimes committed by the CPSU. At the 28th Congress of the CPSU held in July 1990, Yeltsin publicly announced his resignation from the Communist Party with the claim that the reform had failed.

Passive triple transformation

According to some studies, the number of dissidents in the Soviet Union was in the thousands between 1967 and 1968, but by about 1977 the number had been reduced to dozens due to harsh government crackdowns. The dissidents at that time were very weak and widely dispersed (Kimura *et al.*, 2010, pp. 19–28) and their political demands were relatively moderate. However, as the economic reform failed to reach the expected goal, the radical political reform strategy would greatly change the balance of political power within and without the established Soviet system. Through the increasingly more open and more liberal media, the opposition very soon won wide support from the public and the general population; meanwhile, the opposition turned to making more and more radical reform demands. Moreover, there had been established all kinds of official and non-official organizations, including the opposition party, with such well-known and politically savvy leaders as Yeltsin.

The opposition had to support Gorbachev in his reforms and help him overcome resistance from the conservatives before they could gain and expand their space for legal activities and increase their political impact. As a

Political leadership and transformation 115

result, while the splits within the party brought huge damage to the CPSU's cohesion, Gorbachev as the top leader was still able to maintain widespread political support. But such a situation did not last very long. As the economy kept worsening and with social order in chaos, dissatisfaction with Gorbachev increased rapidly not only among the conservatives but also among the ordinary people. On the other hand, when the opposition gained their legal space for political activities, they would either play the opposition in parliament or organize activities in the streets such as parades and demonstrations, demanding that the Soviet authorities promote Western-style democracy and marketization in ways even more radical than those of Gorbachev's reform goals.

Gorbachev asked for cooperation and support from the opposition by making major compromises over the radical reform demands (Shiokawa, 1994, p. 111). To reach this goal, he reiterated his stance of promoting social democracy in an essay published in November 1989, and, in another essay published in February 1990, he explicitly expressed his support for the multi-party system. Around the summer of 1990, Gorbachev even agreed to a plan of privatization. In July 1991, the draft of the newly revised Communist Party Program explicitly proposed building a socialist democracy. About the same time, Gorbachev gave tacit consent to the decree promulgated by Yeltsin, which ordered the separation of the Party and the administration in certain state government organizations.

Therefore, while Gorbachev made use of powerful political initiatives to actively promote the first-stage moderate reform within the system as well as the second-stage reform of radical liberalization, after 1989 when the balance of political power underwent major changes, Gorbachev increasingly succumbed to pressure from the opposition and continued the promotion of Western-style democracy in a passive manner. For example, under the pressure of assembly and demonstration by the opposition, Gorbachev and the CPSU Plenary made a decision on March 11 to submit a proposition to the Congress of People's Deputies of the Soviet Union for a revision of Article 6 of the Constitution.

With all the compromises and concessions made by Gorbachev, things did not develop in the direction he had anticipated. In particular, Yeltsin attempted to launch a final political campaign against Gorbachev by weakening the power of the central government. On January 14, 1991, Yeltsin announced the decision to sign a 'Quartet Treaty' – involving politics, the economy, ethnicity, and culture – between the republics of Russia, Belarus, Ukraine, and Kazakhstan. On February 19, 1991, Yeltsin gave a televised speech that demanded the immediate resignation of Gorbachev and called on the people not to cooperate with the central government. Facing a situation where the political and economic outlook was further deteriorating and the Union was risking disintegration, the conservatives allied themselves with those forces that aimed to maintain the unity of the Soviet Union. And in order to maintain the unity of the Soviet Union as well as his personal political power, Gorbachev started to distance himself from the radical reformists within the Party and assign conservatives to important positions.

116 *Political systems and diplomacy*

On August 19, 1991, Vice President Yanayev of the Soviet Union and others launched a coup d'état and put Gorbachev under house arrest. The State Committee for the State of Emergency headed by Yanayev stated in the *Open Letter to the People of the Soviet Union* that the reform process led by Gorbachev had run into a dead end and that the 'special operation' was for the purpose of saving the country and maintaining the unity of the Union and the leadership of the Communist Party. At that time, public opinion in general tended to attribute the cause of the stagnation to the existent politico-economic system, and to attribute the failure of the reform to resistance from the conservatives and the incompleteness of Gorbachev's reform measures. Consequently, the coup not only met with strong counter-attacks from the opposition headed by Yeltsin, but also failed to win wide political support, including that of the armed forces. Soon after the coup failed, Yeltsin took the political leadership from Gorbachev. Yeltsin was in charge of the disintegration of the Soviet Union, and he also tried to promote marketization and privatization by implementing 'shock therapy'.

Before he resigned from the presidency at the end of 1999, Yeltsin had been the only strong man in Russian politics. But compared with the top leaders of the Soviet era, Yeltsin had no solid power base. First, from day one when Russia inherited power from the Soviet Union, it was the result of adopting Western-style democracy. The presidency and the parliament were created through competitive direct elections, and the people had broad freedom of speech, press, assembly, and demonstration. This meant that the Russian system would be different from that of the Soviet Union – the political power was not monistic but pluralistic, and the Russian Communist Party and other forces of opposition could impose serious restrictions on Yeltsin's power through parliamentary politics, elections, and street activities. Second, the failure of the economic reform, characterized by shock therapy, was a heavy blow to Yeltsin's personal political prestige. Because of significant differences over a series of important issues – economic reform, revision of the Constitution, the Russian political system, foreign policy, etc. – Yeltsin was involved in a fierce power struggle over political dominance with Aleksandr Rutskoy, the vice president, and Ruslan Khasbulatov, the chairman of the Supreme Soviet. In October 1993, Yeltsin used force and suppressed the opposition in parliament, and finally established his personal political dominance.

According to system transformation theory, when a country succeeds in democratization, the political transformation process will enter a period of 'democratic consolidation'. In the case of the Soviet Union and Russia, however, it not only paid the heavy price of state disintegration, economic recession, political instability, and social disorder in its democratization process, but it also faced a lot of problems in the democratic consolidation. Although President Yeltsin safeguarded the democratic system, he in his political operations frequently resorted to anti-democratic and authoritarian means. When Putin succeeded him as president, he not only strengthened the centralization of power, both in the system and in political practice, and exercised more control over the

Political leadership and transformation   117

media, but he also suppressed the opposition highhandedly. As a result, although Russia had on the whole restored basic order in politics, the economy, and social life, democratic politics had not been consolidated, and even regressed in certain aspects. Therefore, many scholars consider the current Russian political system to be a 'competitive authoritarian system' (Levitsky and Way, 2010).

Conclusion

Before they undergo reform, by their control over organizational resources and strict management of the media and publications, and through everyday political and ideological education of the people by various channels, socialist countries have much power in political leadership and social control, while the political opposition is weak and dispersed in society. As a result, systemic reforms in socialist countries originate mainly from a sense of crisis within the established system caused by the stagnancy of politico-economic development, rather than from the political pressure of the opposition. And due to the highly centralized power system in socialist countries, the top leader has the final say over important issues. Therefore, the top leader's attitude towards reform has a decisive impact on whether to carry on the reform and what strategy is to be taken for the reform. At the first stage of the reform, as the opposition had the least power while the government had strong political dominance, both China and the Soviet Union chose a moderate reform line with its major goal of economic development.

However, once a reform strategy is implemented, both the dominant political power and the reform strategy may change as well as interact with each other. Specifically, reformists may adjust their reform strategy and their alliance relationship in the reform according to the development of the reform in the previous stage and the consequent changes in the balance of political power. Meanwhile, other political forces may also influence the reform process through all kinds of efforts and may even attempt to gain political dominance. Therefore, changes in political dominance and adjustments to the political reform strategy turn into a process of interactions. Based on the reform process in China and that of Soviet Union, the following two aspects of reform results are the most important intermediate variables that impact the changes in political dominance and adjustments to the political reform strategy.

The first factor is whether or to what extent the reform will promote economic development. Generally speaking, a reform with substantial achievements will help reformists to consolidate their political dominance while a failed reform will weaken the political clout of reformists. In the transformation theory proposed by O'Donnell *et al.* (1986), the strategy in the transformation mainly refers to the political decisions made by the elites, and the participation of the people is considered to be merely the result of their mobilization by the elites. At the early stage of reform in many countries,

118 *Political systems and diplomacy*

those who initiate or participate in transformation movements are mainly members of the elites. However, what we want to emphasize here is that once a strategy is put into practice, the soundness of the reform strategy, that is, the success or failure of the reform – whether living quality is improved, whether social order is kept, whether public services improve, etc. – will directly affect the personal interests of the population at large. As a result, this situation will reinforce, to different degrees, their stance and attitude towards the reform strategy and push them to take an active part in activities related to the reform; meanwhile, these attitudes and activities of the general public will accordingly impact the struggle for political dominance.

The second factor is the pace of liberalization and the capacity of the government to adapt to it. On the one hand, liberalization by its nature means to increase political freedom and political rights, which goes in the direction of developing democratic politics. On the other hand, liberalization means that the opposition has more free space for speech and social activities, the balance of power between state and society sways in favor of the latter, and the government faces more pressure from the opposition when making and adjusting the reform strategy. Therefore, the key issue is not whether or not the government should promote liberalization, but how the government can control the pace of the course of liberalization and adapt to the process of liberalization by enhancing its governance ability. Generally speaking, in the course of moderate liberalization, due to its slower pace, there is limited space provided to the opposition within a given period of time, and it is therefore easier for the government to adapt to the gradually changing political environment and maintain its political dominance. On the other hand, radical liberalization not only leads to rapid and substantial changes in the balance of political power but also leads to strong resistance from the conservatives within the system, and this, therefore, is not good for the government in maintaining its dominant position in the reform.

When Gorbachev first started to reform the Soviet Union, his intention was also to increase the vitality of society by reform within the system, so as to promote economic development. But as the reform failed to achieve the expected goal, there emerged increasing impatience both within and outside the system, and the reformers readily put the economic failure down to resistance by the conservatives. In their eager pursuit of the concepts or the final goal, they neglected the fundamental importance of carefully planning periodic goals and reform programs based on reality. The promotion of radical liberalization, democratization, and marketization catered to the mood of Soviet society, but it failed to bring about good economic results due to a lack of rational policies, and led to the disintegration and restructuring of the political forces. Subsequently, the radical reformists headed by Gorbachev within the CPSU, the opposition represented by Yeltsin, and the conservatives within the CPSU all promoted their own political concepts and reform goals, yet all of them focused their energy mainly on the struggle for political power and lacked any feasible reform plan or capacity to promote the reform

Political leadership and transformation 119

process effectively. Although the opposition headed by Yeltsin finally won political dominance, and the Soviet Union/Russia completed the transformation of its political and economic systems as well as a restructuring of the sovereign state, the 'triple transformation' was more a result of a series of political developments beyond the expectations of the political leaders, rather than the successful completion of a carefully designed plan.

Notes

1 O'Donnell and Schmitter define liberalization as the redefinition and extension of rights. They propose the idea that though liberalization and democratization are different in nature, the former may create opportunities for the latter and there is a mechanism to spread out the transformation process, and, therefore, liberalization is defined as the preliminary stage of political system transformation. As perceived by the author of this study, however, liberalization as defined by O'Donnell and Schmitter (1986) belongs to radical liberalization and thus differs greatly from the moderate liberalization defined in the present study.
2 After Stalin's death, the CPSU also worked on rehabilitation and the repudiation of such injustices. But it did not do a thorough job.

References

Brown, Archie (1997) *The Gorbachev Factor*, Oxford: Oxford University Press.
Kimura, Hiroshi, Shigeki Hakamada and Toshihiko Yamauchi (2010) *Gendai Roshia wo miru me: 'Puchin no junen' no shogeki* [A Viewpoint on Current Russia: The Impact of 'Putin's Decade'], Tokyo: NHK Publishing Inc.
Kotz, David M. and Fred Weir (1997) *Revolution from Above: The Demise of the Soviet System*, London and New York: Routledge.
Levitsky, Steven and Lucan A. Way (2010) *Competitive Authoritarianism: Hybrid Regimes After the Cold War*, Cambridge: Cambridge University Press.
McFaul, Michael (2001) *Russia's Unfinished Revolution*, Ithaca, NY: Cornell University Press.
O'Donnell, Guillermo and Philippe C. Schmitter (1986) *Transitions from Authoritarian Rule: Tentative Conclusions About Uncertain Democracies*, Baltimore, MD: Johns Hopkins University Press.
Oshima, Azusa and Kazuo Ogawa (2000) *Saishin Rosia Keizai nyumon* [Primer of Up-to-Date Russian Economy], Tokyo: Nippon Hyoron Sha (in Japanese).
Shiokawa, Nobuaki (1994) *Soren towa nan dattaka* [What Was the Soviet Union?], Tokyo: Keiso Shobo (in Japanese).
Wu, Enyuan (2000) 'Lun Geerbaqiaofu de "Jiashu fazhang zhanlvu"' [Consideration of Gorbachev's Acceleration Strategy] *Zhongguo shehui kexue* [Chinese Social Science], no.5 (in Chinese).

7 The political consequences of peace
China's retreat for survival, 1988–91

Yoshifumi Nakai

Survival by default

China has survived a series of national crises. The survival went very well. The Chinese Communist Party (CCP) not only avoided the fate of its Soviet counterpart but also became the largest party organization in the world. Its membership reached almost 80 million in 2012 and has been increasing by almost 2 million a year. The success of the Chinese national economy is now history. The Chinese economy has kept on growing for more than twenty years since the early 1990s and its total gross domestic product (GDP) surpassed Japan's in 2010. China has become the number-two great power in the world, at least in terms of its size.

The rise of China was just a symbol when Chairman Mao Zedong declared that 'China has risen' at the Gate of Heavenly Peace in October 1949. The newly born People's Republic of China (PRC) was a huge but poor country. The national unity of China, the key goal of the nationalist revolution in 1911, was not yet realized. Tibet, Macau, Hong Kong, and Taiwan were under non-communist rule. The foreign relations of the New China with the two traditional great powers in Eurasia, Russia and India, began with high hopes in the 1950s. Since the early 1960s, however, their relations have kept on deteriorating. The PRC came to engage in serious border clashes, first with India in November 1962 and then with the Soviet Union in March 1969.

By the late 1990s, however, the rise of China had become a reality. What happened? When did the turn-around begin? How did these changes occur? In order to answer these questions, we need to look into three historical facts. First, China faced a series of crises in the late 1980s and early 1990s. All of the communist regimes experienced great turbulence in those years. Few survived, notably Cuba, North Korea, and China. Second, the rise of China coincided with the fall of the Soviet Union. The Soviet Union was far ahead of China in terms of political reform. This reversal of positions happened in the three years between 1988 and 1991. While the Soviet Union dissolved into a group of loosely governed political entities, China maintained its multi-ethnic governing structure. Third, the peace persisted, at least among those three great powers in Eurasia, throughout the so-called post-Cold War years.

China's retreat for survival, 1988–91 121

In October 2004, China and Russia agreed to settle the disputes over their national borders. In 2005, China and India agreed to maintain the status quo over their disputed territories.

This chapter first describes the sequence of events and decisions made by the CCP leaders in the three years between 1988 and 1991. The Chinese leaders happened to make a series of 'critical choices' (Pierson, 2004) in those three years. Those decisions kept on framing the range of later choices of the Chinese leadership. Those three years, therefore, deserve careful scrutiny.

Second, this chapter focuses on a comparison of the two political structures of the Soviet Union[1] and the PRC: the complex pseudo-federal state system, and the party–government ruling system. Why did the Soviet Union and the Communist Party of the Soviet Union (CPSU) dissolve so quickly and definitely? Why not the PRC and the CCP? Was the dissolution of the Soviet Union due to its 'unique federal structure' (Shiokawa, 2007a, p. vi.) as a leading Japanese scholar has indicated? Was the 'unified multi-national state structure' (Mouri, 1998, p. 33) of China the reason for the PRC's resilience? These two structures will be compared in this chapter, not in their legal-theoretical forms but in their actions.

Third, the chapter attempts to describe the relationship between the progress of reform and the collapse of one-party rule. There are two foci: the sudden dissolution of the CPSU in late 1991; and the political implications of its demise for China. China abandoned most political reforms before the Tiananmen incident in June 1989; while China abandoned reform, the Soviet Union proceeded with it. Was reform the key factor?

The first default: perestroika in Tibet

Gorbachev's Vladivostok speech in July 1986 shook China. It looked too good to be true. Since the border clash in March 1969, China had deployed more than 70 percent of its land forces to the border zones. Gorbachev's proposal included the unilateral withdrawal of most of the Soviet forces from the Mongolia–Chinese border zones. The Chinese authors of a semi-official history of the PRC could not conceal their astonishment. They wrote that Gorbachev's proposal was an 'important and unprecedented proposal for the improvement of bilateral relations' (Liao, 1991, p. 990). In August, Chinese foreign minister Wu Xueqian met the Soviet liaison ambassador in Beijing. Wu declared that China admired Gorbachev's initiative and promised to consider the proposal carefully and comprehensively.

When the Soviet forces began withdrawing from Afghanistan in October 1986, the rapprochement between the Soviet Union and China accelerated. In February 1987, both countries resumed their talks over the disputed territories along their national borders. Such talks had been suspended since 1978. In December 1987, Chinese foreign minister Qian Qichen paid a visit to Moscow. The last visit to Moscow by a Chinese foreign minister had been in 1956. Qian was a Soviet specialist and had spent a few years in Moscow as a

122 *Political systems and diplomacy*

young trainee. Qian confirmed with his Soviet counterpart that Gorbachev's formal visit to China should take place in the first half of 1989. On that occasion, both countries would declare the normalization of diplomatic relations.

China appreciated Gorbachev's perestroika. The rapprochement between the Soviet Union and China reduced the threats to the mainland from the north and the west, the hot spots in traditional geopolitical thinking. China could expect positive developments in other bilateral relations in the Eurasian continent, above all with her traditional arch-rival, India.

Gorbachev hardly placed his priority on geopolitics, however. According to Dmitri Trenin, director of the Carnegie Endowment for Peace in Moscow, Gorbachev almost single-mindedly pursued his political goal of ending the Cold War (Trenin, 2011, p. 9). In order to accomplish this goal, Gorbachev argued, the arms race with the United States must end. The arms race had brought stagnation to the Soviet economy. In order to revive the Soviet economy, therefore, the Soviet Union had to talk to the United States and agree to reduce the military forces.

Gorbachev was fortunate. His counterpart, US president Ronald Reagan, turned out to be a staunch proponent of nuclear arms reduction. The ever-rising maintenance cost of the nuclear arsenal was becoming a burden on the already-stagnant US economy. In December 1987, the United States and the Soviet Union signed a comprehensive ban on mid-range nuclear weapons. Keeping this early harvest in their pockets, Gorbachev and Reagan started moving towards mutual recognition of the end of the Cold War.

China's senior leaders, on the other hand, looked at the unfolding of Gorbachev's perestroika with great concern. What bothered them most was perestroika's 'pro-Western and liberal contents' (Deng, 1993, p. 178). These senior leaders knew too well that the Chinese youth and intellectuals were likely to be enticed by Western liberalism. They might have detected the real motive behind Gorbachev's perestroika. Socialism was in bad shape in the Soviet Union as well as everywhere else, and without bold reforms it could not survive.

Gorbachev's 'pro-Western and liberal contents' proved to be very powerful, as feared by Chinese senior leaders. Quite a few leading intellectuals in China, including some of the top CCP leaders, not only supported Gorbachev's perestroika but also tried it at home. One of them, the physicist Fang Lizhi, became a symbol of Chinese perestroika.

Turbulence in Tibet became the first stumbling block to perestroika in China. A semi-official Chinese document revealed the perplexity of the Chinese liberals (Liao, 1991, pp. 984–85). The document described the Lhasa incident as a process of recovering law and order in a rebellious province. According to the document, on March 5, 1989, the city of Lhasa, capital of the Tibetan self-governing province, descended into chaos when some Tibetan Buddhist monks marched through the streets with banners demanding Tibet's independence. Violence continued the next day. On March 7, Premier Li Peng declared martial law in Lhasa. The CCP general secretary of Tibet, Hu Jintao, implemented this martial law. On March 9, the document reported that Lhasa had returned to normal, although martial law remained effective until May 1990.

This description ignores two key aspects of the Lhasa incident. First, the document refused to discuss why those Tibetans had taken to the streets. There were inconvenient facts about Tibet: Tibet was an independent kingdom before 1949; India recognized Tibet as an independent nation between 1947 and 1954; massive protests had taken place in Tibet incessantly since the Chinese occupation in 1951; and the spiritual leader of the Tibetan Buddhists, the fourteenth Dalai Lama, was alive and active in exile.

Second, the writers of this document treated the Lhasa incident as an act of treason which had nothing to do with perestroika. All protest movements had to be described as vicious attempts at separatism. All patriotic Chinese had to support the central government and the CCP. This acceptance of the formal position of the Chinese government by liberal Chinese intellectuals cost them dearly. Three months later, it was their turn. All those civilians who got together in and around Tiananmen Square were violently dispersed by the People's Liberation Army (PLA) and were persecuted as anti-government vandals.

The Dalai Lama's June 1988 proposal for the self-government of Tibet had cornered the Chinese leaders. The Dalai dropped the demand for independence of Tibet in his proposal to the European Congress. Instead, he demanded 'high-level self-government' for Tibet. The Dalai may have borrowed the idea of high-level self-government from the agreement between Great Britain and China over the political status of Hong Kong (Mouri, 1998, p. 300).

Did the Dalai Lama have a chance? In retrospect, he had little chance. China devised the so-called one-country, two-systems concept and promised Hong Kong 'high-level self-government' in order to entice Taiwan into a 'peaceful unification with the motherland' (Xu, 1993, pp. 217–18). As Tibet was already a part of China, there was no positive reason to make any concession.

There were, however, at least three hopeful signs that China might concede to the Dalai Lama's proposals. First, Gorbachev's perestroika had changed the political landscape of Europe. The Soviet Union's grip on Eastern Europe was apparently loosening and the large-scale dismantling of the Cold War structure was taking place. The second sign came from Beijing. The general secretary of the CCP, Hu Yaobang, visited Tibet in May 1980 and made a series of concessions. Hu admitted that the Chinese rulers had committed serious mistakes during the Cultural Revolution. He approved the rebuilding of the Buddhist temples and promised freedom of religious belief. Hu opened Tibet to foreign tourists. In short, Hu Yaobang initiated a Chinese version of perestroika earlier than Gorbachev.

Hu's soft policy toward Tibet ended abruptly in early 1987 when he was dismissed from his post. The Dalai Lama still maintained his optimism, however, because Zhao Ziyang then took over as CCP general secretary. Zhao knew the Hong Kong scheme. As premier, he was in charge of the negotiations with British premier Margaret Thatcher over Hong Kong and had signed the December 1984 Joint Declaration. One of Zhao's brains trust

124 *Political systems and diplomacy*

people, Yan Jiaqi, was the designer of the 'one-country, two-systems' scheme (Mouri, 1998, p. 302). In short, Zhao Ziyang represented a peaceful approach toward the question of sovereignty.

The third positive sign was subtle but important. The paramount leader, Deng Xiaoping, delivered a speech in June 1988, a few days before the Dalai Lama's proposal. The title of Deng's speech was 'China must learn from international experience'. In the speech, Deng offered a compromise: China would be willing to extend the transition period of Hong Kong from the present 50 years to 100 years, if necessary (Deng, 1993, p. 267).

China responded favorably to the Dalai's June 1988 proposal. In September, the Chinese delegation agreed to meet the representatives of the exiled Tibetan government. In October, they tentatively agreed to meet in Geneva in January 1989. In early November, the director of the Office of the United Front, Yan Mingfu, confirmed that there was such an agreement.

Then, sometime in mid-November, China changed its mind. On November 18 China presented a counter-proposal. The Chinese proposal offered no room for concession: the Chinese delegation would never meet the close associates of the Dalai Lama, to say nothing of the Dalai himself; and the Tibetan delegation would have to accept the principle of a 'unified motherland' as a precondition for talks. Thus in March 1989 a massive demonstration broke out in Lhasa.

China had faced a similar critical choice right before its own declaration of independence. In September 1949, the PRC declared that it would implement a system of 'self-government by nationalist districts' (Mouri, 1998, p. 44). China chose a different system from the Soviet Union. Why did Premier Zhou Enlai and Chairman Mao decide not to introduce a Soviet-style federal system to China? Zhou found four reasons:

- Federalism was risky because it must admit greater authority to renegade provinces.
- China should not worry too much about the independence movements among the minorities. China had a much smaller minority population than the Soviet Union: as of 1949, the proportion of minorities in the Soviet Union was 47 percent and in China, 6 percent.
- The Han Chinese, the largest body of loosely defined Chinese people, must become the core of the PRC in order to defend the motherland from foreign interventions.
- The establishment of the self-governing district in May 1947 by the pro-CCP Mongolian Wulanfu succeeded in integrating the most populous part of Inner Mongolia into China.

In short, a federal structure would be susceptible to the threat of separatism. That was why, Zhou continued, the PRC did not assume such a structure (Mouri, 1998, pp. 42–43).

This decision in 1949 became the first default. It had a narrow policy goal: to install a pro-CCP government in the regions where the Han Chinese were a minority. The PRC must defend itself against foreign interventions. The decision represented a Chinese version of wartime communism and socialism according to the one-country principle.

Why did this decision have a lasting influence? Succeeding events fortified it. First, the Korean War broke out. The PRC had to suspend plans for the unification of Taiwan, Macau, and Hong Kong. The unification remained an elusive goal and the anti-separatism campaign continued. Second, the growing tensions between the PRC and the Soviet Union and India stirred the suspicions of the Chinese leaders over Xinjiang and Tibet, in particular. The Dalai Lama's exile into India in 1959 caused the Chinese leaders to believe that the Indian government was backing the independence movement in Tibet. Third, the hysterical xenophobia that was a feature of the Cultural Revolution wiped out not only the cultural heritage but also the nationalist minority leaders in Inner Mongolia, Xinjiang, and Tibet. Lastly, this decision resulted in a massive inflow of Han Chinese into those regions. In the late 1960s, responding to the directive of Chairman Mao, more than 16 million youths moved to the countryside to learn from the peasants. Most of this influx happened, however, in the form of legal investment and immigration after the death of Chairman Mao in 1976.

The accumulation of these successes in the 40 years since independence made the makeshift decision in 1949 a solid primary setting, a default. This default began to show its age by 1989, when the Cold War was ending. PLA forces remained in Inner Mongolia, Xinjiang, and Tibet. They looked clumsy and repressive. As Sergei Rogianin, vice-director of the Far Eastern Institute in Moscow, pointed out, the Chinese system of self-government by nationalists was fundamentally inflexible to local variations.[2] The political conditions were widely different in those regions. The success of self-government in one place could not guarantee the success of the same system elsewhere.

Despite these deficiencies, the first default had staying power for three reasons. First, inertia set in. The Chinese leaders considered that their system of self-government was working fine and that therefore there was no need to change it. They hoped that the massive inflow of Chinese capital and people would dampen the local movements for self-rule or independence. Second, reform of the defaults became increasingly difficult. The Chinese leaders regarded perestroika as the source of all troubles. The dissolution of the Soviet Union made this assessment a conviction. Third, Deng Xiaoping's authority gave this 1989 decision strong legitimacy. Deng chose Jiang Zemin and Hu Jintao to succeed Hu Yaobang and Zhao Ziyang. Both Jiang and Hu took a tough position against domestic insurgency.

The second default: Gorbachev in Beijing

Gorbachev's visit to Beijing in May 1989 marked another point of departure. The visit exposed the wide gap between China and the Soviet Union. While Gorbachev was trying to end the Cold War, Deng Xiaoping and other elder

126 *Political systems and diplomacy*

CCP leaders were trying to sustain it. While perestroika gained momentum in the Soviet Union, its Chinese version went down the drain.

China began a crackdown of the pro-perestroika activists in late 1986, when some Chinese students demonstrated on and off campus, demanding more freedom. The so-called anti-bourgeois liberalism campaign reached a climax when the reformist general secretary, Hu Yaobang, was dismissed in January 1987. Hu's dismissal meant that the majority of the CCP leaders feared and resisted perestroika (reform) and glasnost (dissemination of information). Deng Xiaoping did not hide his intolerance of Western liberalism (Deng, 1993, p. 284).

Deng Xiaoping and other elder CCP leaders had a precedent for dealing with such a problem. In March 1979, they had crushed the so-called Beijing Spring movement. They arrested the leaders of the movement, most notably a former PLA soldier, Wei Jingsheng. They prohibited the publication of pro-democracy pamphlets and wall posters. They succeeded in repressing the pro-democracy movement before it could appeal to the masses. They used traditional Chinese tactics: kill the chicken (the leader) to scare the monkeys (the masses).

This default did not work so well in 1987 for three reasons. First, the magnitude of the opposition was far greater this time. Some of the top CCP leaders had become proponents of democracy, although the definition of the concept varied greatly. Hu's successor, Zhao Ziyang, was not supposed to initiate either glasnost or perestroika in politics. But Zhao turned out to be too ambitious to distance himself from perestroika. Zhao's 1987 proposal for administrative reform dangerously resembled one of the central themes of perestroika (Nakai, 2012, pp. 272–75). The CCP elders eliminated two top leaders in a row. The removal caused political instability among the leading elites of the CCP.

The second reason that the 1979 default did not work was Gorbachev. The CCP elders had no control over Gorbachev. He looked sharp and reasonable. His reputation as a reformer grew day by day. The progress of perestroika and glasnost in the Soviet Union overwhelmed both Chinese intellectuals and the CCP leaders. By the time of his China visit, Gorbachev had become a symbol of reform and the savior of socialism. It was extremely difficult for the CCP elders to discredit Gorbachev and his perestroika.

Third, the coincidental sequence of events helped the political opposition. Hu Yaobang died on April 15, 1989, a month before Gorbachev's visit. Infuriated by the shabby condolences offered by the CCP, Hu's supporters got together in Tiananmen Square, where a formal reception was planned. The number quickly reached more than 100,000. The foreign press happened to be there in Beijing to cover Gorbachev's historic visit. Their TV crews had a field day covering the massive demonstrations and hunger strikes. For the first time in the PRC's history, ordinary citizens in Beijing showed up on the TV screens of ordinary citizens in New York, Tokyo, and elsewhere.

According to Yevgeny Bazhanov, president of the Russian Diplomatic Academy and one of Gorbachev's foreign policy advisors, the Soviet leader

China's retreat for survival, 1988–91 127

encountered a few surprises during the visit.[3] The first surprise came when Gorbachev met Deng and other CCP elders. They all looked so unhappy. Deng kept on spitting grumpily. One of the elders, Bo Yibo, openly criticized perestroika.[4] Gorbachev's request for a press conference was flatly rejected. They also refused to keep a record of the meeting. There was no glasnost.

A second surprise followed. Soon after Gorbachev arrived, he found himself very popular among the reform-minded people in Beijing and received a hearty welcome from the demonstrators on the street. Moved by the passionate welcome of the demonstrators, Gorbachev was said to have proposed a meeting with the student leaders. The Chinese officials responded firmly: if such a meeting were to take place, China would immediately suspend the summit and expel the Soviet delegation. Just before the Soviet leader was due to leave the country, a high-ranking Chinese official, most likely Deng Xiaoping himself, told Gorbachev that China would solve this problem immediately after his departure.

On May 20, two days after Gorbachev's departure, martial law was declared in Beijing. On the morning of June 4, PLA brigades entered Beijing and cleared the city. According to the government, about some 200 plus people were killed, including tens of soldiers and an unknown number of students and citizens. CCP general secretary Zhao Ziyang and three Politburo members were dismissed from their positions at the CCP Central Committee meeting of June 23. The Committee accused Zhao of having committed a mistake in supporting the riot and splitting the CCP.

The violent crushing of the demonstrators was a replay of the Lhasa incident three months before. This time, a new factor was added to the first default: China abandoned perestroika and glasnost in politics. The combination of suppression and intolerance constituted the second default. In retrospect, there was no need for massive military interventions in either of these cases. The demonstrations in Beijing were dying down. Most of the foreign press corps left Beijing with Gorbachev. But the powerful influence of successful precedents skewed the decisions. A crisis of socialism was looming, or so the CCP leaders felt. Anyone who protested against the CCP would become the target of repression. The Tiananmen incident of June 1989 marked the end of Chinese glasnost and perestroika.

The third default: coup in Moscow

By the end of 1989, it became obvious that the Cold War was heading towards a crashing end. A massive exodus of the citizens of East Berlin took place in August 1989. The Baltic countries declared their independence from the Soviet Union in the same month. In September in Poland and in October in Hungary, non-communist governments took office. In November, the Berlin Wall fell. The Cold War in Europe ended quickly and quietly, without much violence. Bad news for China continued; in October 1989, the Dalai Lama was awarded the Nobel Peace Prize.

128 *Political systems and diplomacy*

How could China survive in this changing international environment? How did China manage its foreign relations? Deng and the CCP old guard happened to have a precedent. Back in 1978, Deng had broken China's isolation with his visits to Japan and the United States. The normalization of diplomatic relations with the United States in January 1979 had secured China's position in the international community. Later, in 1982, Hu Yaobang, then general secretary of the CCP, summarized the basic position of Chinese foreign policy as all-dimensional diplomacy. The fundamental feature of this position was its emphasis on national interests. China would try to maximize its national interests while disregarding ideology and history. China would make decisions on a '*zeze hihi* (case-by-case) basis' (Okabe, 2002, p. 205).

The perception of crisis and isolation caused Deng to revive this pragmatic posture. After 1989, China made a series of makeshift decisions based on a calculation of national interests. Those 'case-by-case' decisions and the results were as follows:

- The decision to side with the United Nations against Saddam Hussein's August 1990 invasion of Kuwait.
- The PRC refrained from using its veto at the UN Security Council against Iraq in November 1990. The European Community (EC) and Japan dropped their economic sanctions against China in the same month.
- The decision to build formal diplomatic relations with former 'enemies', notably Saudi Arabia and Singapore in 1990, the Baltic countries in 1991, and the former Soviet republics, Israel, and South Korea in 1992.

These renewed relations helped China out of its position of isolation. They also helped to narrow the international space of the rival, Taiwan:

- The decision to expand ties with Japan and the European Community
- China welcomed Japanese prime minister Kaifu in August 1991 and decided to invite the Japanese emperor the next year. China's foreign minister Qian Qichen indicated that this decision was based on 'long-term strategic considerations' (Qian, 1992, p. 2).
- The decision to sort out foreign relations based on concrete national interests.
- The PRC distanced itself from North Korea and approached the regional frameworks in Asia. China started joining the meetings of ASEAN and became a member of APEC in November 1991 with Taiwan (Chinese Taipei) and Hong Kong. China's trade with the ASEAN nations and South Korea dramatically increased.

Mikhail Gorbachev did not share Deng Xiaoping's concerns. The end of the Cold War brought three favorable consequences for Gorbachev. First, his personal reputation as a reformer reached a climax when, in 1990, he was awarded the Nobel Peace Prize. Second, Gorbachev realized large-scale

Table 7.1 China's diplomatic relations 1989–1997

Year							
1989	Bahrain	Micronesia					
1990	Namibia	Saudi Arabia	Singapore				
1991	Estonia	Latvia	Lithuania	Brunei			
1992	Uzbekistan	Kazakhstan	Ukraine	Tajikistan	Kyrgyz	Turkmenistan	Belarus	Israel
	Moldova	Azerbaijan	Armenia	Slovenia	Croatia	Georgia	Korea
1993	Czech	Slovakia	Eritrea				
1994	Andorra						
1995	Monaco	Bosnia					
1996							
1997	Bahamas	Cook Islands					

Source: Radio Press (2011) China Directory, p. 552.

130 *Political systems and diplomacy*

disarmament. The Soviet forces stationed in Eastern Europe began withdrawing in 1989 as the threat from the West diminished. In the five years since 1989, the Russian military forces shrank from 3 million to 1 million (Trenin, 2011, p. 75). The disarmament proceeded quietly. According to Dmitri Trenin, there was a consensus among mid-level military officers that Soviet forces should concentrate on the defense of the Soviet Union and not on missions in foreign countries.[5] The Soviet military bases in Cuba and Vietnam were closed. Third, Gorbachev could count on economic assistance from the West for the rehabilitation of the Soviet economy.

Despite these favorable developments, Gorbachev's Soviet Union dissolved within two years after the end of the Cold War. Gorbachev faced three challenges after 1989. The first was domestic opposition to his rule. Perestroika legalized the voice of the opposition. In March 1990, the Soviet Congress decided to abolish the dictatorship of the CPSU, to introduce a multi-party system, and to allow private ownership of property. At the same Congress, Gorbachev made himself president of the Soviet Union, expecting to stay at the pinnacle of the federation. Soon, most of the Soviet republics set up their own presidents. Perestroika resulted in the 'inflation of presidents' (Shiokawa, 2007a, p. 61). In June, Boris Yeltsin was elected as president of the Russian Republic. Popular elections made Gorbachev vulnerable because he had never been popularly elected.

The second challenge came from the Persian Gulf. The unfolding of Saddam Hussein's Kuwait campaign showed that the Soviet Union could play only a minor role in the world of realpolitik. Gorbachev could not stop Saddam from engaging in a fatal invasion of Kuwait. Neither could he prevent George H. Bush and other Western leaders from initiating a war against Iraq. Gorbachev was busy keeping his own house together. While Deng's China took advantage of the occasion and returned to the world community in 1990, Gorbachev's Soviet Union made a diplomatic retreat. To make matters worse, Eduard Shevardnadze, Soviet foreign minister since 1985 and Gorbachev's right-hand man, quit the government in December 1990. Gorbachev lost one of the most important assets of diplomacy: consistency.

The third challenge, the so-called federation issue, turned out to be a fatal blow to Gorbachev. According to Shiokawa, up until the end of 1989, Gorbachev succeeded in holding down the federal republics' demands for independence (Shiokawa, 2007a, p. 56). Gorbachev's intention to tighten central control, however, suffered a serious setback in 1990. In some Soviet republics, non-communists won the majority in the popular elections for the supreme soviets. Some of them demanded outright independence. Some of them demanded greater self-rule. Three Baltic countries declared their independence in February and March. In June, Russia declared its own sovereignty. Georgia, Moldova, and Armenia soon followed. The successive declarations of sovereignty, the 'parade of sovereignty' (Shiokawa, 2007a, p. 61), greatly increased the centrifugal force of departures from the Soviet orbit.

Recent studies have revealed that the dissolution of the Soviet Union was neither inevitable nor coincidental. Shiokawa Nobuaki, a Japanese researcher,

China's retreat for survival, 1988–91 131

argues that the dissolution was the result of human drama, which was played out by the major actors in the short period of November–December 1991 (Shiokawa, 2007b, pp. 551–73). Kawato Akio, a former Japanese diplomat, concluded that the dissolution was the result of the political plot designed by Boris Yeltsin. Yeltsin succeeded in depriving his rival Gorbachev of his political base by dissolving the Soviet Union and banning the CPSU (Kawato, 2013, p. 134). Dmitri Trenin, a Russian researcher, contended that the Soviet Union had suffered a 'sudden death' (Trenin, 2011, p. 36). This death was caused by four preceding injuries that were inflicted in the latter half of 1991: the August coup; the referendum for the independence of Ukraine in December; the December agreement between Russia, Ukraine, and Belarus on the dissolution of the Soviet Union; and Gorbachev's decision to resign on December 25, 1991.

Deng Xiaoping and the CCP leaders did not have time to ponder over the root cause of these developments. They had to deal with the immediate problems. First, the August coup in Moscow made it clear that Gorbachev was in big trouble. Should China take advantage of it? Second, China had to find a way to communicate with Boris Yeltsin. Was Yeltsin a friend of China or a foe? Lastly, China needed to defend itself against a Soviet-style dissolution. Could China stop the tide of self-rule and independence that had flooded Eastern Europe and Central Asia? A simple application of the previous defaults would not do because these were new problems.

Deng Xiaoping made three adjustments to the existing defaults. The modified defaults did what they were supposed to do: they kept the machine working. First, Deng applied the no-perestroika default to the future generation of CCP leaders. He made sure that there would be neither a Gorbachev nor a Yeltsin in the CCP leadership. Deng chose the low-key CCP official Jiang Zemin as general secretary. Jiang would listen to the party (Deng, 1993, p. 317). The CCP old guard continued to participate in important Party meetings. Jiang Zemin faced the first test in April 1990 when several hundred Uyghur Muslims protested against the Chinese government in the Xinjiang-Uyghur Self-Autonomous Region. Jiang mobilized the PLA forces and suppressed the anti-government movement quickly. He passed the test.

Second, Deng added some practical directives to the case-by-case principle of foreign policy. The timing of this addition was crucial. Such a practical direction was most needed when the external environment was rapidly changing. The case was the August 1991 coup in Moscow. When Gorbachev was detained in the Crimea, some CCP leaders might have welcomed his fall. The *People's Daily* of August 20, 1991 reported on its front page that Soviet vice-president Yanaev had taken over Gorbachev's job. The *People's Daily* explained that Gorbachev's health problem was the reason for this change. Gorbachev's downfall looked certain. On August 21, however, the *People's Daily* changed its tone. A spokesperson for the Chinese foreign ministry declared that the changes in the Soviet Union belonged to the internal matters of that country. The *People's Daily* also reported that Russian president Yeltsin stood against Yanaev. This objective attitude continued on August 22. The *People's Daily* on that

132 *Political systems and diplomacy*

day reported that Gorbachev had come back to Moscow and taken control of the capital. By August 23, ordinary Chinese citizens came to know that there had been coup in Moscow and that it had failed.

At the most critical moment of the coup, China held back. It was quite likely that Deng made this decision. Later, in 1992, Foreign Minister Qian Qichen mentioned in his closed-door speech that Deng had given timely advice to Chinese diplomats at critical moments since 1989 (Qian, 1992, p. 11). Deng's words were put into print in 1993, in the third volume of *Selected Writings of Deng Xiaoping*. By the time of his death in 1997, some of Deng's words were compiled into 16-to-24-Chinese-character directives and became the leading guidelines of Chinese foreign policy (Nakai, 2009, pp. 155–58).

The third modification concerned the economy. Deng let perestroika in the economy go. He had tried his economic pragmatism twice in the past, both in times of crisis. First, in the aftermath of the Great Leap Forward of 1958, Deng initiated a so-called adjustment policy in agriculture. He gave the peasants limited freedom to plant and sell their produce. Agricultural production shot up and China was able to escape famine. Chairman Mao thought this policy was reactionary. In 1966, Mao scrapped both the policy and Deng. After Mao's death in 1976, Deng tried again. This time, he built four special economic zones in the coastal areas near Hong Kong and Taiwan in 1980. The scheme was spreading and Chinese GDP was increasing when the political turbulence of 1989 broke out.

Deng did not have to reset all the economic policies. He just needed to continue what he had been trying since 1980. The scheme of selling land-use rights for 40–50 years to foreign investors was already in place. What China needed was an endorsement and an authorization of such a move from the top. China also needed a competent manager of the economy and not an advocate of political reform. The chaotic nature of the Soviet economy since 1990 convinced Deng and other CCP leaders of this.

Like reformist emperors in the past, Deng looked for a loyal subordinate who could manage his empire. He found an ideal person in the spring of 1991. That person was Zhu Rongji, then mayor of Shanghai. Zhu had no chance of becoming the number one of the CCP. He had suffered political persecution for the anti-rightest campaign in 1958 and returned to his official job only in 1975. In 1987, Zhu just made it as a candidate member of the Central Committee of the CCP. He became mayor of Shanghai in April 1988. During the turbulent years from 1988 to 1991, Zhu proved himself a competent manager. Shanghai remained relatively calm during the Tiananmen incident. Shanghai's stability became an asset for economic development.

In April 1991, Zhu was appointed vice-premier of the PRC. His promotion through the party ranks soon followed. At the Fourteenth Party Congress in 1992, Zhu became a member of the Standing Committee of the CCP Politburo. Although his power was checked by the more powerful members of the Standing Committee, notably Jiang Zemin and Li Peng, Zhu was given a powerful position to pursue perestroika in the economy.

Zhu received the full backing of the emperor, Deng Xiaoping. In January 1992, Deng traveled from Shanghai to Shenzhen, one of the special economic zones he had created in 1980, and gave a powerful endorsement of his version of perestroika in the economy. What Deng meant by his words, *gaige kaifang* (reform and openness), could be translated into two kinds of action: general and specific. At the most general level, it meant the adoption of universal standards of economic management and the market economy. In short, China embraced a capitalist economy. At the most concrete level, it meant encouraging the inflow of foreign direct investment (FDI) into China and sales of land-use rights to foreigners. In short, China became like South Korea or Taiwan. Deng advocated this perestroika and Zhu prosecuted it. Figure 7.1 shows the result of this joint action.

Backward toward empire

In the turbulent years from 1988 to 1991, China battled for survival. Deng Xiaoping was a survival expert. He had survived at least three personal crises caused by Chairman Mao. This time, Deng faced three critical moments. The first came in late 1988 when China refused to concede to the moderate demand for self-rule in Tibet. The refusal triggered anti-government protests in March 1989. The violent repression in Tibet became a critical precedent. The second critical moment came in May 1989 with Gorbachev's visit to Beijing and the dismissal of the reformist leaders. The third critical moment came in August 1991 with the coup in Moscow marking the beginning of the crisis. The Soviet Union as a political structure took a heavy blow (Shiokawa, 2010, p. 4). After the failed coup in Moscow, the disintegration of the Soviet Union accelerated.

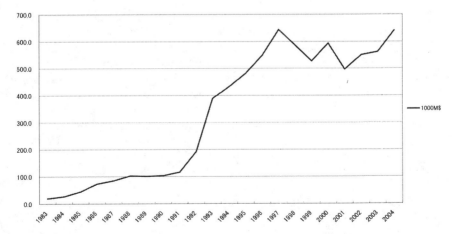

Figure 7.1 FDI in China actual
Source: National Bureau of Statistics (2005).

134 *Political systems and diplomacy*

In all these three critical moments, the Chinese leaders did not have much time to ponder. Nor did they have complete information. In all three cases, mass demonstrations broke out and soon became out of control. In all these events, the future was so murky that no political leader seemed able to take control of events. In these uncertain circumstances, it was extremely useful for such leaders to have a set of policies that were guaranteed to work.

Facing crisis, Deng Xiaoping and his close associates reinstated the precedents. Their goal was not to implement something innovative but to restore order. They looked for policies that had worked before. They found a number of primary settings. Those settings looked rusty and old-fashioned, but they at least were 'tried and true' policies that could be implemented immediately by their subordinates.

These primary settings, the defaults, had fatal deficiencies, however. They shunned innovation. The major purpose of the defaults was to make the given machine work. In order to guarantee the most basic functions of the machine, all add-on features had to be deleted. The functions they could restore were the bare necessities. These primary settings could restore only those parts of the machine that were old fashioned, out of date, wasteful, and clumsy. The PRC survived the crises all right, but the political system of the PRC came to show the traditional tenets of past empires. The wholesale revival of the past and dismay about reform were the political consequences of this peace.

Gorbachev and Yeltsin, on the other hand, tried to operate the old machine with a new and efficient operating system. The old Soviet machine was so huge and complex that it did not respond to the new software. The Soviet machine broke down into pieces. The new machine, the Russian Federation, was assembled by some of the usable parts of the old machine. The new machine looks somewhat like an old machine because they share the same parts. The new machine, however, would not work under the old operating system. The new machine only responds to the new operating system written in a universal language and based on universal standards.

Today's Russia is, in short, post-empire (Trenin, 2011, p. 72). Today's Russia has a democratic constitution, popular elections, and all the democratic institutions. The imperialistic way of thinking, which was so pervasive in the Soviet days, lives only in the culture, memory, and history of the Russian people. Russia is not likely to return to empire because, for most Russians, today's Russia is much more comfortable. Post-imperial Russia, first of all, does not have to take pains to expand its territory and maintain order in rebellious provinces. Second, foreign relations are easy to operate because it is no longer necessary to get along with a country if it does not feel like doing so. Finally, in post-empire, the role of the military remains minimal. This means it is not necessary to fight and die for the defense of vital national interests.

Today's China looks like it is heading backward toward empire. First, China is replacing socialism with nationalism. Today's slogan, the 'resurrection of greater China' indicates that the political goal of the PRC is to push back the situation about one hundred years to 1911. Second, China is departing from its default position. All the defaults were revived and used by Deng Xiaoping in times of national crisis. As China was able to escape these crises, there would be little reason to stick to those defaults. China's assertive diplomacy surfaced in 2009.

Back in the 1950s, the Soviet Union was China's model in many respects. 'Today's Russia is tomorrow's China' was a popular slogan in those days. In the 1960s, Chairman Mao stopped learning from Russia and went on building his own empire. In the 1980s, Deng Xiaoping did the same. Every empire is destined to fall. The fall of the Soviet Empire was chaotic and painful. But the Soviet Union went down quietly and peacefully. There are still some lessons for China to learn from Russia.

Notes

1 This author relied on three non-Russian sources regarding the Soviet Union. The first was a Chinese source written by Chinese researchers and government officials. The second was a Japanese source by Japanese researchers. Shiokawa Nobuaki's works on the dissolution of the Soviet Union were most helpful. The third was an English source including both documents and interviews. Dmitri Trenin's recent works were indispensable. The author conducted a series of interviews with Russian experts on foreign affairs and on Chinese studies in Moscow in March 2012. All the quotations from these interviews, including the anonymous ones, are identified in the endnotes. The author would like to thank all interviewees for their insightful comments, Mr. Keiji Ide, Chief Councilor of the Japanese Embassy in Moscow, and Mr. Akio Kawato, an independent researcher, for their help in arranging these interviews, and to the Slavic Research Center of Hokkaido University for financing the research trip. The author is responsible for all errors and mistakes in translation and interpretation.
2 Interview with the author in Moscow, March 15, 2012.
3 Interview with the author in Moscow, March 13, 2012.
4 Bo Yibo's son, Bo Xilai, became a Politburo member of the CCP and a party chief of Zhongqing city in 2007. Bo Xilai's fortunes abruptly ended in 2012 when he was arrested for bribery. He was sentenced to life imprisonment in September 2013.
5 Interview with the author in Moscow, March 14, 2012.

References

Ando, Masashi (2010) *Gendai chugoku nenpyo 1941–2008* [Annals of Contemporary China 1941–2008], Tokyo: Iwanami Shoten (in Japanese).
Deng, Xiaoping (1993) *Deng Xiaoping wenxuen di san juan* [Selected writings of Deng Xiaoping, Volume 3], Beijing: Renmin Chubanshe (in Chinese).
Gorbachev, Mikhail (1988) *Perestroika: New Thinking for Our Country and the World*, New York: HarperCollins.
Kawato, Akio (2013) *Bei Chu Rossia kyozo ni obieruna* [USA, China and Russia: Looking Beyond Phantoms], Tokyo: Sanyosha (in Japanese).
Liao, Gailong (1991) *Dandai zhongguo zhengzhi dashidian* [Almanac of Chinese Politics], Changchun: Qilin Wenshi Chubanshe (in Chinese).
Mouri, Kazuko (1998) *Shuen kara no chugoku: minzoku mondai to kokka* [A View from China's Periphery: The State and Nationality Issue], Tokyo: Tokyo Daigaku Shuppankai (in Japanese).

136   *Political systems and diplomacy*

Nakai, Yoshifumi (2009) 'Taito Chugoku to America: keizai hatten no tameno retorikku' [Rising China and the United States: Rhetoric for the Economic Development], in Nakai Yoshifumi, ed., *Taito Chugoku no taigai kankei* [Foreign Relations of the Rising China], Tokyo: Ochanomizu Shobo (in Japanese).

——(2012) 'Tousei bunri no seiji katei: Chu-So hikaku no kokoromi' [Political Process of the Division Between Party and Government: China–Soviet Comparison], in Hishida Masaharu, ed., *Chugoku kyosanto no sabaibaru senryaku* [Survival Strategy of the Chinese Communist Party], Tokyo: Sanwa Shoseki (in Japanese).

Okabe, Tatsumi (2002) *Chugoku no taigai senryaku* [China's Foreign Strategy], Tokyo: Tokyo Daigaku Shuppankai (in Japanese).

Pierson, Paul (2004) *Politics in Time: History, Institutions, and Social Analysis*, Princeton, NJ: Princeton University Press.

Qian, Qichen (1992) 'Guanyu danqian guoji xingshe de jige wenti' [On Several Questions of the International Situation Today], *Lilun Duntai*, vol. 1040, October, pp. 1–17 (in Chinese).

Shiokawa, Nobuaki (2007a) *Kokka no kochiku to kaitai: taminzoku kokka soren no kobo II* [The Construction and Dissolution of a State: Rise and Fall of the Multi-National Soviet Union, Part II], Tokyo: Iwanami Shoten (in Japanese).

——(2007b) 'Soren kaitai no saishu kyokumen' [The Final Stage of the Dissolution of the Soviet Union], *Kokka Gakkai Zasshi*, vol. 120, no. 7–8, pp. 551–73 (in Japanese).

——(2010) *Reisen shuen nijunen: nani ga, donoyouni shite owattanoka* [Twenty Years Since the End of the Cold War: What and How Did It End?] Tokyo: Keiso Shobo (in Japanese).

Trenin, Dmitri (2007) *Getting Russia Right*, Moscow: Carnegie Endowment for International Peace.

——(2011) *Post-Imperium: A Eurasian Story*, Moscow: Carnegie Endowment for International Peace.

Xu, Jiatun (1993) *Xu Jiatun xianggang huiyilu xiang* [Xu Jiatun's Hong Kong Memorial, Volume 1], Taibei: Lianhebao (in Chinese).

8 India's pragmatic diplomacy with major powers

A comparative study of the strategic partnership with the US, China, and Russia

Toru Ito

Introduction

Since the advent of the twenty-first century, more and more practitioners as well as scholars have firmly stressed the importance of India in contemporary international relations. India itself has harbored ambitions to be a global power and has gained great self-respect as a regional power since its independence in 1947. On the one hand the first prime minister, Jawaharlal Nehru, who inherited Mahatma Gandhi's great legacy of non-violence, led the global non-alignment movement, which was a grand vision of world peace and independence from colonialism in the midst of the Cold War. On the other hand, however, India's actual sphere of influence was confined to the subcontinent of South Asia, a marginal area far from the West. There was a wide gap between the ideal and the real in India.

The situation, however, has changed completely since the end of the Cold War. India's burgeoning economic development after the liberalization in 1991 and its nuclear tests and nuclearization in 1998 have elevated its hard power to a global level. The fact that most Western major powers have wooed 'the largest democracy in the world' is encouraging its political and diplomatic elites. In fact, India has been recognized as a regional power with the potential to be a 'global power' since the US president Bill Clinton's visit to New Delhi in 2000.

India is now sensing the opportunity to realize its great ambitions. Recent Indian diplomacy has set itself the goal of securing a 'regional power' position in Asia and Eurasia and ultimately becoming a 'global power' beyond the subcontinent. First of all, further economic growth is essential for this end, considering that its neighbor, China, has obtained a much larger scale of economy. It is quite logical that India has strengthened its economic diplomacy to draw more investment from the West, and to stimulate trade by concluding free trade agreements with major and emerging powers. India has also raised an objection to the suggestion of setting legally binding targets for cuts in greenhouse gas emissions, which might hamper economic growth. Neither has its government any intention of doing away with its policy on nuclear energy – even after the Fukushima accidents – making a series of agreements on nuclear power in order to cater for greater energy demand.

138 *Political systems and diplomacy*

On the military front, India devotes its energy to arms procurement. Weapons and arms systems in India, which depended heavily on Soviet Russia during the Cold War, are gradually diversifying. In 2012, the Indian Air Force selected the French firm Dassault Aviation as a negotiating partner for the acquisition of its Rafale fighter in pursuit of a deal for 126 medium multi-role combat aircraft, after severe competition among aircraft companies in the US, Russia, Europe, and elsewhere. The Indian Navy, upon which not much weight had been put, is now boosting its military capabilities in the wake of the Chinese PLA Navy's activities in the Indian Ocean. It is unfolding its ambitious plan to upgrade to a 'blue-water navy' by 2022, which includes three aircraft carriers. Each of India's armed forces is also proactive in military exchanges such as joint exercises and high-level talks with major powers.

Politically, India is becoming very enthusiastic about its entry as a permanent member of the United Nations Security Council, which is regarded as a symbol of being a major global power. At all bilateral summits the Indian prime minister never fails to confirm that his delegate will stand for Indian membership. Moreover, India seems to be striving for final legitimization of its possession of nuclear weapons, seeking admission to multilateral export control regimes such as the Nuclear Suppliers Group (NSG) and Missile Technology Control Regime (MTCR) without signing the Nuclear Nonproliferation Treaty (NPT).

As its approach to realizing the above objectives, India is adopting strategic partnership diplomacy with major and emerging powers. This diplomacy is intended to build and strengthen each bilateral relationship based on frequent or regular summits and high-level official consultations on economy and security, boosting trade and investment, and significant military exchanges, going beyond the sphere of friendly relations. Nevertheless, this will never amount to any alliance that might hamper its diplomatic freedom, its 'strategic autonomy' (Khilnani *et al.*, 2012, p. iii). It is seen, therefore, as an extension rather than a negation of the traditional non-alignment policy.

In this respect, we should note the fact that India has declared strategic partnerships with all major and emerging powers: with the US in 2004, the UK in 2004, France in 1998, Germany in 2001, Japan in 2006, Russia in 2000, China in 2005, South Africa in 1997, Indonesia in 2005, Brazil in 2006, and so on. We can easily find Indian partners comprising all the influential powers in the post-Cold War world, including the West and the former Eastern bloc as well as the developing countries of the Global South, which might be called 'omnidirectional strategic partnership' diplomacy.

Even so, is there any difference among these many partnerships?[1] How does India locate each relationship in its concrete aim of becoming a 'global power'? This chapter will clarify the different characteristics among India's strategic partnerships with the US, China, and Russia, by paying attention to the different issues on which India places significance today. Finally, we would like to see how India regards the role of each partnership in furthering its major goal of becoming a 'global power'.

Increasing closeness of India's relationship with the US

The US was an estranged power during almost the entire period of the Cold War, even though it was not a direct enemy of India. On the one hand, the US had established a cooperative relationship with two of India's enemies, Pakistan and China, especially since the 1970s. On the other, the fact that India had developed a relationship with an imagined enemy of the US, that is to say, the USSR, made India an estranged country even from the viewpoint of the US.

The collapse of the Cold War structure, therefore, cleared away the greatest obstacles to Indo–US relationship-building. Cutting off its military assistance to Pakistan in 1990, the US embarked on an approach to India. Nevertheless, from the US viewpoint, India was not regarded as an essential strategic partner at that time because of its initial stage of economic reform as well as the overwhelming US presence in the post-Cold War world. Above all, the first Bill Clinton administration, in which a policy of nonproliferation continued to dominate US foreign policy in South Asia, was lukewarm about engaging a non-NPT India.

The second Clinton administration in the late 1990s, however, started to recognize the strategic value of India amid the rising economic and security tensions with China. While India's nuclear tests in 1998 under the Atal Bihari Vajpayee (BJP) administration might have disappointed the US for some little time, '[i]ronically, India's nuclear tests shattered US policy, with its single-minded focus on proliferation, and forced a reconsideration of relations with New Delhi' (Cohen, 2001, p. 292). India, which had already acquired nuclear power, was accepted as a US strategic partner to be engaged with and brought over, not a regional power to be refused. The US decided to enter into strategic dialogue with India just after the nuclear tests. The dialogue framework between US deputy secretary of state Strobe Talbott and the Indian minister of external affairs Jaswant Singh resulted in Clinton's visit to New Delhi in March 2000, which was the first US presidential visit in twenty-two years. The visit indicated the US's gradual departure from its balancing policy between India and Pakistan. The president stayed in India for five days, and in Pakistan for merely five hours.

The US trend of attaching importance to India was continued and strengthened by the George W. Bush administration. The policy recommendation report for the presidential election of 2000 published by the RAND Corporation proposed a 'decoupling' policy between India and Pakistan, describing India as a major Asian power and therefore assuming it to be a US partner (Carlucci *et al.*, 2000, p. xiii). As a matter of fact, the Indo–US relationship was enhanced, whereas the US came close to Pakistan again after the September 11th terrorist attacks in 2001. Ashley J. Tellis, who served as senior adviser to the ambassador at the US embassy in New Delhi, boasted that this was a result of 'dehyphenation' between India and Pakistan by the Bush administration (Tellis, 2008). The Indian side, the Vajpayee government, also valued the relationship with the US. India welcomed the US's role as a

140 *Political systems and diplomacy*

'facilitator' to manage the crisis between India and Pakistan in 2001–02 and honored a request by the US to reduce tensions with Pakistan. Next Steps in Strategic Partnership (NSSP) announced by Prime Minister Vajpayee and President Bush in January 2004 expanded bilateral cooperation in more sensitive and strategic areas such as civilian nuclear activities, space programs, and high-technology trade, nuclear, space, and military activities, which aimed to enhance the Indo–US relationship.

The Manmohan Singh (Congress) administration, which came to power after India's general election of May 2004, also adhered to the previous administration's policy of developing a closer relationship with the US. The terms of the Civil Nuclear Agreement, the so-called 123 Agreement, were concluded in July 2007. The Bush administration pushed very hard not only to amend domestic law but also to persuade reluctant members of the International Atomic Energy Agency (IAEA) and NSG to exempt India from their rule of prohibiting trade with non-members of the NPT in spite of lingering concerns and criticism in the international community as well as in the US itself. The Singh administration reciprocated Bush's effort by its decision to discard non-cabinet allies and communist parties, which took strong exception to the nuclear deal with the US, in order to complete the process. As a result, India was granted special exemption from the NSG Guidelines as a non-member of the NPT in September 2008, which enabled India to enter any bilateral negotiations for civil nuclear cooperation. India had a great sense of euphoria, assuming it was tolerated as a nuclear power as a matter of practice. The contribution of the US was highly appreciated in this regard.

Just after the change of guard in the US to the Barack Obama administration, there was a rising chorus of concern in India. First, his vision of 'a nuclear-free world' might tear up India's special exemption. Second, his 'Af-Pak' policy might actually include India and it might be the US's intention to play a more active role as a mediator for resolution of the Kashmir issue between India and Pakistan rather than as a facilitator for crisis management. Third, his policy toward China, which seemed to attach weight to 'engagement' rather than 'hedging', might dilute the strategic value of India from the US viewpoint.

Each concern was addressed in steps by the practical actions of the Obama administration. President Obama's visit to New Delhi in November 2010 was of decisive importance. Admitting India to be a 'nuclear power', the president announced the lifting of controls on export of high-technology items to India and supported its full membership in multilateral export control regimes such as the NSG and MTCR. Justifying his Af-Pak policy as tackling the terrorism problem, he avoided associating it with Indo–Pakistani relations. He said that the US would be ready to play any role in the Kashmir issue if both countries so desired, and there was no imposing of a solution. He also criticized Pakistan for exporting terrorism.

In addition, stating that 'I look forward to a reformed United Nations Security Council that includes India as a permanent member', Mr. Obama showed the most affirmative stance of US presidents on India's entry as a permanent member of the UNSC. The US started annual strategic ministerial-level dialogue with India in 2010, just as it had done with China. The Indian side had a sense of security at last, having been convinced that the Obama administration would never make light of India.

What factors have made India and the US come closer to each other? It is often said that the relationship of both democratic nations has developed into one of 'natural allies' now that the structural obstacle of the Cold War has been removed. However, why is it that every cross-party administration of the US, Clinton, Bush, and Obama, has taken pains to tolerate India's nuclear power in spite of domestic and international concerns about sending the wrong message to Iran and North Korea as well as its long-held policy of adhering to nonproliferation? Why is it that the Singh administration, which could barely hold on to power with communist non-cabinet support, has taken the risk of losing power in order to deepen the strategic relationship with the US?

Economic considerations can be found on either side. The billion-consumer Indian market with its enhanced purchasing power based on a growing middle-income and young-generation group must be attractive to any economic power, including the US. It has also been presumed that the arms and nuclear energy markets, both of which are essential industries of the US, will expand in India. India has been seen as an economic partner with a different twist by China in the circumstance of a world-wide slowdown and catch-up by emerging powers. From India's viewpoint, the huge US market and capital markets are crucial for its further development even though its power is growing relatively weaker. The US has been the largest export counterpart and one of the largest providers of foreign direct investment (FDI).

However, the motivation behind addressing the common concern in China that India and the US are being encouraged to move closer to each other is a strategic one. China, which defeated India in 1962 and has been flexing its military muscle in the field of naval as well as army force, has undoubtedly been seen as a threat in India. It is essential for India to compensate for its weakness in relation to China by cooperating with an overwhelming military power, the US (Mohan and Ayres, 2009, p. 317). The US itself has started to increase its vigilance regarding China in the wake of the Taiwan Strait Crisis of 1995–96. In this situation, it is logical for democratic India with its military potential to become a security partner of the US.

However, there remains a huge divide between India and the US in spite of some common interests. The most salient is the issue over the global political and economic order. India, which has long been committed to the NAM, tends to assume a critical attitude toward any move to dominate the world and to meddle in internal affairs by undermining sovereignty, regardless of ideological inclinations, even now. Even the BJP-led Vajpayee administration that was so proactive in approaching the US rejected a request to send troops to Iraq, alleging that military action 'lacks justification'. The subsequent congress-led Singh administration disappointed the US by not supporting the

142   *Political systems and diplomacy*

attempted US military intervention regarding the Iran nuclear crisis and the Libyan Civil War. The two nations contended with each other in the Doha development round of the World Trade Organization (WTO) and conference of the parties to the United Nations Framework Convention on Climate Change (UNFCCC), which has deterred progress in global negotiations. In the US, there seems to be widespread feeling of disappointment with India, which is sticking to the moldy tradition of emphasizing 'strategic autonomy' and 'developing country' (Tellis, 2012; Miller, 2013; Gilboy and Heginbotham, 2013).

India's relationship with China consisting of 'engagement' and 'hedging'

The relationship between India and China has undergone great changes that might be said to be more drastic than those between India and the US. Having fought each other in the border war in 1962 and thereafter continued a long adversarial relationship, India and China have established strategic-partnership relations today.

The path to improved relations was opened with the ending of the Cold War by Indian prime minister Rajiv Gandhi's visit to Beijing in December 1988, which was the first visit in thirty-four years of an Indian prime minister. Based on the summit agreement, a joint working group on the boundary issue was established, and summit diplomacy began to be actively undertaken. While the Indian nuclear tests in 1998, whose excuse was the 'China threat theory', inflamed China and sent the improving relationship into a tailspin for a moment,[2] the relationship got back on a recovery track, which led to the declaration of the 'Strategic and cooperative partnership for peace and prosperity' in April 2005.

The result of the improved relations can be seen in the expansion of bilateral trade. In spite of neighboring countries, the amount of trade between India and China remained in a near-null state until Gandhi's visit. However, it was in 2008 that China became the largest trading partner for India, surpassing the US, although the trade balance with China is highly unfavorable to India. It is a pressing issue for India to realize further market opening of China in the competitive Indian areas of IT, pharmaceutical agents, and agricultural products. In contrast to the expansion of trade, the scale and flow of investment between India and China still remains low. The biggest factor is India's distrust of China. India tends to discourage any Chinese investment in the areas of telecommunications, harbor infrastructure, and so on.

This is because China has been regarded as a bigger threat to India than Pakistan in terms of regular war. India's first concern is the unresolved border issue that caused the war. There is no prospect for a solution to the contentious boundary question between India and China, although the framework of the special representatives' talks established in 2003 has been maintained. What is worse, the political and military tensions have sometimes escalated along the unclear Line of Actual Control (LAC).[3] The second is the expanding Chinese military influence over India's neighbors. Pakistan could not have developed nuclear and missile technologies without help from its 'all-weather friend', China. It is also well known that China has built a series of huge ports that might be diverted for military use around the Indian Ocean in its so-called string of pearls strategy. A change of 'Indian Ocean' to 'Chinese Ocean' would be untenable in terms of nationalism as well as security. It is the active Chinese movement of the Chinese People's Liberation Army (PLA) Navy that is goading India to strengthen its naval power these days (Integrated Headquarters, Ministry of Defence (Navy), 2007, p. 41). The Chinese side sees not Indian military power as a threat but Indian military cooperation with the US and other Western nations. China reacted sharply against the large-scale joint naval exercise in the Bay of Bengal with the participation of India, the US, Japan, Australia, and Singapore in September 2007.

India and China are competing against each other over energy sources. India suddenly closed in on the Myanmar military regime at the end of the 1990s so as to promote a natural gas pipeline project following China. India's agreement with Vietnam for joint oil exploration around the disputed Spratly Islands has drawn fire from China. Whereas India and China declared that they would engage in a survey and exploration of petroleum and natural gas resources in a third country during Wen Jiabao's visit to New Delhi in April 2005, India has been strongly disaffected by Chinese practical action to dominate really valuable energy sources. India has failed to enter a large part of Africa for resources except Sudan, and in Central Asia, China took a big lead (Chellaney, 2006, pp. 95–100; Sachdeva, 2006, pp. 23–34).

China is also regarded as the largest political barrier to India becoming a global power. In fact, China has given merely reluctant support for India's inclusion in the UN Security Council as a permanent member, repeating its past position that the Chinese side 'understands and supports India's aspiration to play a greater role in the United Nations, including in the Security Council'[4] even during Wen's December 2010 visit to New Delhi just after Obama's expression of more articulated support. It is known that China stuck up for India in endorsing its exemption from the NSG Guidelines in 2008. China is believed to have a mindset of confining India to South Asia, because India might be a rival in Chinese global strategy in the future, and the rise of a democratic India might pose a challenge to the communist regime (Pant, 2011, p. 241).

Nevertheless, it is necessary for India to engage China today. First of all, this is because China is seen as essential to India's further economic development. Cooperation with China is significant in the field of multilateral regimes rather than bilateral trade and investment. It is well known that India and China have worked together in the conferences of the parties to the UNFCCC in order to prevent their legally binding emissions reduction targets from being imposed, which might deter growth of both 'developing countries' with huge populations and lands. In the liberalization negotiations at the Doha round of the WTO, both came into line in that developed

144 *Political systems and diplomacy*

countries should reduce protectionist measures so as to defend their own domestic farming and infant industries. They share a mutual interest in establishing a more equitable world economic order and overhauling the existing international monetary system based on the key currency: the US dollar. Some issues have already been addressed in the framework of the BRICS.

To a lesser extent, India's and China's interests coincide in the ideal global political order in which a multipolar world would be realized, sovereignty respected, and military intervention withheld. India took a positive approach to trilateral strategic dialogue with China and Russia (RIC) when the US during the Bush administration pursued a unilateral path. The annual meeting of RIC was established at foreign-minister level in 2002 and at summit level in 2006. India also decided to attend the Shanghai Cooperation Organization (SCO) as an observer in 2005. The joint statement issued during Manmohan Singh's visit to Beijing in January 2008 clearly expressed that '[a]n international system founded to tolerance and respect for diversity will promote the cause of peace and reduce the use, or threat of use, of force' and 'the continuous democratization of international relations and multilateralism are an important objective in the new century'.

However, India, which takes pride in being 'the largest democracy in the world' cannot put the noninterference principle before democracy and human rights without reservation. India tends to support UN sanctions and resolutions against undemocratic regimes, which will not lead to use of force. At the beginning of 2012, India voted for a UNSC resolution on Syria and a UN Human Rights Council (UNHRC) resolution on Sri Lanka, to both of which China and Russia were adamantly opposed.

Some Indian strategists indicate a need for China's engagement in terms of regional foreign and security policy (Mohan, 2006, p. 30). India could increase its freedom of policy on Kashmir and Afghanistan should it knock a wedge into the 'all-weather friendship' between China and Pakistan. Nevertheless, this cannot be a main motive for India's engagement of China because of the persistent skeptical view about Chinese actions.

India's 'time-tested' relationship with Russia

The relationship with Russia/USSR has not undergone great changes since the Cold War as compared to those with the US and China. The USSR was the only reliable and powerful partner in the areas of politics and security during the Cold War, above all, after the conclusion of the Indo–Soviet Treaty of Peace, Friendship and Cooperation in 1971. The collapse of the USSR, therefore, definitely had a major impact on India. On the one hand, whereas the successor, Russia, signed a new diluted treaty with India, it paid little attention to India in the 1990s as a whole, occupied as it was with reordering of its economy and approaching the West. On the other, the Indian side was absorbed in its economic management after liberalization and attached importance to building a multifaceted economic diplomacy by establishing a bridgehead in Southeast Asia. India manifested no interest in the Indo–Russian–Chinese trilateral strategic initiative put forward by the Russian prime minister Yevgeny Primakov during his visit to New Delhi in December 1998.

It was under the Vladimir Putin administration that Russia embarked on approaching India in earnest. President Putin valued relationships with non-Western countries, aspiring to rebuild a sufficiently 'strong Russia' to confront the West. Just at the same time, India recognized the necessity to modernize its weapons in the wake of the Kargil War with Pakistan in 1999. As a result, President Putin immediately upon assuming office paid a visit to New Delhi to establish 'a strategic partnership' in October 2000. While his visit was half a year later than Clinton's, Russia was the first among the three to declare a strategic partnership with India. The process of annual summits has been established and completely maintained between India and Russia since then, which cannot be seen in Indo–US and Indo–Chinese relations. The relationship with Russia has been based on a long-standing trust since the era of the Cold War.

It is in the spheres of weaponry and energy where the close Indo–Russian bilateral relations are most obvious. India's arsenal has long depended on the former USSR. Russia is the largest supplier of defense equipment for India, and India has been the largest customer of the huge Russian armament industry since 2007 (Sachdeva, 2011, p. 216). Russia has never provided state-of-the-art weaponry and technology to China, furnishing India exclusively with them. Underpinned by strong relations of trust, the bilateral cooperation has evolved from a purely buyer–seller relationship to joint research, design development, and production in recent years of items such as the BrahMos cruise missile and fifth-generation fighter aircraft.

Russia has also been an old partner in nuclear cooperation for India. Russia not only provided India with fuel but also built facilities, which pushed cooperation into suspension by 2004 under international criticism for breach of the NSG Guidelines. Russia signed a bilateral nuclear pact with India no sooner than India's special exemption from the NSG Guidelines was granted. The agreement made clear that India possessed the rights to reprocess spent fuel and transfer enrichment technology, and ensured uninterrupted fuel supplies, none of which has been clearly guaranteed in the 123 Agreement with the US. Russia has already started to construct more power plants in Tamil Nadu. Russia has also invited India to its Sakhalin energy project.

In terms of politics and security, Russia has certainly been the most reliable partner for India since the start of the Putin administration. It was Russia that gave the most unequivocal support for India's entry as a permanent member of the UNSC and full membership of multilateral export control regimes such as the NSG as early as 2000. India took sides with Putin's Russia standing against the US tendency to unilateralism, which resulted in substantializing the trilateral initiative of RIC. The Joint Communiqué of the trilateral meeting of foreign ministers held in New Delhi in February 2007 emphasized the need for 'democratization of international relations' centered around the UN to build 'an increasingly multi-polar world order'. India also

146 *Political systems and diplomacy*

expected the trilateral initiative to soften the pigheaded Chinese stance on UNSC reform with Russian help.

India and Russia share a common interest in their regional strategy. Both hold a common concern about their rapidly rising neighbor, China, in spite of the framework of RIC, although their respective relationships with China might have improved. Russia has also consistently denounced Pakistan's strategy of exporting terrorism and maintained the case against intermediation of a third party regarding the Kashmir dispute, siding with India. Both share mutual interests in the situation in Afghanistan after the withdrawal of US troops, measures to deal with the nuclear issue in Iran, and suppression of extremism in Central Asia.

Nevertheless, from the Indian viewpoint, the significance of Russia tends to be reduced in comparison, even in traditionally closely related spheres, because relations with the US and other Western countries have been established and strengthened. As Ollapally (2010, p. 246) puts it, 'while Russia will be an important partner for India, it will be unlikely to regain a pivotal position in the foreseeable future'. Russia is no longer the only option for India. It was the US that India counted on to end the 1991 Kargil War and 2001–02 crisis with Pakistan, and to exert pressure on Pakistan to dismantle the terrorist organizations after the 2008 Mumbai attacks. India did not choose Russia but France as its partner for the planned installation of 126 medium multi-role combat aircraft in 2012. The strategic significance of RIC regarding the global political order has been reduced since the end of the Bush administration. To be sure, it was not until 2009 that the Indian prime minister attended the summit of the SCO held in Russia. This was reputed to be 'a triumph for Russian diplomacy' (Radyuhin, 2009), but it was possible on the back of de-anti-Westernization of the SCO itself in the wake of the end of the Bush administration. The cooperation between India and Russia in the arena of international economic order formation in the WTO and UNFCCC is not as salient as that between India and China.

Indo–Russian bilateral economic relations have been limited in trade as well as investment. Since the Soviet collapse, economic relations have not been restored even to the level that held during the Cold War (Sachdeva, 2011, pp. 216). The Indo–Russian trade total in 2010 remains at 5 billion dollars compared to Indo–US trade of 45 billion dollars and Indo–Chinese trade of 63 billion dollars. FDI from Russia remains at a negligible level. Economic relations, except for energy and weaponry, between India and Russia can be said to be practically naught.

The different significance of three 'strategic partnerships'

As described above, India has established 'strategic partnerships' with the US, China, and Russia since the new century. However, we can find close collaborative partners or estranged or competitive countries, depending on the issue. Let us look at the table below.[5]

Each rating in Table 8.1 should be seen as comparative. In addition, we should keep in mind that the issue area recognized as significant depends on the international situation surrounding India first of all and on domestic discussion to a lesser extent. As described earlier, the issue area of international political order loomed as critical during the Bush administration after the outbreak of Iraq War, which generated domestic argument over the significance of the strategic triangle of RIC.[6] As the multipolar world translated into reality with the start of the Obama administration, however, it became less significant. The values of domestic politics such as democracy and pluralism tend to be emphasized as a counter-ideal in order to express solidarity with the US or Russia when the sense of threat from China or extremism increases in India (Muni, 2009, pp. 12–15). India has proclaimed itself to be one of 'the world's two largest democracies' along with the US on the one hand, and 'the largest multiethnic, multilingual, and multireligious States' to a lesser extent with Russia on the other. In contrast, India has never made mention of placing value on domestic politics in the joint declaration or statement with China despite emphasizing shared interests as 'the world's two largest developing countries'. We should also note that the significance of the value placed on domestic politics might be leveraged as a dependent variable of regional strategy to a considerable degree.

Considering these aspects, we can find three salient facts from the table. First, India has no affinitive or cooperative partner in every issue area, but no estranged, competitive, or conflictual country in every issue area, either. Second, India can expect affinity or cooperation from at least one country in every issue area, and two in most cases. Third, India has no conflicting point but an affinitive or cooperative point in every issue area with Russia except

Table 8.1 Image of relations with the US, China and Russia from the Indian viewpoint in 2012

Issue area	US	China	Russia
Value on domestic politics (democracy, pluralism)	O	×	Δ
International political order (multipolar world, respect for sovereignty)	×	O	O
International economic order (WTO, UNFCCC, etc.)	×	O	Δ
India as a global political power (UNSC reform, membership of NSG, etc.)	O	×	◎
Regional strategy (Kashmir dispute, Af-Pak, China, etc.)	O	×	◎
Military cooperation (import and development of weapons, joint exercise)	O	×	O
Trade and investment	◎	O	×
Energy and resources	O	×	O

Notes: ◎ Close affinity or cooperation.
O Affinity or cooperation.
Δ Mixed relations.
× Estrangement, competition, or conflict.

148 *Political systems and diplomacy*

for weak trade and investment relations. Nevertheless, even without Russia, India can expect affinity or cooperation from either the US or China.

How does India see each relationship as a result? To be sure, the US as an old and overwhelming power is in an adversarial relationship with India as a new rising power in the issue areas of international political and economic order, but an essential partner for India to resist China and Pakistan, to become a permanent member of the UNSC, and to achieve further economic growth. That is to say, the US is regarded as useful for raising the status of India within the existing framework.

China as India's larger neighbor is seen as a major security threat to India. It is not only seen as a political barrier to India's permanent membership of the UNSC and NSG, but also as a competitor for energy and resources. China is therefore a rival to India within the existing international framework. However, India and China form a united front to create economic circumstances favorable to emerging powers, such as in the arenas of the UNFCCC and WTO. Moreover, in the case of the US propensity toward unilateralism or use of force without respecting sovereignty, both cooperate against such moves in the UN, RIC, and SCO. In this respect, China is also a compeer as an emerging power, which speaks for revision of the existing international order.

India continues to sustain a virtually good and close relationship with Russia as its oldest friend. But it is undeniable that post-Cold War Russia possesses less overall national power than the US and China. As mentioned above, complementarity is secured in India's relationships with the two powers, the US and China, by themselves. As a result, the relationship with Russia basically occupies merely a backseat in India's diplomacy. Nevertheless, on the one hand, Indo–Russian deep 'time-tested' ties are 'insurance' against times when India's relations with the US and Russia might plunge into crisis, and on the other, it is also India's 'leverage' for developing relationships with the US and China in its favor. Keep in mind that Russia preceded the US, whose companies hesitate to enter because of India's nuclear liability law[7] in constructing nuclear plants since concluding the bilateral agreement, and there might be signs of China softening its stubborn stance on India's permanent membership of the UNSC through cooperation within the framework that includes Russia.

Conclusion

The situation in which the USSR is the only reliable partner of India has completely changed since the end of the Cold War, especially since the advent of the twenty-first century. India has developed 'omnidirectional strategic partnership' diplomacy to establish and strengthen relationships with every power including the US, China, and Russia. Importantly, what India expects from each partnership is not the same. Above all, India strives to derive advantage either from the US as an old power or China as a new emerging power, in pursuit of its goal of becoming a 'global power' that sustains both relationships.

India might seem to be oscillating between major powers, approaching the US at times, and coming close to China and/or Russia at other times. However, given the fact that India has no strategic partner that coincides with its own interests on every issue area, except for Russia whose power is less than that of the US and of China, it is unpractical and unlikely that India will become completely intimate with one, and antagonize the other. Instead, India will approach one in a particular issue area, but depend on the other in another area. That is to say, without any reliable and powerful partner that is cooperative in every issue area, it is pragmatic for India to adopt 'omnidirectional strategic partnership' diplomacy in which the power on which to rely varies according to the issue area.

How long will India be able to continue such diplomacy? We should note that an international environment favorable to India, which has enabled 'omnidirectional strategic partnership' diplomacy, was not only a result of growth of the national strength of India itself but also a result of diplomacy among the US, China, and Russia with a power shift in the post-Cold War world. The fact that each top leader of P5 paid a visit to New Delhi in only the last half year of 2010 and that each country gave a favorable response to India's first success in test-launching Agni-V, an intercontinental ballistic missile, in 2012, are expressions of favorable situations in which each power has a mind to attract India to its own side.

However, India's edge might be lost in a future scenario of further global power transition. What will happen if joint hegemony such as G2 emerges or a new cold war between the US and China emerges with the latter's rise in power, and what is worse, if a more powerful China seriously damages India in the field of energy and security? 'Omnidirectional strategic partnership' diplomacy might not be sustainable under such circumstances.

Notes

1 The Foundation for National Security Research (FNSR, 2011) published an intriguing report to attempt a comparative analysis of India's strategic partnerships with major powers. Each strategic partnership with the US, Russia, France, Japan, and Germany is rated by each area of politics, economy, and defense. In this previous work, however, the issue area is so limited that cooperation in the fields of energy and international economic order is not considered. Moreover, China is excluded from comparison. Nadkarni (2010) examines and describes the three bilateral strategic partnerships among Russia, India, and China, mainly focusing on their impacts on the regional and global contexts.
2 While Indian defense minister George Fernandes did not hesitate to publicly call China the 'number-one enemy' even just before the tests, Prime Minister Vajpayee sent US president Bill Clinton a letter just after the tests in which he mentioned 'an overt nuclear weapon state on our borders, a state which committed armed aggression against India in 1962', that is to say, China, as an impulse for India's nuclearization.
3 According to the Indian media, Chinese 'incursions' into the Indian side have occurred frequently, especially in 2009 and 2013.

150 *Political systems and diplomacy*

4 Some analysts indicate signs of flexibility of the Chinese stance based on the fact that the term 'Security Council' has been added to the summit joint statement since 2008.

5 The idea of analyzing each relation according to the issue area was suggested to me by Professor Takako Hirose when I made a presentation at the 2013 East Japan Meeting of the Japan Association for Asian Studies (JAAS) held at Dokkyo University. Each assessment of Table 8.1 is based on discussion and comments at the JAAS Meeting, some previous works by the FNSR (see note 1) and the Institute for Defence Studies and Analyses (Gupta and Azad, 2011), and the tone of the local press and magazines, as well as not a few interviews with Indian researchers and officials.

6 Pant (2008, pp. 39–62), however, sees the strategic triangle as merely 'rhetoric', because of the different interests and the significance of the relations with the US among India, Russia, and China.

7 India's Nuclear Liability Law, enacted in 2010, includes provisions on certain responsibilities of manufacturers and suppliers of nuclear reactors in the case of accidents, which has caused concern in the US.

References

Carlucci, Frank, Robert Hunter and Zalmay Khalilzad, co-chairs (2000) *Taking Charge: A Bipartisan Report to the President-Elect on Foreign Policy and National Security: Transition 2001*, Santa Monica CA: RAND.

Chellaney, Brahma (2006) *Asian Juggernaut: The Rise of China, India and Japan*, New Delhi: HarperCollins.

Cohen, Stephen P. (2001) *India: Emerging Power*, Washington, DC: Brookings Institution Press.

FNSR Group of Experts (2011) *India's Strategic Partners: A Comparative Assessment*, New Delhi: Foundation for National Security Research.

Integrated Headquarters, Ministry of Defence (Navy) (2007) *Freedom to Use the Seas: India's Maritime Military Strategy*, New Delhi: Ministry of Defence.

Gilboy, George J. and E. Heginbotham (2013) 'Double Trouble: A Realist View of Chinese and Indian Power', *Washington Quarterly*, vol. 36, no. 3, pp. 125–42.

Gupta, Arvind and Sarita Azad (2011) *Evaluating India's Strategic Partnership using Analytic Hierarchy Process*, www.idsa.in/idsacomments/EvaluatingIndiasStrategic PartnershipsusingAnalyticHierarchyProcess_agupta_170911.

Khilnani, Sunil, Rajiv Kumar, Pratap Bhanu Mehta, Lt. Gen. (Ret.) Prakash Menon, Nandan Nilekani, Srinath Raghavan, Shyam Saran and Siddarth Varadarajan (2012) *Nonalignment 2.0: A Foreign and Strategic Policy for India in the Twenty First Century*, New Delhi: Center for Policy Research.

Mohan, C. Raja (2006) 'India and the Balance of Power', *Foreign Affairs*, vol. 85, no. 4, pp. 17–32.

Mohan, C. Raja, and Alyssa Ayres (2009) 'Situating the Realignment', in Alyssa Ayres and C. Raja Mohan, eds, *Power Realignments in Asia: China, India, and the United States*, New Delhi: Sage, pp. 307–27.

Miller, Manjari Chatterjee (2013) 'India's Feeble Foreign Policy: A Would-Be Great Power Resists Its Own Rise', *Foreign Affairs*, vol. 92, no. 3, pp. 14–19.

Muni, S. D. (2009) *India's Foreign Policy: The Democracy Dimension*, New Delhi: Foundation.

Nadkarni, Vidya (2010) *Strategic Partnerships in Asia: Balancing without Alliances*, New York: Routledge.

Ollapally, Deepa M. (2010) 'The Evolution of India's Relations with Russia: Tried, Tested, and Searching for Balance', in Sumit Ganguly, ed., *India's Foreign Policy: Retrospect and Prospect*, New Delhi: Oxford University Press, pp. 226–50.

Pant, Harsh V. (2008) *Contemporary Debates in Indian Foreign and Security Policy: India Negotiates its Rise in the International System*, New York: Palgrave Macmillan.

——(2011) 'India's Relations with China', in David Scott, ed., *Handbook of India's International Relations*, London: Routledge, pp. 233–42.

Radyuhin, Vladimir (2009) 'A Triumph of Russian Diplomacy', *Hindu*, June 15.

Sachdeva, Gulshan (2006) 'India's Attitude towards China's Growing Influence in Central Asia', *China and Eurasia Quarterly*, vol. 4, no. 3, pp. 23–34.

——(2011) 'India's Relations with Russia', in David Scott, ed., *Handbook of India's International Relations*, London: Routledge, pp. 213–22.

Tellis, J. Ashley (2008) 'The Merits of Dehyphenation: Explaining U.S. Success in Engaging India and Pakistan', *The Washington Quarterly*, vol. 31, no. 4, pp. 21–42.

——(2012) *Nonalignment Redux: The Perils of Old Wine in New Skins*, Washington, DC: Carnegie Endowment for International Peace.

Part III
History

9 Autonomous regions in the Eurasian borderlands as a legacy of the First World War

Yoshiro Ikeda

The empire-state was the basic unit of international order in nineteenth-century Europe and Eurasia. During the first decades of the twentieth century, however, this order was radically changed, first by the collapse of the Qing dynasty in 1911 and then by the downfalls of the Romanov, Habsburg, Hohenzollern, and Ottoman empires due to the First World War. What was the impact of this breakdown of empires on the world in the following decades and today? To answer this question, in this chapter I will focus on autonomous regions as idea and form in Europe, and then in Eurasia when the analyses concern Russia and, to the lesser extent, China.

Juridically, an autonomous region is an intermediary stage of statehood between state and province of a state (Jellinek, 1896, p. 11), though in practice the difference between these types is often unclear. They were indispensable components of an international system before the First World War. As mentioned above, this system consisted largely of empire-states, which were distinguished by highly multiple subjects in ethnic, confessional, historical, and other terms. This was especially so in the land empires, such as the Habsburg, Russian, Ottoman, and Chinese empires. In these empires, the territory spreading over a vast landmass with heterogeneous cultural communities contributed to preventing the nation-building process for the 'core' nationalities, and, correspondingly, the integrating function of the dynasties was preserved more persistently than in maritime empires such as the British Empire, where a relatively homogeneous core region was separated from its colonies by the sea (Barkey and von Hagen, 1997; Miller and Rieber, 2004). More often than not, autonomous regions lay at the edges of these land empires, where dynasties and imperial governments bestowed autonomous status, as a privilege, on some peripheral parts of their territory specific in one or another regard.

The objective of this chapter is to trace the development of the autonomous regions in the European and Eurasian borderlands, starting from the first half of the nineteenth century through the First World War to the 1920s, with special reference to the Russian Empire and the Soviet Union. Focusing on the situation in Russia allows us to expand our scope beyond the separation of Europe and non-Europe, analyzing how the changes in various regions

156   *History*

of the world interrelated with each other. Besides, the experiences of Russia also attract our special attention because the country, together with China, has preserved till today some features of traditional empire in its multiethnic composition. In the following, I will show how this succession of 'imperialness' in Russia through the Revolution of 1917 had particular significance for the problem of stability in the Eurasian borderlands.

Autonomous regions in Europe before the outbreak of the First World War

In modern European history, empires had long had a natural affinity with various types of autonomy defined as privileged status, because the ruling dynasty of an empire had traditionally secured the loyalty of various cooperative bodies by giving each of them different respective prerogatives. So, up to the middle of the nineteenth century, establishing an autonomous region was an act of a dynasty bestowing privilege on a particular group, or groups, of subjects, as with the case of the Grand Duchy of Finland, which was founded as an autonomous entity of the Russian Empire in 1809 (Kappeler, 2001, pp. 94–98); or, it was an act between a ruling dynasty and an obedient dynasty, as was the case of the Principality of Serbia, which came into being as a result of a compromise between the Ottoman Empire and the rebellious Obrenović dynasty in 1817 (Jelavich and Jelavich, 1977, pp. 36–37).

This situation began to change in the second half of the nineteenth century, as the rising tide of nationalism, which up to that time had been suppressed more or less successfully by the collective actions of the European powers, became so strong that many governments began to seriously consider the possibility of exploiting, or making a compromise with, that movement. The ruling elites of the empires soon found that autonomous regions were a convenient device for this aim, the theoretical discrepancy between the dynastic principle and modern nationalism notwithstanding. At the forefront of this trend was the Habsburg Empire, which had experienced a windstorm of nationalist protests during the 1848 Revolution, and which then suffered military defeat by the forces armed with nationalism. First, the loss in the war of 1859 with Sardinia led to a reform that resulted in an autonomous Galicia with the dominance of the Polish nobility at the expense of the Ruthenians by 1871 (Wandycz, 1982, pp. 82–86). Second, after the humiliating defeat by Prussia in 1866 brought about the *Ausgleich* (compromise) between Vienna and Budapest, the Kingdom of Hungary, now one-half of the Dual Monarchy, granted a certain degree of autonomy to Croatia in 1868 (Kohn, 1961, p. 46).

The European powers also used territorial autonomy as a device to regulate their competition for the sphere of influence (Yavuz, 2011, p. 29). Following the Russo–Turkish War and the Treaty of San Stefano, the Congress of Berlin in 1878 became a milestone in this regard. In the capital of the German Empire, diplomats of the Great Powers reached the decision to concede, besides the independence of Romania, Serbia, and Montenegro, to the establishment of an autonomous principality of Bulgaria, with a large reduction in its territory stipulated in the Treaty of San Stefano by carving out another autonomous polity, Eastern Rumelia, under the suzerainty of the sultan (*Sbornik*, 1952, pp. 181–206).

Moreover, responding in part to lobbying by the Armenian communities inside and outside of the Ottoman Empire, the Great Powers decided to force the Sublime Porte to promise administrative reform in the Ottoman provinces with a high percentage of Armenians, with the prospect of giving them a certain level of autonomy (Reynolds, 2011, p. 15). Thus, the autonomous regions became a focal point where the Great Powers' vying for spheres of influence became intertwined with the political aspirations of the minority groups living in the borderlands of the empires.

For many national movements at the turn of the century, an autonomous region was not at all a compromise, or a surrogate, for independence. On the contrary, for most national movements in Europe before the First World War, territorial autonomy was a highly esteemed goal per se, insofar as the independence of minor nationalities had not been thought sustainable, and the continuing persistence of empires was one of the basic premises for any political consideration.[1] It is only after the fates of several empires became gloomier at the later stage of the Great War that many national movements both within and without Europe came to have a clear orientation towards political independence, often finding Woodrow Wilson's fourteen points to be a straight call for that goal despite the American president's more limited intentions (Manela, 2007). In contrast, before the outbreak of war, the collapse of empires in Europe seemed, with the possible exception of the Ottoman Empire, to be an unrealistic supposition. So, during the years of turmoil of the Revolution of 1905–07, a wide range of peripheral regions of the Russian Empire raised their voices calling for territorial autonomy, which, in combination with the federalization of the empire, was regarded as an optimal form of national self-determination (*Programmy*, 1995, pp. 76, 166–69, 186–89).

Though the tsarist government had successfully suppressed these movements by 1907, political activists and jurists of the Russian Empire continued to elaborate theoretical problems of autonomy. They were greatly inspired by the development of the British Empire, during which its white settler colonies came to obtain, after the Imperial Conference of the same year, the official status of 'dominion' with much wider political rights than those enjoyed by the autonomous regions of other empires. For Russian left-liberals, the British Empire with its metropole–periphery relations structured on nearly equal terms indicated a path for their own empire to follow (Korf, 1914, pp. 447–49). However, not all British colonies acquired the status of dominion, and for Russian center- and right-liberals, a more restricted self-rule, such as was stipulated in the third Irish Home Rule Bill and fully satisfied no one, was sufficient. It might even be applicable only to Poland, while other peripheral regions were, besides Finland with its constitution, to remain as ordinary provinces of the empire, with the right to use the native language guaranteed in school, law court, and other public facilities (*S'ezdy*, 2000, p. 178; *Programmy*, 1995, pp. 329–30). In any case,

158 *History*

learning about other empires in their practice of autonomy by politicians, administrators, and political activists is an important, but uninvestigated, theme in the study of inter-imperial relations before the First World War.

Empires and autonomous regions in Europe during the First World War

The outbreak of the First World War brought about radical changes in the interrelations between the imperial governments and the political movements of ethnic (more precisely, ethno-confessional) minorities. Let us look at various aspects of these changes, focusing mainly on land empires and especially on Russia.

First of all, after the outbreak of war, imperial governments one after another began to cooperate with ethnic minorities in and out of their territory much more eagerly than before. Of course, their choice of targets was selective: Istanbul cooperated with paramilitary organizations of the Kurds in suppressing the Armenian subjects, whereas Petrograd put on an affable face to the Poles, treating the Ukrainians in the western region of the empire and occupied Eastern Galicia rather coldly (Üngör, 2012; *Narody i oblasti*, 3-4-5, 1914, p. 4; *Natsional'nye problemy*, 4, 1915, p. 40; Hagen, 2007, pp. 37–42). For the governments, the immediate motive behind this cooperation was strategic: to ensure domestic security and to undermine adversaries from within. This was especially true given that ethnic groups lived, as was often the case, on both sides of the borders between antagonistic empires.

However, the cooperation between the imperial capitals and the various minority groups also proceeded against a backdrop of more general changes caused by the total war in each belligerent country. Generally speaking, waging total war necessitates the heightened political consciousness of the inhabitants, not only on special occasions (manifestos, meetings, etc.), but also and especially in everyday life. More often than not, in multiethnic empires, common people in everyday life used the local languages, adhered to local customs, and belonged to their own confession, which differed from those of the officials and ruling classes. The more total the mobilization became and the greater the number of subjects drawn into the endeavor of war was, the more deeply the governments had to depend on local leaders with their knowledge of life in their regions, and the more considerate the mobilization politics had to become towards the mores of the minority communities. Therefore, total war inevitably incited governments to stimulate local nationalisms.

Promises of territorial autonomy were among the standard methods of the imperial governments to promote cooperation with the local communities. Most such promises turned out to be empty, but under the conditions of the total reshuffling of inter-imperial relations, they sounded quite likely. The logic of conferring territorial autonomy was still dynastic in its essence, as a privilege given by the grace of the emperor. The proclamation of the supreme commander-in-chief of the Russian army to the Poles is a well-known case, in which Grand Duke Nikolai Nikolaevich (Figure 9.1) opined that the time had come for the Polish nation to 'be reunited under the scepter of the Russian tsar' and that under it 'Poland will be reborn, free in her faith, language, and self-government' (Golder, 1927, 1964, p. 37).

Polish communities in the Russian Empire welcomed this proclamation, though with a preponderance of the principle of national self-determination

Figure 9.1 Grand Duke Nikolai Nikolaevich
Source: *Ekonomicheskoe vozrozhdenie Rossii* [The Economic Renaissance of Russia], No. 6–7, 1915, cover.

over the principle of dynasty, as follows: 'The Poles ... have always believed in the triumph of self-determination of the nation' (*Narody i oblasti*, 3-4-5, 1914, p. 37). The discrepancy between the two principles could be laid aside for some time, at least at the first stage of war. An analogous declaration was made by the Hohenzollern and Habsburg dynasties guaranteeing the resurrection of the Polish kingdom (Fischer, 1967, pp. 271–73). Maritime empires did not fall behind, as was shown by the case of the British Empire officially recognizing the desirability of furthering self-government in India in August 1917 (Manela, 2007, p. 83).

The local leaders of ethnic communities did not just accept these promises passively. On the contrary, they were quite eager to exploit the competence of the empires, promoting their own scenario for repartition of the occupied regions. To cite an example, on August 22, 1914, a deputy of the State Duma (Russian legislative body) from Lithuania, Martynas Ichas, submitted a manifesto of Lithuanian public organizations to Grand Duke Nikolai Nikolaevich and other high officials of the Russian Empire, calling for the annexation of the Lithuanian lands in East Prussia: 'We believe that our foreign brothers by blood will be taken from under the German yoke and be reunited with us, since the historical mission of Russia is to be the liberator of nations' (Voina i litovtsy, 1914, p. 22). The expansionism of the imperial governments and the nationalism of the ethnic minorities were thus in complicity.

Territorial autonomy was a traditional way for the activists of ethnic communities to save the fate of their compatriots living on the other side of the border. Armenian public figures living in the Russian Empire were especially active in this regard, because of the desperate hardships their brothers in the Ottoman Empire had to suffer during the war. These public figures envisioned the founding, with the help of the Russian Empire, of an autonomous Armenian region in the Ottoman lands. The publicist A. K. Dzhivelegov insisted on the establishment of such an autonomous region, which would be put under the aegis of the tsar and guaranteed by a treaty of the Allied Powers, like, possibly, the Treaty of Berlin (Kirakosian, 2007, p. 194). This claim inevitably came into collision with the reunification plans of other ethnic groups. The Georgian G. Gvelesiani, for example, criticized Dzhivelegov's autonomous Armenia plan since it included Lazistan, which, according to Gvelesiani, was 'a purely Georgian region both geographically and ethnographically' (Gvelesiani, 1915, p. 11).

Those who were in favor of the nationalist cause did not hesitate to resort to the institutions deriving from the dynastic principle.[2] For example, as a way to secure an autonomous Armenia, the Russian jurist Maksim Kovalevskii proposed a 'real union' between the Russian Empire and the latter, modeled on relations between the Russian Empire and the Grand Duchy of Finland (Kovalevskii, 1915, p. 269). Dynastic forms were used not only for territorial autonomy, but also for independence. In the latter half of 1915, when the forces of the Central Powers succeeded in occupying a wide stretch of the Russian western border, some Belorussian nationalists began to turn their orientation from Petrograd to Berlin, proposing to the German forces the establishment, under the aegis of the Hohenzollern dynasty, of a 'Grand Duchy of Lithuania', in analogy to the medieval polity stretching over a large portion of the eastern Slavic lands (Stashkevich, 2002, p. 352). Reference to these dynastic forms did not mean that their followers were willing to establish an archaic order; they just sought an optimal form of statehood that was more realizable in consideration of imperial realities.

The downfall of the Romanov dynasty in the spring of 1917 radically changed the context in which the local elites of the Russian Empire found themselves in relation to the capital. In all corners of the country, national movements began to gain momentum, openly demanding not only democratization of the regime in general, but also its decentralization in particular. As had been the case during the 1905 Revolution, territorial autonomy combined with the federalization of Russia appeared as a widely accepted objective for many nationalities. The two republican federations commanded considerable attention: the 1874 Constitution of Switzerland was translated with commentaries, while the political system of the USA was popularized through cheap pamphlets (*Soiuznaia Konstitutsiia*, 1917; Kazmin, 1917). Many ethnic minority parties found an ideal model of a new democratic Russia in these federations. So, around April of 1917, the Latvian Democratic Party based in Petrograd passed a resolution calling for an autonomous Latvia to join a 'Democratic Russian Federative Republic' like a canton of Switzerland or a state of the USA. The Estonian Radical Democratic Party alike insisted that Russia be a 'federative democratic republic' consisting of each nationality as a state (Dimanshtein, 1930, pp. 229, 255).

A unique venue for raising these and other demands was the Congress of Nationalities convened by the Ukrainian Central Rada from September 8 to 15, 1917 in Kiev, with eighty-four delegates of the Ukrainian, Belarusian, Georgian, Estonian, Jewish, Cossack, Latvian, Lithuanian, Moldovan, Russian, Tatar, and Turkic peoples. The resolution of the congress insisted that 'Russia must be a federative-democratic republic', calling to convene, besides the All-Russian Constituent Assembly, regional constitutional assemblies as well, which would decide 'the norms of relations of regions with central organs of the federation', and 'inner organization of the autonomous institutions of a given nationality or region' (*Ukrains'ka tsentral'na rada*, 1996, pp. 288, 303–4, 308, 310).

It should not be overlooked that, with the exception of Poland, even after the downfall of dynasty, almost all the national movements on Russia's periphery that were aiming to obtain some kind of statehood pursued it, not in the form of independence, but of autonomy. Those with special knowledge of constitutional law made clear the difference between an autonomous region, which is ordinarily founded by the decision of the central government, and a member-state of a federation, which owes its existence to its own decision (*Ukrains'ka tsentral'na rada*, 1996, pp. 297–98). But, more often than not, the distinction between them remained vague, as is clear from the above-mentioned

162 *History*

resolution of the Kiev Congress. Likewise, a council of socialist parties of various nationalities in Russia in late May 1917 adopted a stance favoring 'political self-determination' implemented through either ethnic-territorial autonomy, ethnic-personal autonomy, or federation with Russia (Dimanshtein, 1930, pp. 451–52).

Territorial autonomy thus remained the goal for the majority of the national movements on Russia's periphery. It was only with the Bolshevik take-over of power in Petrograd that the local elites finally decided to detach themselves from the politics of Russia proper to declare independence (Stankevich, 1921, pp. 15–16).

Autonomous regions in the Eurasian borderlands after the First World War

The Great War led to the extinction of a number of autonomous regions in Europe, together with their host empires. From the ruins of these empires rose a new Europe, which mainly consisted of nation-states. Some of the former autonomous regions, such as Finland and later Ireland, succeeded in obtaining independence. Others, like Galicia, were incorporated into successor states, which pretended to a 'national' right to these regions. However, the autonomous region as form and idea never disappeared in post-war Europe. Insofar as the successor states remained multiethnic, voices were still heard seeking territorial autonomy among the ethnic minorities in the former Habsburg and Ottoman lands, as with the case of the Slovaks or the Kurds, to name but a couple of examples (Krajčovičová, 2011; Yavuz, 2001, p. 7).

Moreover, there were places where autonomous regions were established anew, and what was more, in an updated form of 'autonomous republic'. They saw the light in the Russian Soviet Federative Socialist Republic (RSFSR), and then in the Soviet Union. The first of the autonomous repub-lics established under the 1918 Bolshevik Constitution, the Bashkir Autono-mous Soviet Socialist Republic, was created during the Civil War, in March 1919, as a result of the compromise between the Bolsheviks and the Bashkir national movement (Smith, 1999, pp. 94–98). Then, many peripheral regions of the former Russian Empire underwent an analogous process. The autono-mous republic was a unique amalgam of historical trends. On the one hand, 'autonomous' meant that Bolshevik Russia inherited some characteristic fea-tures of imperial governance, especially the way of granting special status to a particular region, one by one. On the other hand, 'republic' was a time-tested device from the era of the French Revolution to turn subjects of the monarch into politically active citizens, in response to the necessities of total war.

The practice and concept of the autonomous republic also had importance in the international arena. Especially in the Eurasian borderlands, the Soviet autonomous republics played a conspicuous role as actors of geopolitical competence, side by side with other intermediary polities. In contrast to Europe, where many autonomous regions had disappeared because of the

Great War, in Inner Eurasia, there remained, besides the Soviet autonomous republics, various intermediary statehoods. The reasons were that (1) the war had shaken the British Empire's hold on its periphery, (2) some autonomous regions of the Russian Empire remained unincorporated into Soviet Russia, and (3) the Republic of China, which came into being in 1912, was also unsuccessful in integrating all the lands of the former Qing Empire.

Among various intermediary polities in the Eurasian borderlands, active diplomatic efforts distinguished the Emirate of Afghanistan (Figure 9.2), an autonomous polity whose foreign affairs had been controlled by the viceroy of British India. When the Emirate began an independence war against the British Empire in May 1919, the Bolsheviks, in search of partners in their isolated struggle against the imperialists, sought to reach out to Afghanistan via the Turkestan Autonomous Soviet Republic, an improvised state encompassing the former Government General of Turkestan which, being obedient to Moscow, had to operate virtually at its own risk due to lack of communication during the Russian Civil War. However, with the prospects for independence looking good (London would recognize its independence in August), Kabul came to take a rather aggressive stance towards Soviet Russia,

Figure 9.2 Central Asia region (1922)
Source: Adapted from Richard Pipes (1964) *The Formation of the Soviet Union: Communism and Nationalism, 1917–1923*, Revised Edition, Cambridge, MA: Harvard University Press, p. 157.

164　History

demanding to have under its protection the Khanate of Khiva and the Emirate of Bukhara, the two autonomous regions of the Russian Empire remaining out of the Bolshevik domain. To avoid this from happening, the emir of Bukhara for his part sought to cooperate with the British Empire and Soviet Russia as well. In the end, with the help of local reformists, the Red Army conquered the Khanate of Khiva and the Emirate of Bukhara in 1920 and reorganized them into the Khorezm and Bukharan People's Soviet Republics respectively, discouraging Afghanistan by this. Thereafter, both statehoods were, together with the Turkestan Autonomous Soviet Republic, disassembled in the process of the ethnic demarcation of Central Asia. A part of the former Emirate of Bukhara was reborn as the Tajik Autonomous Republic, with a view to demonstrating the superiority of Soviet national policy to the Tajiks living on the other side of the border in Afghanistan, quite an imperial practice before and during the First World War in Europe and elsewhere (Panin, 1998, pp. 5, 12, 14, 37, 55, 110–11, 139–45; Hirsch, 2005, pp. 160–86; Cobban, 1969, p. 203).

Having enjoyed autonomous status under the Qing dynasty, some peripheral regions of China were to be especially affected by the idea of the Soviet autonomous republic. The most important case was Outer Mongolia (Figure 9.3), which had declared independence at the end of 1911 with the Bogd Khan, a reincarnated Lama, on the throne, separating itself from the collapsing Qing Empire. Its destiny was, however, dependent on the international

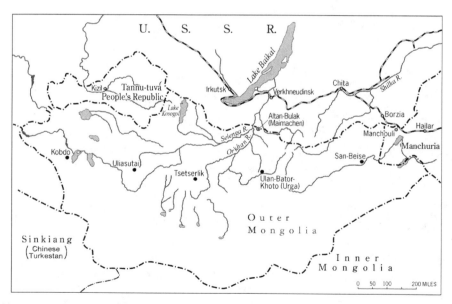

Figure 9.3 Outer Mongolia and Tuva
Source: Adapted from I. I. Serebrennikov (1931) 'A Soviet Satellite: Outer Mongolia Today', *Foreign Affairs*, vol. 9, no. 3, p. 510.

relations of Inner Eurasia, and in November 1913, the Republic of China and the Russian Empire declared together that Outer Mongolia be autonomous under the suzerainty of China (Damdinsuren, 2001, p. 43; *Sbornik*, 1952, pp. 418–20). This was an autonomy given in the traditional, dynastic manner, with the local lords gathering around the Bogd Khan as its trustees.

The collapse of the Russian Empire tempted major Asian forces to extend their political influence over Mongolia. The Japanese Empire invented an abortive 'government of Great Mongolia', while in November 1919 the Republic of China annulled the autonomy of Outer Mongolia. The consequent struggle for a Mongolian statehood was conducted consistently around the notion of autonomy, not independence. First, Baron Ungern-Sternberg, a White Army officer, in February 1921 resurrected the autonomy of Outer Mongolia, putting the Bogd Khan on the throne again. Second, the Soviet government and the Mongolian People's Party alike aimed at autonomy for Outer Mongolia as their immediate goal. In July 1921, the People's Government of Mongolia took the place of the theocratic government; the Bogd Khan remained on the throne, but his political power was significantly restricted and shortly after his death in June 1924, Outer Mongolia was declared a people's republic. Nevertheless, de jure, Outer Mongolia was still autonomous, due to a compromise between the Soviet Union and the Republic of China. On May 31, 1924, both states came to an agreement that recognized Outer Mongolia as a 'component part' of China. By this, an ex-imperial space of the former Qing dynasty was retained for the time being with the connivance of the Bolsheviks. The Republic of China would recognize the independence of Mongolia only after the Second World War in 1946 (Damdinsuren, 2001, pp. 45–46, 49, 52, 55, 65; Sanders, 2010, p. xxxvi; *Dokumenty Vneshnei Politiki* vol. 7, 1963, pp. 333, 709–10).

Thus, for the short period from 1911 to 1924, Outer Mongolia was transformed from a traditional autonomous region based on the dynastic concept to an 'autonomous republic' à la Bolshevik, combining within itself an ex-imperial space with nationalism. Under the impact of the First World War and the Russian Revolution, Mongolia experienced the historical trend of the peripheries of the European empires from the mid-nineteenth century to the early twentieth century in a compressed way.

The idea of the Soviet autonomous republic affected more immediately Tuva (Uriankhai), a small land between the northwest corner of Outer Mongolia and Siberia. After the collapse of the Qing dynasty, the ownership of the territory became a burning question of the region. Regarding the territory as a component part of the Mongolian lands, Outer Mongolia was eager to 'reunite' with it, while the Russian Empire also pretended to the right to hold the territory against the Republic of China, having Russian colonists in Tuva as a convenient foothold. As a result, Tuva came under the protectorate of the tsar in June 1914, and even after the downfall of the Romanovs, its successor Soviet Russia likewise preferred to keep the land under its own aegis despite the will of the Mongolian People's Government to annex it. Thus,

166   *History*

established in August 1921, the People's Republic of Tannu Tuva (from 1926, the Tuvan People's Republic) was again practically an autonomous region Bolshevik-style, under the protectorate of Soviet Russia with the Republic of China having nominal sovereignty over it. By 1925, economic hardships pushed the leaders of the Republic of Tannu Tuva to ask the Mongolian government for unification, but Soviet Russia categorically blocked this, referring to the formal sovereignty of China over both statehoods as an excuse (Shurkhuu, 2001; Baranov, 1913, pp. 19–21). Subsequently, the Second World War provided Moscow with an incentive to bring the fate of Tuva to its logical conclusion: in 1944, the Tuvan People's Republic was officially incorporated into the USSR as an autonomous region (*oblast'*) of the RSFSR, and then in 1961, it was upgraded to an autonomous republic (*Istoriia Tuvy*, 1964, pp. 234–36, 438–39).

So, under the influence of the First World War and the Russian Revolution, the Bolsheviks invented an updated version of the autonomous region, that is, the autonomous republic. Its concept and practice were spread by Soviet Russia deep into Inner Eurasia, and even beyond the borderline, into the periphery of the former Qing dynasty. The autonomous republic was a unique hybrid of the dynastic and the national principles: it enabled the Bolsheviks to keep a heterogeneous, post-imperial sphere almost intact on the one hand and to continue with mobilization depending on nationalism on the other. However, the Soviet autonomous republic and its counterpart on the Chinese periphery could also serve as a destabilizing factor for international relations due to its ambiguous status with intermediary statehood. In the interwar period, both people's republics of Tuva and Mongolia remained unrecognized by the rest of the world, and the latter in particular played a considerable role in local conflicts as the territorial ambitions of the Japanese Empire became fiercer, as in the battles of Khalkhin-Gol in 1939. The awkward existence of these people's republics foreshadowed the 'unrecognized states' and similar statehoods (Abkhazia, Crimea, and so on) on the periphery of the former USSR of the early twenty-first century.

Conclusion

In modern Europe, the properties of the autonomous regions gradually changed. Initially a result of the dynastic principle, these regions, as the tide of nationalism heightened, came to be increasingly regarded both by the imperial governments and the local elites of minority groups as a feasible framework for national self-determination. The First World War significantly intensified this trend.

The collapse of the empires detached the autonomous regions from the dynastic principle as such. But territorial autonomy as form and idea remained a way to realize national self-determination, and was even updated in the form of the autonomous republic in Soviet Russia. Because of the global scale of the Great War, these devices spread deeply into Inner Eurasia and exerted influence beyond the border. As a result, on the periphery of the former Russian and Chinese empires, a number of new autonomous polities came into being. Devoid of full-fledged statehood, but oriented towards nationalist mobilization, these autonomous polities often turned out to be a destabilizing factor in the Eurasian borderlands.

Following the collapse of the Soviet Union, its autonomous republics have been inherited by Russia and other former states of the USSR. Furthermore, the Soviet nationalities policy gave inspiration to the People's Republic of China as well, though Beijing did not grant any statehood to ethnic minorities. Therefore, the practice and idea of the autonomous republic is still essential today in understanding the problem of stability in the Eurasian borderlands.

Acknowledgments

I would like to thank John Horne, Oliver Janz, Yoichi Kibata, and Jay Winter for their helpful comments on an earlier version of this chapter.

Notes

1 Alfred Cobban, it seems to me, underestimates the importance of territorial autonomy as a goal of national movements before the First World War (Cobban, 1969, pp. 13–56).
2 Here, I owe much to Tatsuya Nakazawa, who has stressed the importance of the lingering effect of dynastic principles in understanding modern Slovakian history, especially in analyzing how Slovakian nationalists appropriated the 'crown lands' and other dynastic conceptions in seeking their own statehood within the Habsburg Empire. See Nakazawa (2007). In his recent article written in Japanese on Slovakia during and shortly after the First World War, Nakazawa studies how the Slovakian nationalist discourse of the period depended on such dynastic notions as 'crown lands' and 'kingdom'. See Nakazawa (2014).

References

Baranov, A. (1913) *Uriankhaiskii Vopros* [Uriankhai problem], Harbin: Tipo-lit. Zaamurskogo Okruga Otd. Korp. Pogr. Str. (in Russian).
Barkey, Karen and Mark von Hagen (1997) *After Empire: Multiethnic Societies and Nation-building. The Soviet Union and the Russian, Ottoman, and Habsburg Empires*, Boulder, CO: Westview Press.
Cobban, Alfred (1969) *The Nation State and National Self-Determination*, New York: Crowell.
Damdinsuren, S. (2001) 'Mongol'skaia natsional'no-demokraticheskaia revoliutsiia 1921 goda i Rossiiskii factor' [The Mongolian National-democratic Revolution of 1921 and the Russian Factor], in *Rossiia i Mongoliia* [Russia and Mongolia], pp. 43–69 (in Russian).
Dimanshtein, S. M. (1930) *Revoliutsiia i natsional'nyi vopors: Dokumenty i materialy po istorii natsional'nogo voprosa v Rossii i SSSR v XX veke* [Revolution and the National Question: Documents and Materials on the History of National Question

168 *History*

in Russia and the USSR in the Twentieth Century], vol. 3, Moscow: Izdatel'stvo Kommunisticheskoi Akademii (in Russian).

Dokumenty vneshnei politiki SSSR [Documents of the Foreign Policy of the USSR], vol. 7 (1963), Moscow: Gosudarstvennoe izdatel'stvo politicheskoi literatury (in Russian).

Fischer, Fritz (1967) *Germany's Aims in the First World War*, London: Chatto and Windus.

Golder, Frank Alfred (1927, 1964) *Documents of Russian History 1914–1917*, Gloucester, MA: Peter Smith.

Gvelesiani, Gr. (1915) 'K armianskim obshchestvennym deiateliam' [To Armenian Public Activists], *Natsional'nye problemy*, vol. 3 (in Russian).

Hagen, Mark von (2007) *War in a European Borderland: Occupations and Occupation Plans in Galicia and Ukraine, 1914–1918*, Seattle, WA: Herbert J. Ellison Center for Russian, East European, and Central Asian Studies, University of Washington.

Hirsch, Francine (2005) *Empire of Nations: Ethnographic Knowledge and the Making of the Soviet Union*, Ithaca, NY: Cornell University Press.

Istoriia Tuvy [The History of Tuva], vol. 2 (1964) Moscow: Nauka (in Russian).

Jelavich, Charles and Barbara Jelavich (1977) *The Establishment of the Balkan National States, 1804–1920*, Seattle: University of Washington Press.

Jellinek, Georg (1896) *Über Staatsfragmente*, Heidelberg, Germany: Gustav Koester.

Kappeler, Andreas (2001) *The Russian Empire: A Multiethnic History* (Tr. by Alfred Clayton), Harlow: Pearson Education.

Kazmin, N. (1917) *Chto Takoe Soiuznoe Gosudarstvo (Federativnoe Gosudarstvo)* [What Is the Union State (Federation State)], Petrograd: Muravei (in Russian).

Kirakosian, Dzhon (2007) *Aleksei Dzhivelegov i ego istoriko-publitsisticheskoe nasledie* [Aleksei Dzhivelegov and His Heritage as a Historical Publicist], Erevan: Institut Istorii NAN RA (in Russian).

Kohn, Hans (1961) *The Habsburg Empire, 1804–1918*, Princeton, NJ: D. Van Nostrand.

Korf, S. A. (1914) *Avtonomnye kolonii Velikobritanii* [The Autonomous Colonies of Great Britain], St. Petersburg: Trenke i Fiusno (in Russian).

Kovalevskii, M. (1915) Armianskii vopros [The Armenian Question], *Vestnik Evropy* [Herald of Europe], June (in Russian).

Krajčovičová, Natália (2011) 'Slovakia in Czechoslovakia, 1918–38', in Miluláš Teich, Dušan Kováč, and Martin D. Brown, eds, *Slovakia in History*, Cambridge: Cambridge University Press, pp. 137–56.

Manela, Erez (2007) *The Wilsonian Moment: Self-Determination and the International Origins of Anticolonial Nationalism*, Oxford: Oxford University Press.

Miller, Alexei and Alfred J. Rieber (2004) *Imperial Rule*, Budapest: Central European University Press.

Nakazawa, Tatsuya (2007) 'Slovak Nation as a Corporate Body: The Process of the Conceptual Transformation of a "Nation without History" into a Constitutional Subject during the Revolutions of 1848/49', in Hayashi Tadayuki, ed., *Regions in Central and Eastern Europe: Past and Present* (21st Century COE Program, Slavic Eurasian Studies), Sapporo: Slavic Research Center, 2007.

——(2014) 'Nijusei no teikoku kara "nijusei no kyowakoku" to "okan wo itadaku kyowakoku"e' [From the Dual Monarchy to 'a Dual Republic' and 'a Crowned Republic'], in Yoshiro Ikeda, ed., *Daiichiji sekai taisen to teikoku no isan* [The First World War and the Legacy of Empires], Tokyo: Yamakawa Shuppansha (in Japanese).

Narody i oblasti [Nationalities and Regions], no. 3-4-5 (1914) (in Russian).

Autonomous regions as a legacy of WWI 169

Natsional'nye problemy [National Questions], no. 4 (1915) (in Russian).

Panin, S. B. (1998) *Sovetskaia Rossiia i Afganistan 1919–1929* [Soviet Russia and Afghanistan 1919–29], Moscow and Irkutsk: Izd-vo Irkut. gos. ped. un-ta (in Russian).

Programmy politicheskikh partii Rossii. Konets XIX – nachalo XX vv [Programmes of Political Parties of Russia. From the End of the Nineteenth Century to the Beginning of the Twentieth Century] (1995) Moscow: ROSSPEN (in Russian).

Reynolds, Michael A. (2011) *Shattering Empires: The Clash and Collapse of the Ottoman and Russian Empires 1908–1918*, Cambridge: Cambridge University Press.

Rossiia i Mongoliia: novyi vzgliad na istoriiu vzaimootnoshenii v XX veke. Sbornik statei [Russia and Mongolia: New Perspective on the History of Interrelations in the Twentieth Century. Collected Papers] (2001) Moscow: Institut Vostokovedeniia RAN (in Russian).

Sanders, Alan J. K. (2010) *Historical Dictionary of Mongolia*, 3rd edn, Lanham, MD: Scarecrow Press.

Sbornik dogovorov Rossii s drugimi gosudarstvami. 1856–1917 [Collection of Treaties of Russia with Other States. 1856–1917] (1952) Moscow: Gosudarstvennoe izdatel'stvo politicheskoi literatury (in Russian).

S'ezdy i konferentsii konstitutsionno-demokraticheskoi partii, [Congresses and Conferences of the Constitutional Democratic Party], vol. 3, book 1, *1915–1917 gg* (2000) Moscow: ROSSPEN (in Russian).

Shurkhuu, D. (2001) 'Uriankhaiskii vopros v mongolo-rossiiskikh otnosheniiakh v pervoi chetverti XX veka' [The Uriankhai Problem in the Mongol–Russian Relations in the First Quarter of the Twentieth Century], in *Rossiia i Mongoliia* (2001), pp. 97–117 (in Russian).

Smith, Jeremy (1999) *The Bolsheviks and the National Question, 1917–23*, Basingstoke: Palgrave Macmillan.

Soiuznaia konstitutsiia shveitsarskoi federatsii 29 maia 1874 g. s izmeneniiami, posledovavshimi po 1905 g. [The Union Constitution of the Swiss Federation of 29 May, 1874 with the amendments introduced by 1905] (1917) Tr. by L. M. Magaziner, Petrograd: Muravei (in Russian).

Stankevich, V. (1921) *Sud'by narodov Rossii: Belorussiia, Ukraina, Litva, Latviia, Estoniia, Armeniia, Gruziia, Azerbeidzhan, Finliandiia, Pol'sha* [Destinies of Nationalities in Russia: Beralus, Ukraine, Lithuania, Latvia, Estonia, Armenia, Georgia, Azerbaijan, Finland, Poland], Berlin: Izd. I. P. Ladyzhnikova (in Russian).

Stashkevich, N. S. (2002) 'Revoliutsiia 1917 goda i dva puti natsional'no-gosudarstvennogo stroitel'stva v Belorussii' [The Revolution of 1917 and Two Ways for the Nation-State Building in Belarus], in *Rossiia v XX veke: Reformy i revoliutsii. V dvukh tomakh* [Russia in the Twentieth Century: Reforms and Revolutions. In Two Volumes], vol. 1, Moscow: Nauka, pp. 350–58 (in Russian).

Ukrains'ka tsentral'na rada. Dokumenti i materiali u dvokh tomakh [The Ukrainian Central Rada: Documents and Materials in Two Volumes], vol. 1. (1996) Kiev: Naukova dumka (in Ukrainian).

Üngör, Uğur Ümit (2012) 'Paramilitary Violence in the Collapsing Ottoman Empire', in Robert Gerwarth and John Horne, eds, *War in Peace: Paramilitary Violence in Europe after the Great War*, Oxford: Oxford University Press, pp. 164–83.

Voina i litovtsy [The War and the Lithuanian People], (1914) *Narody i oblasti*, no. 3-4-5 (in Russian).

Wandycz, Piotr S. (1982) 'The Poles in the Habsburg Monarchy', in Andrei S. Markovits and Frank E. Sysyn, eds, *Nationbuilding and the Politics of Nationalism:*

170 History

Essays on Austrian Galicia, Cambridge, MA: Harvard University Press, 1982, pp. 68–93.

Yavuz, M. Hakan (2001) 'Five Stages of the Construction of Kurdish Nationalism in Turkey', *Nationalism and Ethnic Politics*, vol. 7, no. 3, pp. 1–24.

——(2011) 'The Transformation of "Empire" through Wars and Reforms: Integration vs. Oppression', in M. Hakan Yavuz and Peter Sluglett, eds, *War and Diplomacy: The Russo–Turkish War of 1877–1878 and the Treaty of Berlin*, Salt Lake City: University of Utah Press, pp. 17–55.

10 Empires and the shari‘a

A comparison of colonial Islamic legal systems

Jun Akiba

Imperial shari‘a

Many of the nineteenth-century European empires (including Russia) had a large number of Muslim populations in their respective domains. When confronted with Muslim society, these empires did not force the legal system of the metropoles upon their Muslim subjects, but allowed the indigenous social norms, that is, the shari‘a or Islamic law, with certain limitations. Thus, the principle of personal jurisdiction was established, in which metropolitan laws were applied to the colonizers who migrated from the metropoles, and the shari‘a was applied to the native Muslims. This was a means by which a small number of ruling groups could effectively govern an overwhelmingly large population of Muslims and also mitigate the latter's hostility to colonial rule. It should also be remarked that the preservation of indigenous laws was based on the colonizers' understanding that the natives were under-civilized and could not understand the virtue of metropolitan laws. At the same time, it was the principle of difference or discrimination that justified the policy of not giving the natives the same rights as the colonizers.[1]

However, as a result of incorporating the shari‘a legal system into governmental institutions, the imperial powers were obliged to position themselves as protectors of the shari‘a and supported the enforcement of the 'proper' shari‘a. It is somewhat ironic that the Europeans who saw Islam as anti-civilization encouraged the purification of Islam and the application of its fundamental interpretations.

The upholding and protection of the shari‘a by the imperial powers, however, did not lead to the preservation of the shari‘a as it had been. The shari‘a underwent a serious transformation under imperial rule. First, certain legal principles such as slavery and some forms of corporal punishment were abolished or their application was restricted to a considerable extent. Generally, as the penal law of the metropole or its simplified and more severe version was introduced, the validity of the shari‘a was finally restricted to the realm of family law. Second, the administration of justice was centralized and new institutions such as appellate courts were created. Third, through codification of law and introduction of case law, specific legal interpretations became a standard for application, which led to loss of flexibility of the shari‘a. This was in part brought by the imperial powers' concern for the efficiency of the

172   *History*

administration of justice, but it also originated in the authorities' and the Orientalists' understanding of the shari'a as an old and unchangeable law.

A phenomenon similar to the transformation of the shari'a mentioned above can also be observed elsewhere in the colonial powers' attempt to discover and codify the customary law of the indigenous peoples. However, because of the highly developed legal system of the shari'a and the significant social influence of its experts, the imperial governments gave special importance to the shari'a and made considerable effort to learn it. Since the shari'a was in principle the universal law of the Muslims, they always referred to the situation of different regions. Thus, the shari'a politics of each empire is one of the best subjects for a comparative study of empires. Because many empires ruled Muslim societies in various parts of the world, however, it is difficult to study all of them. In this chapter, I take examples from British India, the Volga-Ural regions in Russia,[2] Russian Turkestan, and French-ruled Algeria to investigate the shari'a politics in each region during the late nineteenth and early twentieth centuries and examine their connections.

In the Ottoman Empire, itself a Muslim empire, a similar trend such as curtailment of the jurisdiction of the shari'a court, codification of shari'a-based law, and centralization of the shari'a court system can be observed during the same period. In the latter part of this chapter, I will address the question of how these Ottoman reforms had any relation with the European empires' rule over Muslims.

Historical shari'a

First, it will be helpful to summarize the nature of the shari'a in Muslim societies before the advent of the European powers.[3] The shari'a is generally explained as an all-embracing body of prescriptions that Muslims should obey in this world. Thus, it encompasses a wide range of prescriptions including manners and rules concerning daily prayers, division of inheritance, sales contracts, and the penalty for murderers. However, the shari'a is not a codified law. While only a few concrete legal principles are explicitly indicated in the Qur'an, all the other stipulations that answer to a variety of problems that Muslims face in actual society have been deduced from authorized sources, most prominently the Qur'an and the *hadith*, by generations of Muslim jurists. Islamic law is a whole body of jurists' interpretations that were manifested in the books of jurisprudence. In this sense, Islamic law can be characterized as jurists' law. Because it is composed of interpretations, there is much room for disagreement. During the process of development of Islamic jurisprudence, several schools of law (*madhhab*s) were formed according to the differences in interpretation of law. Among the Sunnis, four schools of law, namely, the Hanafi, Shafi'i, Maliki, and Hanbali, established themselves as authoritative schools.

Exercise of reasoning to find law is called *ijtihad*. By the tenth century, when the four schools of law were established, the notion that 'the gate of ijtihad was closed', had become widespread by which modern scholars assume that creative interpretation of the shari'a stopped at that time. However, Islamic jurists had been engaged in lively discussions and produced various original interpretations, especially when new materials such as coffee or tobacco were introduced, or when there was a demand from society such as in the case of cash *waqf*. Islamic law as jurists' law was originally flexible and changeable (Hallaq, 1984).

In order to enforce the provisions of Islamic law, the *'ulama*, or Islamic scholars who mastered the Islamic sciences, especially jurisprudence, were entrusted with official positions in state and society. The most important among these were the positions of *mufti* and *qadi*. The mufti was a jurist who was entitled to issue a legal opinion called a *fatwa*. Generally, a fatwa was composed in a question-and-answer format. Although this answer was given to a specific question, the use of proper names was usually avoided and it was instead presented as a general rule, which meant that a fatwa could have universal applicability. Fatwas of celebrated jurists would be collected in a book and utilized as a legal manual for lawyers. However, fatwas were in principle legal opinions and did not have binding force.

In contrast, what did have binding force was a verdict given by a qadi, a judge of the shari'a court. Theoretically, a qadi was free to choose certain interpretations when there was a conflict in opinion among the same madhhab. As a corollary to this principle, the shari'a court system had no appellate court and decisions were not valid as precedents. Although in theory qadis were appointed by the ruler, the practice depended on the extent of the central state's authority. In some cases, the duties of qadi and mufti or *imam* overlapped, making it difficult to distinguish one from another. In the Ottoman Empire, however, a hierarchy of the 'ulama was formulated, in which the offices of qadi and professor were arranged in hierarchical order, and the *şeyhülislâm* or the mufti of the empire was placed at the top.

Although the shari'a covered the whole range of human activity in theory, judicial authority did not solely rest on the shari'a courts. To embody the image of the ruler who would redress wrongs and do justice, a '*mazalim* court' was established, which received complaints of the people concerning administrative cases such as the wrongdoings of state officials, on which the ruler or his delegates would give rulings (sometimes commissioning qadis to judge the case) and execute them. In case one would like to raise an objection against the qadi's decision, one could appeal to the mazalim court, which functioned as a kind of a higher court as well. In addition, the mazalim court also had jurisdiction over matters concerning taxation or criminal cases, about which the shari'a did not provide detailed prescriptions.

In actual practice, the theory of mazalim court had justified the rulers' judicial authority that originated from non-Islamic traditions (Darling, 2013, esp. pp. 79–80). In the Ottoman Empire, the Imperial Council (*Divan-ı Hümayun*) in the center and the governors' advisory councils (*divans*) in the provinces corresponded to the mazalim courts in legal theory (Heyd, 1973, pp. 210, 226, 257–58; Darling, 2013, pp. 143–44; Ursinus, 2005). Since Islamic

174   *History*

penal law did not specify the kind or degree of punishment for a wide range of punishable deeds, in actuality, criminal cases were often dealt with politically or administratively by the mazalim court, or by the political powers without recourse to the mazalim court. When the colonial powers subjugated a Muslim state, they often soon assumed jurisdiction over criminal cases. The shift was relatively easy because the political authorities that they overturned had taken charge of criminal justice.

An important problem that arose when colonial powers ruled Muslim societies was *waqf* or pious foundations based on Islamic law. In the system of waqf, the founder could renounce his/her ownership right over his/her property (usually immovable) as a waqf property and assign the revenue accrued from it to certain charitable use. Since the ownership of the property set aside as a waqf property was frozen, the existence of waqf property often caused difficulties when the government tried to take over estates or buildings belonging to waqf, especially in the regions where the practice of waqf founding was widespread. However, we are not concerned here with the problem of waqf, which needs a volume to itself if written properly.[4]

Lastly, it may be worth considering whether the shari'a was a personal statute. Although the shari'a was sometimes described as a personal statute, when we look at its history, only the provisions concerning religious rites can be characterized as a personal statute, while the contract law, property law, and criminal law of the shari'a could be applied to non-Muslims in principle. In the Ottoman Empire, cases in which both parties were non-Muslims can be observed frequently in the shari'a court records. Moreover, some Christians would get a divorce or arrange the division of inheritance before the shari'a judge. In this sense, even family law was not personal but territorial (see also Al-Qattan, 1999).

Protectors and reformers of the shari'a: European rule over Muslims

British India: precursor to colonial shari'a

In India, after seizing control over the Bengal region, the British East India Company introduced there a new judicial institution[5] and established civil courts over which tax collectors (later officials appointed by the Company) presided. At first, jurisdiction over criminal cases rested in the hands of the Mughal rulers, but in 1790 it was abolished and transferred to the Company, which set up the courts presided over by Company officials. Appeal courts for civil and criminal cases were also created. However, the abolition of the shari'a courts did not lead to suspension of the shari'a. Warren Hastings, the first governor of Bengal, believed that the Indian people should be governed in conformity with their own customs and rules. Needless to say, reliance on the existing systems was necessary for the minority foreign ruling class to govern the overwhelming Indian majority. Therefore, it was decided that, 'in all suits regarding inheritance, marriage, caste, and other religious usages or institutions',[6] indigenous norms should be applied to Muslims and Hindus respectively, that is, 'the laws of the Koran' with respect to Muslims and Hindu law with respect to Hindus. Muslim law was also often applied in cases of contract or transaction.

Since the officials of the British East India Company did not have specialized knowledge of the shari'a, Muslim jurists called *maulavis* were appointed as 'law officers' to every civil court, and would respond to the judges' questions concerning Islamic law. Similar specialists in Hindu law were also employed for Hindus, and this practice continued until 1864. In the criminal courts, however, Islamic law was to be applied to all the native residents. Here, again, the qadis and the muftis who had been attached to the shari'a courts were employed as law officers, and the judges would give rulings on the basis of the 'fatwas' the law officers issued. Although the role of the law officers in criminal cases was reduced after 1832, application of shari'a criminal law continued until 1864, when Indian criminal law and the law of legal procedure were issued.

The official abolishment of shari'a courts under the Company's rule may appear radical compared to the practices of Russian or French rule over Muslims mentioned below. However, because the Company was only granted taxation rights and the rights ancillary to it, it may be more appropriate to consider that the Company built their system upon the existing Mughal institutions. According to Mughal studies, in Mughal local society, provincial officials with different areas of authority – administration, taxation, and security – in addition to qadis exercised their respective judicial powers without clear division of jurisdiction.[7] Presumably, it would be more correct to say that the Company inherited one of these provincial officials' roles and put the qadis under their administration. In this sense, the British did not create a new institution but arranged and unified the existing Mughal institutions.

It should be mentioned that the European colonial powers in Muslim countries would normally abolish the enforcement of the shari'a in the sphere of criminal law. The case of British India was an exception to this practice (another exception was British Nigeria) (Peters, 2009). This is probably due to the fact that the Company took over the judicial function of the Mughal provincial officials. It can be assumed that the Mughal provincial officials administered justice according to the local practices partly derived from the shari'a or perhaps even arbitrarily. The British could not base their judicial system in India on informal practices, much less on arbitrary decisions, but even if they had desired to introduce English criminal law, there was no codified criminal law in Britain. Thus, it was necessary to adopt Islamic law in criminal cases (Peters, 2009; Fisch, 1983, pp. 20–24).

However, from the very outset, the British started to learn Islamic law for themselves, in order to prevent the maulavis from monopolizing specialized knowledge of Islamic law, because they did not have trust in the Muslim jurists. In 1791, *Hidaya*, written by the twelfth-century Hanafi jurist Marghinani was translated into English, which was followed by a translation of *Sirajiyya*,

176   *History*

a classic work on inheritance.[8] The British thus now directed their efforts to applying 'proper' Islamic law. Consequently, the role of law officers gradually decreased and the office was abolished in 1864. However, a limited number of translations of classic legal works and legal manuals based on specific classic works led to transformation of the nature of the shari'a. Islamic law, originally characterized by its flexibility based on the jurists' diverse interpretations and the judges' discretionary powers, was now deemed a set of inflexible, fixed and unchangeable rules.

Transformation of the shari'a by the British colonial powers was not limited to this. Especially important was introduction of the doctrine of precedent, which was the basic principle of British common law. The rulings of the judicial committee of the Privy Council in London acquired authority in India. Official publication of law reports began in the 1840s. Thus, in India, an entirely new legal system was generated, which was called Anglo-Muhammadan law.

The Volga-Ural regions in the Russian Empire: integration of the 'Muslim clergy'

Imperial Russia had had a large number of Muslims under its rule since its conquest of the Kazan Khanate in 1552. The Russians adopted a policy of conversion of the Tatars to the Orthodox Church during the late seventeenth and mid-eighteenth centuries and demolished mosques in its course, but the policy was not thoroughly enforced. Until the late eighteenth century, Islamic institutions such as mosques and schools, and Islamic intellectuals and religious figures, basically did not become objects of state administration or control, though they did suffer persecution. In sum, the Russian state neither interfered with the realm of Muslim belief, law, or practices, nor had sufficient knowledge about or interest in them.

The relation between the Russian state and its Muslim subjects underwent a profound change under Catherine the Great, who initiated a policy of religious toleration and established an 'Ecclesiastical Assembly of the Muhammedan Creed' in Ufa in 1789 (Crews, 2003, 2006; Naganawa, 2008). The aim of the Assembly was to organize the Muslim religious leadership into a hierarchical order modeled on orthodox clerical organization and to govern the Muslim population through it. At the head of the Assembly was a mufti, who was regarded as the leader of the Muslim community in Russia. The mufti, with three qadis who assisted him, would grant qualifications to 'Muslim clergy (*mullah*s)', who were appointed to 'parishes'. This formation with the mufti at the top assisted by qadis was in apparent reference to the Ottoman hierarchy of 'ulama (*ilmiye*) headed by the *şeyhülislâm* or grand mufti, and more directly to the institution of the Crimea Khanid annexed to Russia in 1783 (Fisher, 1970, pp. 149–50), which itself was a copy of the Ottoman ilmiye institution. Mullahs were responsible for the conduct of religious rites, marriage, divorce, and inheritance according to the shari'a and also heard cases mainly concerning Islamic family law such as marriage and inheritance.

Integrated into the local administration of imperial Russia, they were entrusted with keeping population registers ('parish registers') and collecting marriage tax among other duties. While these functions of mullahs clearly show the influence of orthodox clerical organization, they were also reminiscent of the Ottoman method of governing the Christian population by means of the clerical hierarchy.

The Muslim Ecclesiastical Assembly had an appellate function for the cases heard by the local mullahs. When a litigant had any objection to a decision of the Assembly, they could appeal to the Ministry of the Interior. The Russian state thus played the role of guaranteeing the implementation of the 'orthodox' shari'a. As in British India, the shari'a became gradually fixed and standardized in Russia. Supported by the imperial authorities, the Assembly and the mullahs began to enforce specific interpretations of Hanafi jurisprudence as the 'orthodox' shari'a. They especially attacked and tried to punish what they regarded as 'abuses' against orthodox Islam (such as bride abduction), in cooperation with the Russian government, which had a shared interest in maintaining the family order (Crews, 2006, pp. 143–66).

The Muslim population, who saw the Russian state as the guardian of the shari'a, now turned to the Russian authorities or even to the czar himself to bring charges against their spouses, their parish inhabitants who would not observe the religious duties, or their political foes who challenged their positions, seeking justice according to what they understood as the orthodox tenets of Islam. Imperial Russia became involved in the struggle over the correct interpretation of the shari'a. The Russian government, concerned with determining the standard shari'a without relying on mullahs or muftis, started to promote Oriental studies and train scholars and officials with specialized knowledge of Islam. By the 1850s, it was not uncommon for the Interior Ministry and the Orientalists who belonged to it to interfere in family disputes and overrule the decisions of the Muslim Ecclesiastical Assembly. During this process, Russian translations of and commentaries on the classics of Islamic jurisprudence were published, thereby contributing to fixing the shari'a by specific interpretations (Crews, 2006, pp. 176–91).

In the case of Russia, in contrast to the case of above-mentioned India or below-mentioned Algeria, the organization of the 'Muslim clergy' was created in the place where there was no hierarchy of 'ulama or institutionalized system of qadi courts. This organization was essentially a mechanism by means of which the state could rule the Muslims in cooperation with the 'ulama who were integrated into the Russian administration. When compared with the British East India Company, which initially had to make use of the existing framework of Mughal institutions, the extent of state intervention seems greater in Russia. However, since the 'ulama organization became an indispensable element of administration, the judicial institutions of the shari'a were given much greater autonomy in Russia. Nonetheless, phenomena common to the case of British India, such as standardization of the shari'a, also occurred in Russia.

178 *History*

French Algeria: 'ulama into government employees

After occupying Algeria in 1830, France encouraged the settlement of French colonists, who encountered the overwhelming majority Muslim population. Islamic law was allowed to survive but the sphere of its authority was gradually narrowed by the 1870s. Criminal law was replaced with the French Criminal Code and the Regulation of 1873 confirmed the application of the principles of French law to land ownership. The French administration put high priority on the matter of land law since it was a device for the French settlers to legally seize lands in Algeria. Consequently, Islamic law remained in force mainly in the realm of family law. Maintenance of Muslim family law was just the reverse side of denial of French citizenship to Muslims. Islamic law, which approved polygamy and unilateral repudiation by husbands among others, was deemed incompatible with the French Civil Code. Muslims would be required to abandon their social practices and institutions and accept the French Civil Code to become 'naturalized', should they apply for French citizenship.[9]

Even though Islamic law was preserved in the realm of family law, it did not remain unchanged, as with the case of India and Russia. Since Algeria was located on the periphery of the Ottoman Empire, the shari'a courts and the judiciary were far less institutionalized than in the core regions of the empire. Qadis were not appointed from Istanbul but by the *dey* of Algeria or his subordinates (*beys*). Inheriting this situation, France set about appointing qadis to large cities, but a major intervention in the Muslim judicial administration began with the Décret of 1854 (Mennesson, 1888, pp. 27–36). At that time, the French needed to establish a structure of colonial administration after pacifying the resistance of Abd al-Qadir and were at the same time compelled to take a conciliatory policy toward the 'ulama to co-opt them when the outbreak of the Crimean War was expected. By the Décret, the judicial institutions of Islamic law were established, which comprised qadi courts and *medjlès* (*majlis*es or councils) composed of a qadi, a mufti, and two members of the 'ulama (*àdels*), which corresponded to the appeal court. The latter had existed during the early years of French rule and had been inherited from Ottoman times. The 1854 Décret also stipulated the number of personnel and the authority of the qadi courts and obliged the courts to take registers, leading to the institutionalization and bureaucratization of the shari'a courts.

However, as a result of opposition from the colonizers who considered the 1854 Décret as conceding too many rights to the Muslims, the medjlès as appellate courts were abolished in 1859. After this, any appeal against a decision of the qadi court was to be addressed to the French courts. The 'ulama strongly objected to this arrangement, which might curtail the legal autonomy of the Muslims. In 1866, a concession was made to the Muslims by accommodating the 'ulama in the appeal procedures; a special chamber was set up at each civil tribunal, composed of three French magistrates and two Muslim associate judges (*asseseurs*) in Oran and Constantine and two magistrates and one assesseur in other places. In Algiers, the Superior Council of Muslim Law (*Conseil Supérieur de Droit Musulman*) composed of five Muslim jurisconsults was to give opinions on matters concerning Islamic law (Mennesson, 1888, pp. 70–83; Christelow, 1985, p. 186). However, these arrangements turned out to be short-lived. The Superior Council was abolished in 1875 and the Muslim members were excluded from the chambers of the tribunals and the Court of Appeal in 1889 (Collot, 1987, p. 182).

In the meantime, Islamic institutions such as the qadiship were gradually incorporated into the colonial government apparatus. Qadis, muftis, and imams now became salaried government employees appointed upon examination. Moreover, the colonial government intervened in the training of 'ulama, by establishing schools called official madrasas (*médersas officielles*), which functioned to train qadis and other Muslim functionaries. This attempt was first made in 1850 and, after the 1870s, the curriculum of the official madrasas included non-Islamic subjects such as French and French law (Kudo 2013, pp. 141–42; Watanabe, 2006).

French rule in Algeria, which incorporated Islamic institutions into the government apparatus, may be compared to the Russian case mentioned above. However, in Algeria, the autonomy of the 'ulama organization was limited to a minimum degree, which was in contrast to the relative autonomy of the Muslim Ecclesiastical Assembly in Russia. The difference was visible in that the French did not create an office of grand mufti. The policy of making 'ulama into government employees may be reminiscent of post-Napoleonic France, where the church was under the control of the state that appointed bishops and paid salaries to the clergy.

The fact that the Court of Appeal (*Cour Impériale*, later *Cour d'Appel*) in Algiers heard appeal cases from the qadi courts opened the way for the intervention of the colonial authorities into questions as to what the proper shari'a was. Schacht (1964, p. 98) comments that the influence of the Court of Appeal was comparable to that of the Privy Council in British India. Since the 1860s, French jurists and administrators had published numerous books and articles on Islamic law (Henry and Balique, 1979). These writings and the related laws and regulations together with legal precedents constituted a new set of laws, which was properly called Algerian Muslim Law (*Droit musulman algérien*). It was a mixture of Islamic law and French law, but since French jurists based their understanding of the shari'a on the classics of Maliki jurisprudence, they often disregarded developments before the nineteenth century and local practices but emphasized a more fundamentalist interpretation of the shari'a. This point had a parallel in the situation observed in British India and Russia.

Development in the late nineteenth century: threat of Islam

The years around 1860 were a period in which imperial powers became convinced of Muslim 'fanaticism' through a series of incidents such as the Great Indian Revolt of 1857–58, the Lebanese Crisis, and the Damascene Affair in

180 *History*

1860. Thus, the colonial administration of Muslims during this period generally reflected the colonizers' distrust of the Muslim religious leaders, that is, the 'ulama. The dissolution of the medjlès in Algeria and the abolition of the office of law officer in British India can be located in this context. Imperial Russia, which faced fierce and prolonged resistance by Imam Shamil in the northern Caucasus, experienced the threat of 'fanatical Muslims' in an earlier period. Having learned from this experience, in Central Asia, Russia adopted a policy of non-collaboration with the local 'ulama, by not granting them any official positions. This policy was attributed to Konstantin von Kaufman, the first governor of Turkestan and known for his 'disregard' (*ignorirovanie*) of Islam. In Turkestan, different from the method applied in the Volga-Ural regions and Crimea, the body of 'ulama was not supervised under a single person or organ. Von Kaufman abolished the office of chief qadi (*kazi*), which was left untouched just after the conquest of Tashkent and introduced the election principle and a fixed term of appointment to the office of qadi while reducing the functions of the qadi courts. Litigants of the qadi courts could appeal to a committee composed of several qadis as well as to Russian courts. These arrangements aimed to weaken the powers of the 'ulama by not protecting or not supporting the Islamic institutions (Sartori, 2009; Morrison, 2008).

However, after the late nineteenth century, the imperial powers in different regions turned to a policy of acknowledging and protecting the authority of the Muslim judicial institutions and at the same time intervening in and administering them. What the colonizers feared during this period was a pan-Islamist movement. They were extremely anxious that movements advocating Muslim solidarity or jihad against foreign powers might occur successively and cause a chain reaction in the area under their rule. The Mahdist movement in Sudan in 1881–98 and the Andijan Uprising in 1898 were sufficient to make them believe that their fears were finally being realized. Also, when the Ottoman sultan, Abdülhamid II, tried to exert his influence over the Muslims of the world by advocating his status as the caliph of the *umma* or worldwide Muslim community, the Great Powers increasingly felt the necessity of coopting and administrating the Muslims so as not to divert their loyalty toward the Ottoman sultan-caliph. At the same time, they could not disregard the consequences of reforms in the Ottoman Empire during the nineteenth centuries, either.

Ottomanized shari'a: judicial reform in the nineteenth-century Ottoman Empire

In the nineteenth-century Ottoman Empire, the range of application of Islamic law became gradually narrower with the development of a body of state law. After the establishment of the commercial court in 1840, the Ottoman judicial institutions underwent a major transformation in 1864–67, when the *nizamiye* courts were created to hear civil and criminal cases according to state law, such as the Ottoman Criminal Code and the Land Code.[10] The

Colonial Islamic legal systems compared 181

instructions of 1888 defined the division of jurisdiction between the shariʻa and the nizamiye courts; the shariʻa courts were to hear cases concerning family law such as marriage, divorce, alimony, and inheritance, criminal law peculiar to Islamic law such as retaliation (*qisas*) and blood money, and civil cases when both litigants agreed to settle in the shariʻa court. Waqf cases were also under the jurisdiction of the shariʻa courts. Thus, the functions of the shariʻa courts were eventually redefined as 'Muslim courts' largely according to the principle of personal jurisdiction. However, it should be noted that since the shariʻa courts still dealt with the administration of inheritance involving heirs who needed guardians and cases concerning orphans' property, the division of jurisdiction was not entirely based on the principle of personal law (Mehmed Şevkî, 1322, p. 229).

One cannot deny that pressure from the foreign powers was one factor that brought about the changes in Ottoman judicial administration. The Great Powers were unwilling to be subject to the Ottoman legal and judicial systems, and criticized certain aspects of the shariʻa that were discriminatory to non-Muslims. It was thus partly due to foreign pressure that the Ottomans developed a legal system that was modeled on the European counterparts and guaranteed the legal equality of non-Muslims with Muslims. However, more essentially, the Ottoman state needed a new legal system in order to administer and make use of its lands and subjects. This rationale can be typically observed in the promulgation of the new criminal code and the land code.

The reforms of the shariʻa court system can be understood in the context of centralization. The Ottoman system of qadiship in the early modern period had been better organized in a centralized fashion, compared to that of other Islamic dynasties. During the eighteenth century, it became general practice for qadis to farm out their duties to their deputies (*naib*s). In the nineteenth century, the qadiships became almost entirely nominal positions and instead the system of naibship was established. After the mid-century, naibs were salaried officials appointed for a specific term (Akiba, 2005). In 1855, a new school for training naibs was created in Istanbul. By 1882, the appellate procedure was firmly established, in which special chambers under the *şeyhülislâm* were to examine appeal cases. Before the nineteenth century, litigants who had an objection to a decision of the shariʻa court could appeal to the Sublime Porte, where the decision would be reviewed by the Imperial Council or by other councils where the grand vizier would refer the case to the *kazasker* (chief judge) or to a high-ranking qadi. After 1838, petitions concerning the shariʻa were transferred from the Porte to the Şeyhülislâm's Office. The reforms during the 1870s and the 1880s institutionalized the existing practices (Heyd, 1973, pp. 225–26, 257–58; Yurdakul, 2008, pp. 33, 117–18). Traditionally, as a mufti, the şeyhülislâm had no judicial power but only gave legal opinions (fatwas). It was only in 1838 that the appellate procedure of shariʻa justice was placed under the organization of the şeyhülislâm. In a sense, by this arrangement, the şeyhülislâm's institution came closer to the organization of the Muslim Ecclesiastical Assembly in Russia.

182 *History*

While new laws and regulations such as the criminal code, commercial law and procedural law were modeled on French law, the Ottoman Civil Code was a codified law based on the shari'a. The Ottoman Civil Code called the *Mecelle* was compiled by a special committee of the government, which mainly codified the stipulations of contract law based on the interpretations of Hanafi jurisprudence. This meant that the state legislated from specific interpretations of the shari'a and fixed its content. Thus, having deviated from the classical understanding of Islamic law, the Mecelle was a peculiarly Ottomanized shari'a (Messick, 1993, pp. 56–57; Deringil, 1998, p. 50). Nevertheless, this is not to say that the pre-nineteenth-century Ottoman state did not interfere in the interpretation of the shari'a. Structuring a career path from madrasa education to the offices of madrasa professors and qadis via apprenticeship was originally motivated by the state's attempt to standardize the interpretation of Islamic law (Tezcan, 2009). The textbooks used in the madrasas were more or less fixed. Also, the legal opinions of the şeyhülislâms were compiled and referred to by legal practitioners as manuals. Thus, standardization of the shari'a took place to some extent even before the nineteenth century.

However, the Mecelle was innovative in that it was a codified law modeled after a modern law and was legislated by the state. It was compiled in order that 'anyone could read [it] easily', as the statement of reasons for legislation declared (Cevdet Paşa, 1300, p. 6). It was designed to be understandable by judges of commercial courts, elected associate judges of the nizamiye courts, or administrators, by simplifying and standardizing the legal stipulations and leaving out conflicting views. Since the Mecelle fixed the shari'a by adopting specific interpretations so as to make it available to those who were not trained in Islamic jurisprudence, this effort of the Ottomans had something in common with the attempt of the colonial powers that tried to fix and simplify the shari'a to make it easy to understand. However, once the Mecelle was put in force, it was generally applied to all Ottoman subjects irrespective of religion in the nizamiye courts. This idea would not occur to the colonial powers, who reduced the shari'a to Muslim personal law.

Encounter between Ottoman shari'a and colonial shari'a

As seen above, the shari'a judicial system in the nineteenth-century Ottoman Empire saw similar developments to those of Britain, Russia, and France in their respective dominions. On the one hand, similarity of the shari'a politics derived from the fact that the Ottoman reforms followed the European model due to the influence of and pressure from the European powers. Although it was unlikely that the Ottomans referred to the shari'a legal system in India or Algeria, it can be said that they shared some of the European attitude toward the shari'a as a result of adopting European systems and the logic behind them. On the other hand, it can be considered that it was an inevitable choice for the Ottomans, who pursued centralization to overcome crises. The

Ottoman Empire also aimed to strengthen its control over its lands and subjects and needed a new legal system to that end. Just as the Europeans brought about the modern state in their colonies, the Ottomans, too, were in the process of transformation into a modern state. The similarity of the results of the legal-judicial reforms was in a sense a logical consequence.

However, this is not to deny influence or transmission. After the late nineteenth century, it was the Ottomans who provided the model for other states. A conspicuous example was the Ottoman Civil Code, the Mecelle. In early twentieth-century Russian Turkestan, the former policy of neglecting Islam was reconsidered and there was serious concern about the codification and standardization of the shari'a. The Russian officials especially referred to the British experiences in India and they found the English translation of *Hidaya* very useful, although it had been translated more than a century before (1791). Based on its abridged version and after consultation with the local *'ulama*, a legal code mainly covering family law was drawn up in 1910. Although it was not enacted, interest in codification of the shari'a persisted, and in 1911 a Russian translation of the Mecelle was published in Tashkent. The Ottoman Mecelle continued to provide Russian officials with a major source of inspiration (Sartori, 2009, pp. 492–94; Morrison, 2008, pp. 274–82). During the same period, a French Orientalist, Marcel Morand, prepared a draft of Muslim family code based on Maliki jurisprudence in Algeria on commission from the French colonial administration. This code, carrying forward the method used in the Mecelle of choosing a specific interpretation from among different views, also adopted opinions of different *madhhab*s at several points. Morand incorporated the stipulations on legal proof from the Mecelle and borrowed many articles from the manual of family law compiled by Muhammad Qadri of Egypt in 1875 (Arabi, 2000).

When the Hapsburg Empire occupied Bosnia and Herzegovina (hereafter Bosnia) in 1878 and Britain ruled Palestine after World War I, both of these states regarded the preservation of the shari'a legal system and the religious autonomy of the Muslims as crucial for smooth administration. The Hapsburgs created an office of *reis-ul-ulema* (head of the 'ulama) and entrusted to him and his advisory council called *Ulema-medžlis* the election of qadis and muftis and the administration of waqf property in Bosnia (Yoneoka, 2011).[11] This was, in a sense, a copy of the Ottoman *ilmiye* institution headed by the şeyhülislâm. In fact, the office of reis-ul-ulema was introduced as a substitute for the şeyhülislâm in order to cut off his influence.

Although the influence of the Bosnian model was not clear, Britain, too, created a Supreme Muslim Council in Palestine and named its head *ra'is al-'ulama* (the Arabic form of *reis-ul-ulema*) (Kupferschmidt, 1987; Huneidi, 2001). The responsibilities of the Council were similar to those of Ulema-medžlis in Bosnia. It is significant that the ra'is al-'ulama was called the grand mufti, which was the English rendering of the şeyhülislâm. In a sense, the administration of the Muslim population in Bosnia and Palestine returned to the Russian system in the Volga-Ural regions, by which the Muslims were

184   *History*

governed through the organization of the 'ulama. This was not only because the imperial powers could not neglect the institutions established in the Ottoman Empire, but also because they considered the shari'a legal system peculiar to the Muslims and believed that they could rule the Muslims through the religious system.

Interestingly, the British officials likened the Muslim administration in Palestine to the *millet* system. What they understood as the Ottoman 'millet system' was presumably that of the late nineteenth and early twentieth centuries, when the autonomous privileges of individual non-Muslim communities (millets) were confirmed as explicitly stated in the Reform Edict of 1856, which was issued under severe pressure from the Great Powers. Following the Reform Edict, a millet organization headed by the *milletbaşı* (the head of the millet) was established in each millet, where communal affairs were administered through the ecclesiastical council and the mixed council of clergy and laymen.[12] The British officials compared the organization led by the Supreme Muslim Council with the millet organization and even referred to the ra'is al-'ulama as the milletbaşı. However, the Muslims in the Ottoman Empire had no millet organization. Moreover, the function of the shari'a courts had been reduced since the nineteenth century and the 'ulama were not the sole representatives of the Mulsim elites. At the time when Britain occupied Palestine, the shari'a courts were under the authority of the Ministry of Justice, by which the şeyhülislâm was deprived of his judicial authority. The provincial elites in Ottoman Palestine or elsewhere not only took part in the local administration but also participated in the state administration and politics by serving as central bureaucrats or being elected to parliament. In addition, the bureaucracy and the parliament were also open to non-Muslims. Together with the millet system that granted autonomy to each religious community, the egalitarian principle constituted the late Ottoman policy of integrating non-Muslims. It was apparent that the framework of the millet system alone was not sufficient to integrate the Muslim population of Palestine under British rule. However, the British policy was conditioned by the European powers' experience of administration of Muslims, their understanding of the shari'a, and the notion of the millet system that was created through their own intervention in the internal affairs of the Ottoman Empire.

Notes

1 On legal pluralism in the empires, see Benton, 2002 and Yamamuro, 2003.
2 Although the Volga-Ural regions were not colonies of Russia, I include them in this analysis of 'colonial Islamic legal systems', since here I use the adjective 'colonial' as a term denoting certain power relations that the modern European empires had with their Muslim subjects.
3 For an outline of Islamic law, see Schacht, 1964, and a more recent work by Hallaq (2009).
4 On the problem of waqf in British India, Algeria, and Russia, see Powers, 1981; Kozlowski, 1985; Naganawa, 2009.

Colonial Islamic legal systems compared 185

5 On the Islamic judicial institutions in British India, see Carroll, 2004; Anderson, 1999; Fisch, 1983; Kozlowski, 1985, pp. 106–31; Hallaq, 2009, pp. 371–83.
6 Cited in Anderson, 1999, p. 67.
7 On the judicial administration in Mughal India, see Jain, 1970; Day, 1969, Ch. 7; Singha, 1998, pp. 4–21; Kumar, 1999, pp. 137–41.
8 For the implications of the act of translation of the *Hidaya* into English, see Hallaq, 2009, pp. 375–76.
9 On the French shari'a politics in Algeria, see Christelow, 1985; Collot, 1987; Powers, 1981; Arabi, 2000; Kudo, 2013.
10 On the Ottoman nizamiye courts, see Rubin, 2011; Akiba, 2012.
11 According to Yoneoka (2011, p. 98), the Hapsburg bureaucrats surveyed Islamic institutions in the Russian Caucasus and French Algeria.
12 For a review of the literature on the millet system, see Ueno, 2010.

References

Akiba, J. (2005) From *Kadı* to *Naib*: Reorganization of the Ottoman Sharia Judiciary in the Tanzimat Period, in C. Imber and K. Kiyotaki, eds, *Frontiers of Ottoman Studies*, London: I. B. Tauris, vol. 1, pp. 43–60.
——(2012) Osuman teikoku no seiteihou saibansyo seido: uramā no yakuwari wo chūshin ni [*Ulema* in the Ottoman *Nizamiye* Court System], in T. Suzuki, ed., *Osman teikokushi no shosō* [Aspects of the Ottoman History], Tokyo: Yamakawa Shuppansha, pp. 294–320 (in Japanese).
Al-Qattan, N. (1999) Dhimmīs in the Muslim Court: Legal Autonomy and Religious Discrimination, *International Journal of Middle East Studies*, vol. 31, pp. 429–44.
Anderson, M. R. (1999) Legal Scholarship and the Politics of Islam in British India, in R. S. Khare, ed., *Perspectives on Islamic Law, Justice and Society*, Oxford: Rowman & Littlefield, pp. 65–91.
Arabi, O. (2000) Orienting the Gaze: Marcel Morand and the Codification of le *Droit Musulman Algérian*, *Journal of Islamic Studies*, vol. 11, no. 1, pp. 43–72
Benton, L. (2002) *Law and Colonial Cultures: Legal Regimes in World History, 1400–1900*, Cambridge: Cambridge University Press.
Carroll, L. (2004) Mahkama, 5. The Indo-Pakistan Subcontinent, in H. A. R. Gibb *et al.*, eds, *Encyclopaedia of Islam*, 2nd edn, Leiden: Brill, vol. 12, pp. 560–66.
Cevdet Paşa, A. (1300 [1882–83]) *Mecelle-i Ahkâm-ı Adliyye* [The Ottoman Civil Code], Istanbul: Matba'a-i 'Osmaniyye (in Ottoman Turkish).
Christelow, A. (1985) *Muslim Law Courts and the French Colonial State in Algeria*, Princeton NJ: Princeton University Press.
Collot, C. (1987) *Les institutions de l'Algérie durant la période coloniale (1830–1962)*, Paris: Éditions du CNRS.
Crews, R. (2003) Empire and the Confessional State: Islam and Religious Politics in Nineteenth-Century Russia, *The American Historical Review*, vol. 108, no. 1, pp. 50–83.
——(2006) *For Prophet and Tsar: Islam and Empire in Russia and Central Asia*, Cambridge MA: Harvard University Press.
Darling, L. T. (2013) *A History of Social Justice and Political Power in the Middle East: The Circle of Justice from Mesopotamia to Globalization*, London: Routledge.
Day, U. N. (1969) *The Mughal Government, AD 1556–1707*, New Delhi: Munshiram Manoharlal.
Deringil, S. (1998) *The Well-Protected Domains: Ideology and the Legitimation of Power in the Ottoman Empire, 1876–1909*, London: I. B. Tauris.

186 History

Fisch, J. (1983) *Cheap Lives and Dear Limbs: The British Transformation of the Bengal Criminal Law 1769–1817*, Wiesbaden, Germany: Franz Steiner Verlag.

Fisher, A. W. (1970) *The Russian Annexation of the Crimea, 1772–1783*, Cambridge: Cambridge University Press.

Hallaq, W. B. (1984) Was the Gate of Ijtihad Closed?, *International Journal of Middle East Studies*, vol. 16, no. 1, pp. 3–41.

——(2009) *Sharīʿa: Theory, Practice, Transformations*, Cambridge: Cambridge University Press.

Henry, J.-R. and F. Balique (1979) *La doctrine colonial du droit musulman algérien: Bibliographie systématique et introduction critique*, Paris: CNRS.

Heyd, U. (1973) *Studies in Ottoman Criminal Law*, ed. V. L. Ménage, Oxford: Oxford University Press.

Huneidi, S. (2001) *A Broken Trust: Herbert Samuel, Zionism and the Palestinians, 1920–1925*, London: I. B. Tauris.

Jain, B. S. (1970) *Administration of Justice in Seventeenth Century India*, Delhi: Metropolitan Books.

Kozlowski, G. C. (1985) *Muslim Endowments and Society in British India*, Cambridge: Cambridge University Press.

Kudo, A. (2013) *Chichūkai teikoku no hen'ei: Furansuryō Arujeria no 19 seiki* [Le mirage d'un empire méditerranéen l'Algérie et la France au XIXe siècle], Tokyo: University of Tokyo Press (in Japanese).

Kumar, R., ed. (1999) *Survey of Medieval India, Vol. 10: Administration, Law and Justice in Medieval India*, New Delhi: Anmol Publications.

Kupferschmidt, U. M. (1987) *The Supreme Muslim Council: Islam under the British Mandate for Palestine*, Leiden: E. J. Brill.

Mehmed Şevkî (1322 [1904–5]) *Taʿyin-i merciʿ* [Designation of the Competent Authority], Istanbul: A. Asaduryan Şirket-i Mürettebiye Matbaʿası (in Ottoman Turkish).

Mennesson, Ch. (1888) *Organisation de la justice et du notariat musulmans en Algérie et législation applicable en Algérie aux musulmans*, Paris: Challamel.

Messick, B. (1993) *The Calligraphic State: Textual Domination and History in a Muslim Society*, Berkeley and Los Angeles: University of California Press.

Morrison, A. S. (2008) *Russian Rule in Samarkand 1868–1910: A Comparison with British India*, Oxford: Oxford University Press.

Naganawa, N. (2008) Roshia teikoku no Musurimu ni totteno seido, chiiki, ekkyō: Tatārujin no baai [Institution, Region, Border Transgression for Muslims in the Russian Empire: The Tatar Case], in T. Uyama, ed., *Chiiki ninshikiron: taminzoku kūkan no kōzō to hyōshō* [Essays on Understanding of Region: Structure and Representation of Multiethnic Space], Tokyo: Kodansha (in Japanese).

——(2009) Teisei Roshia makki no wakufu: Voruga Uraru tiiki to nishi Shiberia wo chūshin ni [Waqf in Late Imperial Russia: Cases from the Volga-Urals Region and Western Siberia], *Isuramu sekai* [*The World of Islam*], no. 73, pp. 1–27 (in Japanese).

Peters, R. (2009) Sharīʿa and 'Natural Justice': The Implementation of Islamic Criminal Law in British India and Colonial Nigeria, in A. Christmann and J.-P. Hartung, eds., *Studies in Memory of Holger Preißler (1943–2006)*, Oxford: Oxford University Press, pp. 127–49.

Powers, D. S. (1981) Orientalism, Colonialism, and Legal History: The Attack on Muslim Family Endowments in Algeria and India, *Comparative Studies in Society and History*, vol. 31, pp. 535–71.

Rubin, A. (2011) *Ottoman Nizamiye Courts: Law and Modernity*, New York: Palgrave Macmillan.

Sartori, P. (2009) An Overview of Tsarist Policy on Islamic Courts in Turkestan: Its Genealogy and its Effects, *Cahiers d'Asie Centrale*, vol. 17/18, pp. 477–507.

Schacht, J. (1964) *An Introduction to Islamic Law*, Oxford: Clarendon Press.

Singha, R. (1998) *A Despotism of Law: Crime and Justice in Early Colonial India*, Delhi: Oxford University Press.

Tezcan, B. (2009) The Ottoman *Mevali* as 'Lords of the Law', *Journal of Islamic Studies*, vol. 20, no. 3, pp. 383–407.

Ueno, M. (2010) Mirretosei kenkyū to Osuman teikokuka no himusurimu kyōdōtai [Historiography of the Millet System and the Non-Muslim Communities under the Ottoman Rule], *Shigaku zasshi*, vol. 119, no. 11, pp. 64–81 (in Japanese).

Ursinus, M. (2005) *Grievance Administration (şikayet) in an Ottoman Province: The Kaymakam of Rumelia's 'Record Book of Complaints' of 1781–1783*, London: RoutledgeCurzon.

Watanabe, S. (2006) Shokuminchiki Arujeria no Arabiago kyōiku seisaku: 1930 nendai – 50 nendai no ishin mondai [Les politiques de l'enseignement officiel de l'arabe dans l'Algérie coloniale: la question de son prestige et la société des années 1930 aux années 1950], *Nihon chūtō gakkai nenpō* [*Annals of Japan Association for Middle East Studies*], vol. 20, no. 1, pp. 87–111 (in Japanese).

Yamamuro, S. (2003) 'Kokumin teikoku ron' no shatei [The Range of 'National Empire Theory'], in Y. Yamamoto, ed., *Teikoku no kenkyū: Genri, ruikei, kankei* [Empire Studies: Principle, Pattern, Relations], Nagoya: Nagoya University Press, pp. 87–128 (in Japanese).

Yoneoka, D. (2011) Hapusuburuku teikokuka Bosunia ni okeru Isurāmu tōchi to sono hannō: Reisu uru Uremā shoku wo megutte [Religious Politics of the Habsburg Monarchy and Reactions from the Islamic People of Bosnia: Focusing on the Establishment of the Reis-ul-Ulema], *Shirin*, vol. 94, no. 2, pp. 89–107 (in Japanese).

Yurdakul, İ. (2008) *Osmanlı ilmiye merkez teşkilâtı'nda reform (1826–1876)* [Reform in the Ottoman Central Ilmiye Organization], Istanbul: İletişim Yayınları (in Turkish).

Part IV
Culture and society

11 Delineating contours
Portrayal of regional powers in British Asian immigrant literature

Hisae Komatsu

Transformation of the sense of belonging in immigrant literature

In the 2000s especially after 9/11, British Asian literature garnered much attention in Britain as it 'reveals the hidden worlds that shine in the darkness' (Manzoor, 2006). There was a tendency to deny or even abhor the traditions and culture of Asia, which were the roots of works published until then. Gradually, a compromise was forged with English culture, and as the new millennium began, Asian culture ceased to be considered inferior or second class.

This paper investigates the works of authors of Indian or Pakistani descent who live in contemporary Britain and examines their sense of belonging, which is inherent in their work, as well as how they position and represent their roots. Young Asians, particularly second-generation Indian immigrants onward, seek to ground their identities in India, but that is the imaginary homeland conceived by Salman Rushdie, and ultimately an India that is an idealized homeland.[1] The India they depict is one that they have imagined, but within that, what is emphasized? How is India written about, or even rewritten? Examining the works of several British Asian authors, I reveal how the concept of 'nation' is presented.

In addition, this chapter provides a general overview of contemporary British Asian literature, especially the young authors, who are not well known in Japan.[2] In introducing their work, I especially establish the following points. The first concerns the symbols of *home* and *homeland*. *Home* is where the authors currently live and make their living. On the other hand, *homeland* is their hereditary land of India, where they have their roots. While making a living in Britain, their *home*, they enthusiastically employ India as a symbol of their *homeland*. However, the majority of modern British Asian authors are second- or third-generation immigrants with no experience of living in India. While they symbolize a world they do not know well, how do they present it, and with what intention? The second point concerns the categorization of these authors and their work. Regardless of the content, their work is evaluated based on the attached label of being 'Indian' or 'Asian'. How do these authors confront such labels, and how do they cope with them? In examining this, I highlight the sense of

192 *Culture and society*

belonging of immigrants portrayed in British Asian literature, and the profile of the 'India' depicted by these immigrant authors.

British Asian literature in English literary circles

Representative authors

Salman Rushdie (1947–) gloriously introduced himself in the 1980s, when he was noticed as a leading Asian figure in English literary circles. Authors such as Rohinton Mistry, Arundhati Roy, Monica Ali, and Indra Sinha, who followed him, are also prominent in the world of English literature; all of them have been recipients of or finalists for the Man Booker Prize, especially in the 1990s. As a multi-ethnic culture became more widely accepted in Britain in the twenty-first century, the activity of young Asian authors born in Britain has become even more pronounced. I am introducing several representative authors here.

The son of a Pakistani father and an English mother, Hanif Kureishi (1954–) is a second-generation immigrant born in England. His initial works, published in the early 1990s, the novel *The Buddha of Suburbia* (1990) and the screenplay *My Beautiful Launderette* (1985), depict the world of Indian immigrants for the first time and greatly influenced many leading contemporary authors who followed him. Kureishi and Rushdie are central figures in British Asian literature and are highly respected in the country and overseas.

Nadeem Aslam, who debuted in 1993 and became famous for his second work, *Maps for Lost Lovers* (2004), is a so called 1.5-generation immigrant who, as a child, moved with his parents to London from their home in Pakistan. In his work, he depicts the Islamic world of the Pakistani, Afghan, and British Pakistani communities. *Maps for Lost Lovers*, which centers on the honor killing of a couple, scrupulously portrays the British Pakistani immigrant community. Monica Ali, born in Dhaka to an English mother and a Bangladeshi father, immigrated to England when she was three years old and made her debut with *Brick Lane* (2003). The book was named after a street at the heart of London's Bangladeshi immigrant community, and the novel depicts the life of an immigrant woman living there. The novel was later adapted into a movie that was fiercely rejected by the Bangladeshi community because they perceived it as unnecessarily propagating a negative image of them. Hari Kunzru, a second-generation Indian immigrant from Kashmir, debuted in 2003. His first novel was set in colonial India, where the young protagonist struggles to discover his identity on a long trip through India, Britain, and Africa. This work, highly praised as a first novel, along with its huge publishing contract, became a popular topic of conversation in Britain.

A special distinction of these 1.5- and second-generation authors is that the majority of them studied at prestigious universities. Furthermore, many are of mixed race, and the women especially had their work portrayed in the media alongside their 'exotic' appearance. It is quite interesting to observe that many of these authors who are credited with telling typically Asian stories are in fact atypical and exceptional. In addition to evaluating the works themselves, I address the greatly animated public opinions of many of their works, accompanied by factors such as fatwas, large amounts of contract money, and backlash from the community.

Circumstances of the emergence of British Asian literature

As previously mentioned, Asian literature in modern Britain saw a remarkable rise. Not only did many literary works receive global acclaim but they also became very successful in the mainstream and were adapted into movies and television dramas. The prospering of Asian literature is also notable in the environment surrounding the writers.

As the largest minority population in Britain, Asians conduct lively cultural activities as a community. Online magazines are merely one of the recent trends. For example, one of the most popular websites for the community, Desi Blitz, established in 2008 with the goal of developing the community, presents a diversity of useful articles and interviews related to Asians. The website frequently introduces new works of Asian literature that are published alongside book reviews and author interviews. Occasionally, the website even publishes special reports on popular British Asian authors.

The Asian Writer (TAW) is a literature website launched in 2007 that specializes in Asian authors; it aims to 'inspire the next generation of British Asian writers and raise the profile of talented emerging writers'. TAW organizes workshops and events for young Asian authors, provides them with a forum for presentations and conducts book reviews and discussions of their work. Furthermore, it also has a print publication and contributes to the motivation of emerging authors by establishing funds and literary prizes. In addition, the non-profit organization Asia House sponsors the Asia House Festival of Asian Literature, employing a philosophy 'to promote informed understanding and the mutual exchange of ideas, building stronger relationships between the diverse communities of Europe and Asia'. The festival celebrates literature for Asians by Asians, and it marked its sixth event this year. Moreover, the DSC South Asian Literature festival held in Jaipur, India, is the largest Asian literary festival, and it is an enormous contributor to the development of Asian literature.

Literary activities in other immigrant communities

The Indian immigrant community includes vibrant literary activities such as the festivals mentioned above that establish literary prizes as well as websites that fuel the well-being of writers. However, intriguingly, one rarely sees such activities among other immigrant communities.

A primary reason for this may be that no ethnic minority in Britain comes close to the population of Asians. There has been the prominent immigration of Russians, for example (that is, people from Russia or countries comprising the

194　*Culture and society*

former Soviet Union), after the collapse of the Soviet Union in the early 1990s. According to a report from the International Organization for Migration (IOM, 2007), there are approximately 300,000 Russians presently living in Britain.[3] Although Russians have a large population in terms of numbers, their history of immigration is extremely short, and as of the mid-2000s, an active community was almost non-existent (Byford, 2012, p. 725).

Next, we consider Chinese immigrants. Their numbers are recorded to have increased in Liverpool since the early nineteenth century, but by the mid-twentieth century the population of their community barely exceeded 10,000 (12,523 people, according to the 1951 census). According to the 2009 census, British Chinese constitute merely 0.8 percent, or 500,000 people, of the entire British population. On the other hand, Asians account for half the ethnic minority population, or 6 percent of the entire British population (3,160,000). Thus, unlike other ethnic groups, a separate British Chinese community never developed. While there exists a Chinatown in London, second-generation immigrants claim that there is a lack of things that they can share as a community (BBC News, 2002). This differs greatly from Asian communities, which include religious institutions such as mosques, Sikh temples (gurdwaras), or Hindu temples, where people can gather. These religious institutions fulfill the functions of a community center. Thus, not having any community center, Chinese descendants do not have a place to share and affirm their traditional culture. Consequently, they do not share a group identity as 'British Chinese' and lack uniformity and solidarity as a community. Furthermore, this lack of solidarity is most likely the obstacle to forming strong voices in the community in the form of flourishing minority literature.[4]

However, second-generation immigrants possess different values from their parents' generation. One example of this is the Chinese community website launched in 2001, Dimsum (www.dimsum.co.uk). Dimsum related British Chinese culture to the outside world with the aim of inspiring unity in the community. It introduced various cultural activities such as fashion, food, lifestyle, movies, and music, and established a platform to discuss various issues such as intergenerational opposition, racial discrimination, and cultural friction. Until now, there has been no particular emphasis on supporting cultural development. However, considering that the website has sponsored two film festivals, the focus may shift in future to the development of literature.

Regardless of the numbers, socially and economically, the presence of the Russian and Chinese communities has grown in Britain. There are obvious signs of change as we enter the twenty-first century. Currently, British Chinese exceed every other ethnic minority in terms of education levels, school attendance, and economic levels, even surpassing Whites. Moreover, China as a nation has a growing economic and political influence. Thus, this may have changed the image of Chinese immigrants in Britain. Likewise, Russians have seen some movement. The current Russian elite enjoys a freedom and wealth in London that is unheard of in their home countries. Previously, the clichéd Russian image was 'All Russian women are potato pickers', but recently this has transformed into 'All Russian women are beautiful. They all wear fur. They're wearing diamonds. They have yachts' (*Forbes*, 2005). Ascending the economic ladder has elevated the image of Russians, and the same may be said about the Chinese. While both have an economic and political influence on par with the Asian community, each community's future changes in terms of literary and cultural activities will be noteworthy.

Changing consciousness of second-generation immigrants – from rejection to acceptance and pride

The second section examined and compared conditions surrounding Asian literature in different immigrant communities. In the third section, I consider how Asians are actually represented, and how they represent themselves in literature.

I shall examine the transformation of the representation of Asians in literature from a historical perspective. The history of Asian migration to Britain is long. According to records of the East India Company, in the seventeenth century, thousands of people were brought to Britain every year as sailors, laborers, and servants to British families (Visram, 1986, p. 34; Visram, 2002, pp. 1–37). There were many Asians living in Britain before the Second World War, but most of the immigration from India, Pakistan, and Bangladesh occurred in the 1950s and 1960s. Many recent first-generation immigrants had jobs involving hard physical labor, such as construction and farm work.

The second generation was born and raised through the 1970s and 1980s, when racial discrimination in British society was widespread. Kureishi reflects on his 1970s childhood in an essay that narrates the severe racial discrimination he experienced from the skinheads and teachers, as well as their bigotry against Asian culture (Kureishi, 1996, p. 73). The image of Asians as 'nothing but effete cowards' was propagated in society through media such as television shows. However, the mid-1980s witnessed changes, and British-born Asians began rejecting the 'otherness' forced upon them by Whites (Mills, 2004, p. 19). They were different from the first generation, who arrived in Britain with great optimism and ambition. The second generation grew up sensing their rejection by mainstream British culture. Unable to completely merge with the mainstream culture, they recognized themselves as an ethnic minority, leading to an outpouring of their internal conflict. Among them, Kureishi became a pioneer. He began to 'write back' against mainstream culture by depicting the immigrant society for the first time. Thus, from the late 1990s, the representations of urban immigrant culture diversified.

As part of such change, even representations of immigrant culture within immigrant literature were gradually transformed. Many immigrants arrived from abroad alone, entering unknown territory. They struggled to build a life for themselves in spite of being tormented by loneliness. They longed for the culture of their *homeland* and 'their culture' was something to protect. However, the second generation, born and raised in England, know nothing except their *home*, and thus have no nostalgia for their *homeland*. They are not

196   *Culture and society*

familiar with the culture of their *homeland* that their parents and grand-parents hold so dear, and thus cannot truly consider it as 'their culture'. Each generation holds different thoughts on culture. This 'gap' between the two cultures is the source of the discord that shapes the identities of the second generation and beyond. Thus, many Asian authors have incorporated this as a theme. In their work, they depict characters who gradually accept themselves as 'second-generation immigrants' by overcoming the discord surrounding mixed cultural identities.[5]

However younger generations have recently begun contradicting the culture of their *home*, and representations of pride in the superiority of their *homeland*'s culture are emerging. This 'superiority' is sometimes connected to a return to tradition or fundamentalism, which leads to exclusivity, transforming their characters from one who is rejected to one who rejects others. For example, in a short piece by Kureishi called *My Son the Fanatic* (1997) or in Monica Ali's *Brick Lane*, this exclusivity is represented as Islamic fundamentalism. Kureishi's character Ali abruptly finds his faith in the middle of the story, criticizes Western culture, and denounces his father for 'innumerable violations of Koranic law' (Nakamura, 2004, p. 100). Ali also tells his father that 'he and *his people*' are sick of Western materialism and the corrupt, depraved world. In fact, Ali had never left England, and he had never visited and knew nothing about Pakistan. A character from Monica Ali's work, a young Muslim named Karim, also experiences a major transformation in the middle of the story. Karim, a lover of the heroine who wants to radicalize the local community against a racist White group, has thrown his jeans off and put on a skullcap and ethnic costume instead. He becomes a leader of local young Muslim group and begins to laud the superiority of Islamic culture. Ali and Karim are second-generation immigrants who are depicted as fundamentalists in these novels. Being excluded from the White-dominated mainstream British culture of their *home*, they lose sight of where they belong, and grow up feeling bitterly disillusioned with their peripheral status. Thus, to establish their own identity, they deny the culture of their *home* and adopt an exclusive cultural identity grounded in the teachings of Islam and the culture of their *homeland*. Through this, they attempt a reversal of their values; this is where their *homeland* carries great significance for them.

Homeland of the imagination or 'my India'

One's *homeland* is always an abstract concept as it is physically distant. Thus, numerous versions of 'my India' exist in the work of these authors. What do they desire from their 'motherland' that does not exist 'here'? When concretely considering the representations of *home* and *homeland*, we can consider the example of works that appeared in 2006 by three active young male Asian authors. They are second-generation immigrants in their thirties, living on the outskirts of London, and for two of them, we investigate their debut work.

Investigating orthodoxy: Gautam Malkani (1976–)

Born to an Indian mother of Ugandan descent in Hounslow on the outskirts of London, Malkani worked as an editor for the *Financial Times* after graduating from Cambridge University. *Londonstani* (Malkani, 2007) received acclaim from multiple media sources, for example: 'Artful, thought-provoking and strikingly inventive. An impressive, in some respects brilliant, first novel'. In addition, the large publishing contract he received became a popular topic of discussion before the novel was even published.[6]

Londonstani is the coming of age story of the main character, Jas, a 19-year-old growing up in Hounslow. Jas is an ex-honor student who joins a mixed group of Hindu and Sikh juvenile delinquents. He struggles to establish himself in the group by becoming a 'proper' desi. Contentions with the group, relationships with friends, love, illegal business, and family troubles are all narrated in the first person. Desi is an important keyword that emerges often in *Londonstani*. The original Hindi word means 'one's native land' or 'home territory' and refers to people living on or associated with the Indian subcontinent. The characters in the book constantly contemplate being or becoming 'proper' desi and strive to flaunt their desi-ness to their friends. Therefore, from the various elements – fashion, music, mobiles, or language – desi is the most emphasized cultural peculiarity in the book. Through Jas, the author most emphasizes the speech used by a 'proper' desi (Malkani, 2007, pp. 45–46). This speech is replete with street slang that has thrust aside proper English grammar and elevated vocabulary, and desi-ness is measured by the degree to which it is used.

Based on thorough field research, Malkani forges this unique writing style meticulously. Rather than simply incorporating slang borrowed from Indian languages and rap, the writing style also includes abbreviations used on the Internet and mobile communication along with references to various Indian movie stars and fashion brands. Furthermore, *Londonstani* does not explain or italicize these non-standard terms.[7] As printed below, these are used not only in dialogues but also in narrative descriptions. Most book reviews address this, and the majority applaud the realistic and lively representation of modern Asian youths:[8]

[sample 1] to a comrade he dislikes. (p. 22):
'Wat's wrong wid'chyu, sala kutta? U 2 embararass'd to b a desi? Embarrass'd a your own culture, huh? Thing is, u is actually an embarrassment to desis. Bet'chyu can't even speak yo mother tongue, innit.'

[sample 2] A monologue by Jas after successfully asking someone out on a date, which he practiced for hours before a mirror (p. 149):
Proud a me? You fuckin should be. I practiced that line a hundred times in front a my bedroom mirror an a hundred fuckin times in front a the bathroom mirror. Sometimes I practised it as Johnny Depp, sometimes as Pierce Brosnan, sometimes as Brad Pitt. But in the end I went with this cross between Andy Garcia an Shah Rukh Khan cos it just worked for me.

198 *Culture and society*

Jas is a member of an Asian gang and strives to become a 'proper' desi. Consequently, the reader obviously recognizes Jas as Asian. However, at the end of the story, it becomes clear that 'Jas' is really 'Jason'; he is not Asian, but White. Thus, the desi culture transcends ethnicity and proposes that the White mainstream high culture is not absolutely superior. In this work, 'India' and 'Indianness' stem from a powerful culture that can overturn values or collapse the cultural order, and as participants of this culture, the characters presented search for authenticity.

Seeking one's place: Nirpal Singh Dhaliwal (1974–)

Dhaliwal was born in Greenford to first-generation immigrant parents. After graduating he worked as a journalist and now contributes to the *Times* and the *Guardian* as a freelancer. He has also made visits to India and contributed to a local magazine there for the last three years.

His debut novel, *Tourism* (Dhaliwal, 2006a), depicts the journey of the self-discovery of a second-generation immigrant, Bhupinder. The novel presents the diversity of modern urban culture in Britain and the cultural life of second-generation immigrants through the protagonist's frank narration on race, sex, and social disparity. The narrator and protagonist is an anti-hero in his late twenties who indulges in sex, drugs, and alcohol. He retreats from his life in the immigrant community with no hope of progressing and schemes to associate with the elite class by using a wealthy woman. In what has been called a 'bracing debut that sizzles with sexual and racial tension. A terriffic book', the narrator frequently treats the rich White people around him as objects of ridicule.

For example, the protagonist takes advantage of the rich White woman Sophie, and with her connections and economic power, enjoys the upper class culture that he had no access to until then. Yet, he considers Sophie as a fungible host to take advantage of and for whom he has no feelings. Moreover, Bhupinder brags that the sex with her is boring:

> She was a nice girl, but she bored me. Fucking her already felt like a chore. – She didn't rock my world. – I thought about what I might do when I left Sophie. There weren't many options. – The only alternative were to find another woman who'd go nuts over me.
>
> (Dhaliwal, 2006a, p. 179)

Then, in the park, he observes a white man doting on his child, and he agrees with the comments of his black friend:

> White chicks love dark cock, – When spades, the Pakis, and the rest of them got off the boat with their big dicks and their beautiful faces, the white boys shit themselves. That's why they bring their women cups of tea in bed, and listen to their bullshit. It's the only way they can get laid. – Niggers don't have to do that.
>
> (Dhaliwal, 2006a, p. 160)

What is noteworthy here is the main character's attitude toward middle-class White people. He looks down on them, especially sexually, excessively flaunts his masculinity and rejects the Asian image of inferior 'otherness' that is thrust upon him. Thereby, he discriminates against the discriminators and transforms himself from an inferior immigrant to a 'handsome ethnic'. Furthermore, Asians tend to be represented as having an extremely close connection to their families and community, but Bhupinder distances himself from them in order to join the world of the upper class. Therefore, he poses as a drifter, calling himself a 'tourist' who does not belong anywhere. However, it is revealed in the second half that this is simply a front. He flees the country and roams abroad to escape various troubles. However, gradually, the journey becomes a mission to find out where he belongs. While on this journey, Bhupinder comes to his senses through meditation and yoga, rediscovers his love for his mother, and develops a deep interest in his mother's homeland, that is, India (Dhaliwal, 2006a, p. 254).

For him, India is a land overflowing with pure and spiritual love. More importantly, it is where he finds and warmly accepts his roots and ultimately discovers his need to return to 'Mother India'. For the protagonist, being a 'tourist' who does not belong anywhere was initially a point of pride. However, he eventually finds the true place he belongs to. He is unable to single out the place in his *home*, England, and as a result of continued searching, 'discovers' it in his *homeland*. Bhupinder's image of India – Yoga, meditation, spirituality, etc. – completely overlaps with the general image of India held by the White people whom he had been ridiculing up to that point. If you consider this together with the writer's own wavering sense of belonging in Chapter 5, it is exceedingly interesting.

Affirmation of camaraderie: Bali Rai (1971–)

The debut of the second-generation immigrant Rai was the earliest of the three, and unlike the others, he did not embark on the path of journalism shortly after graduating from university. For several years he worked various jobs in places such as supermarkets and nightclubs. After *(Un)arranged Marriage* (2001), he began receiving awards and became modern Britain's foremost young adult novelist. The main theme of his work is the coming of age of Asian boys and girls.

Published in 2006, *The Last Taboo* is the story of a romance between a young Indian girl Simran and a young black boy Tyrone, set in a secondary school. The protagonist Simran grows up in the Asian community, which considers love with a black person as taboo. She faces a lack of understanding and rejection from the people around her.

Rai's story is set primarily in a ghetto, where young Asian kids grow up facing issues such as poverty, drugs, prostitution, violence, and racism. *The Last Taboo* also depicts racism and its resulting violence, but what is noteworthy is that the perpetrators in this work are an Asian gang called the Desi

200   *Culture and society*

Posse, Simran's family, and Indian classmates who obstinately reject the interracial love. Her Indian classmates combine to violently eliminate outsiders. In the novel, the 'outsiders' are Blacks as well as Indians who interact with Blacks and Whites, such as Simran. In many of his novels, Rai depicts Asians not only as the victims of violence from racial discrimination but also as the aggressors.[9] Furthermore, by having the protagonist as close friends with people of a different race, such as Whites and Blacks, in several of his works, he warns against racial discrimination and the antagonism between racial groups from camaraderie based on race. Even in *The Last Taboo*, 'India' is depicted as the cornerstone of the aggressors' sense of 'We'. However, as mentioned before, even though he may depict characters with such beliefs, the author himself denies the concept of brotherhood through exclusivity. Simran is criticized by her Indian classmates for deepening her friendship with non-Indians – 'It's just that you seem to think you're different to the rest of us – It's like you're not proud to be Indian or something'. You can clearly gather Rai's view on a sense of belonging in her reply to this:

> Who are 'us'? – I'm British, I wasn't born in India so how can I be Indian?

> (Rai, 2006, p. 203)

The author's sense of belonging: British or Indian?

This section considers the author's individual sense of belonging. How is it determined or influenced? I consider this bearing in mind the marketplace as well as the creative process.

What kind of person am 'I'?

British Asian literature pioneer Kureishi is a second-generation immigrant; however, he dislikes such categorization.[10] He contends that although he may be South Asian, he is British. On the other hand, Dhaliwal emphasizes his roots as 'an Indian, born and raised in London', and maintains that his 'mother's Indian values nonetheless gave him a platform on which to build his life' (Dhaliwal, 2008). This is part of an essay he wrote immediately after he began living in India, but interestingly, after four short months, Dhaliwal's wavering sense of belonging emerged with his acknowledgment that he is 'very British'.[11] While Dhaliwal's example is extreme, most British Asian novelists, whether they acknowledge or deny it, are very aware of their roots and continue to grope for belonging.

When discussing a sense of belonging, it is important to consider the writers who have Islamic heritage. In the many novels published in Britain in the 2000s by Muslim authors, the self-awareness of being Pakistani or Muslim emerges very strongly. For instance, Sanfraz Manzoor is a journalist of the same generation as the three authors discussed in the fourth section above. In his memoir, *Greetings from Bury Park* (2008), it is evident that Manzoor is constantly aware of his Pakistani heritage. This is especially true for his father, who came to Britain as an migrant. His pride as a Pakistani and sense of belonging does not waver.[12]

On the other hand, the same author, who is the second-generation son, naturally accepts the mainstream culture of his *home*, Britain, where he was raised, and thus wishes to become British. However, he frankly admits that 'I had never really felt as if I truly belonged here', after which he understands his British Asian identity, which wavers between *home* and *homeland* (Manzoor, 2008, p. 265). What is noteworthy about his portrayal is the sense of belonging of the third generation. This generation (which is in its teens and twenties) rejects its identity as British Asian; these young people say that they 'did not want to be part of this thing called "Britain"'(ibid.). Moreover, some of these young people dream of Islamic countries, that is, their *homeland*, and seek to destroy their *home*, Britain, through acts of terror. For them, their sense of belonging to their *homeland* is unrelated to geography and, in a sense, it is grounded in a global sense of religion. In the Western world after 9/11, widespread Islamophobia intensified the 'othering' of Muslims. Therefore, believers in Islam were compelled to deal with their religious identity unrelated to their country of origin. Further investigation is required to identify how these conditions influence literary work.

Who is writing and who is selling?

The questions regarding who is writing and who is selling elicit a subtle disparity; the former involves the issue of the sense of belonging, while the latter is tied to marketing. As seen thus far, the ranks of Asian authors are teeming, and with the coexistence of many cultures, the Asian brand is thriving in the market. In addition, as seen in the second section above, with the establishment of media such as websites, literature festivals, and exclusive Asian awards, the brand is making remarkable progress, even in British society. However, this label has polarized opinions among Asian authors.

The majority of authors reject the label. Concerning exclusive Asian awards, Dhaliwal is against the 'special quota' (Dhaliwal, 2005). Furthermore, regarding how book reviews commented on his origin rather than only the contents of his book, Malkani does not conceal his repulsion and says in one article: 'I hate it when reviewers talk about me and not the book. Would they have said the same things if it was a middle class English man who went to Cambridge, worked for FT and wrote the same book?' (Malkani, 2006). Rather than being overly positive, writers who agree with the label undoubtedly apply it as a publishing strategy to survive as writers.

Naturally, the attitudes of these writers regarding the label are not necessarily consistent. Here I focus on Dhaliwal's view, which supposedly rejects the label of Asian. Through *Londonstani*, Malkani was called the 'voice of the young Asians'; however, Dhaliwal rejects this epithet: 'how [can] a nice Cambridege graduate ... possibly know what Hounslow homeboys are thinking[?]' (Roy, 2006). Thus, although Dhaliwal rejects the notion of being labeled as

202 *Culture and society*

Asian, he is dissatisfied with anyone else being reviewed as the voice of Asians. Furthermore, he attacks fellow Asian writers. He claims that they are elitist, come from the middle class, and graduate from first-rate universities. He declares that although these authors claim to depict the reality of the streets, they write novels merely to obtain the attention of Whites. By contrast, Dhaliwai insists, he himself writes from the street level, that is the coalface of British multiculturalism, therefore he is the very person that can really represent the British Asian community (Dhaliwal, 2006c). Even though he rejects the label 'Asian', he claims his authenticity as an 'Asian writer'.

Rethinking 'migrant literature'

In their style, convictions, and even backgrounds – where they live, their religion, economic/social position, degree of education, etc. – British Asian writers are truly diverse. As a matter of convenience, the fourth section presented three authors and their work divided into three major categories. However, these cannot be clearly categorized. There are also cases in which several factors are included in a piece, and representations within the body of work of even the same author may differ. In addition, as with Dhaliwal, the writer's sense of belonging may change with time or through experience. First-generation immigrant Rushdie said this about British Asian authors: 'British Indian writers are not all the same type of animal', and urged readers to note the variety of characteristics among authors (Rushdie, 2010, p. 16). It has been nearly thirty years since he made this statement. The immigrant community has progressed, and traveling between *home* and *homeland* has never been easier. Moreover, there is an ever-widening diversity among Asian writers. When discussing Asian writers in the future, a group which is by no means monolithic, how useful will their *homeland* and cultural heritage be? As seen in the conclusion of the fifth section above, the sense of belonging of the already numerous Muslim authors is being displaced from a connection to location toward a connection to religion. Furthermore, it is difficult to predict the establishment of a group identity in the Chinese and Russian communities, which are also growing in prominence.

The label 'migrant literature' is used to distinguish it from 'orthodox' English literature, and it is externally applied. However, what will happen to the label as the line between future generations of immigrants and 'citizens' becomes increasingly blurred? As this chapter has suggested, will the categorization reinvent itself as authors shift from a division based on their *homeland* to one based on a religious identity, or would this lead to fragmentation? Or will the label become meaningless? This is the time to redefine the British Asian label, and even the entire 'migrant literature' genre.

Notes

1 Their ideas of India conflict with the representation by the American Katherine Mayo. Mayo was sent to India by the British authorities at the beginning of the

British Asian immigrant literature   203

twentieth century, and her 'traveler's journal' repeatedly justifies British governance and excessively emphasizes the backwardness of India. This 'uncivilized' India that she writes about can be considered as completely negated by the British Indian authors of the twenty-first century. In particular, see my notes in Komatsu 2013, pp. 83–100).

2　The inhabitants of Britain generally referred to as 'Asian' are those from the Indian subcontinent and their offspring. They may also include those from the Asian diaspora who dwell in the Caribbean and/or the East Africans and their descendants.

3　International Organisation for Migration (2007, p. 6).

4　Naturally, in this context, there are various members who do not fit in the category of 'Chinese'. People from the Chinese mainland comprise merely 12 percent of the community. Other included groups are Chinese from Malaysia, Singapore, Vietnam, and Hong Kong. Thus, they probably would not easily form a homogeneous identity. The same could be said for the 'Asian' category, which will be mentioned later.

5　An exemplary case can be seen in two young adult novels: Bali Rai's *(Un)Arranged Marriage* (2001) as well as Narinder Dhami's *Bindi Babes* (2003). In the first half of the stories, the teenage protagonists cannot accept the culture of their *homeland*. In the second half, they accept the culture of their *homeland* and learn to compromise with a hybrid cultural identity.

6　More high praise for the work is shown below:

Undoubtedly the biggest British Asian novel of the millennium.

(Asiana magazine)

Captivating … London's second-generation Asians are given the Trainspotting treatment.

(New Yorker)

Artful, thought-provoking and strikingly inventive. An impressive, in some respects brilliant, first novel.

(Los Angeles Times)

7　There is no glossary attached to the British or Indian editions, but the American edition has one on the last page of the book.

8　What I want to highlight here is that the only criticism has come from a fellow Asian writer. Nirpal Singh Dhaliwal, who we consider next, has criticized the writing style: 'the writing is complete nonsense. Where in the world did the author meet such strange kids?' (Dhaliwal, 2006b).

9　In particular, after the novel *What's Your Problem?* (2003), in which the sole Asian kid in school is forcefully removed by the White people around him, Rai creates the opposite version in *Them and Us* (2009), in which a White youth is eliminated by attacks from Asians. Thus, Rai shows that the role of the 'other' can easily be changed, and that the line between victim and assailant is truly vague.

10　Kureishi rejects the label 'second-generation immigrant'. 'I am not an immigrant, but a first generation British Asian.' In an interview by Kazue Nakamura (2004, p. 100).

11　Interviewed for the *Asian Writer* in August 2008.

12　Mazoor's father advises him after he has indulged in Western culture, 'Pakistan is the only country that will not betray you. The only home you will ever have is Pakistan' (Manzoor, 2008, p. 254).

204   *Culture and society*

References

BBC News (2002) 'Chinese Britain: How a Second Generation Wants the Voice of Its Community Heard' (http://news.bbc.co.uk/hi/english/static/in_depth/uk/2002/race/chinese_britain.stm)

Byford, A. (2012) 'The Russian Diaspora in International Relations: Compatriots in Britain', *Europe-Asia Studies*, vol. 64, no. 4, p. 725.

Dhaliwal, N. S. (2005) 'Gosh, Brown and Talented? Super', *Times Online*, April 16.

——(2006a) *Tourism*, London: Vintage Books.

——(2006b) '*Londonstani* by Gautam Malkani (Fourth Estate, GBP 12.99): Nitwits on Nokias', *Evening Standard* (London), 11 April, 2006 (via Thomson Dialog News Edge).

——(2006c) 'A Real Page-Turner, Interview by Stacy-Marie Ishmael', *KAL Magazine* (www.kalmagazine.com/features/print.php?id=60. Site has been deleted; last accessed April 8, 2010); Interview by Sam Leith, Notebook, *Telegraph* April 3.

——(2008) 'How the West Will Be Won', *Tehelka,* vol. 5, issue 13.

Forbes (2005) 'Welcome to Londongrad' (www.forbes.com/forbes/2005/0523/158.html).

International Organization for Migration (IOM) (2007) *Russia: Mapping Exercise*. London: International Organization for Migration.

Kureishi, H. (1996) 'The Rainbow Singh', in Hanif Kureishi, *My Beautiful Laundrette and Other Writings*, London: Faber and Faber, p. 73.

Komatsu, H. (2013) 'America jin ga egaita 20 ceiki hajime Indo no rinkaku: Mother India (1927) wo yomu', in Naoji Okuyama, ed., *Contact Zone no Jinbungaku*, issue 4, Koyo Shobo, pp. 83–100 (in Japanese).

Malkani, G. (2006) *DNA* May 20 (www.dnaindia.com/).

——(2007) *Londonstani*, New Delhi: HarperCollins.

Manzoor, S. (2006) 'Why Do Asian Writers Have to Be "Authentic" to Succeed?' *The Guardian*, April 30.

——(2008) *Greetings from Bury Park: Race, Religion and Rock 'n' Roll*, New York: Vintage Departures Original.

Mills, A. (2004) 'Monica Ali's Brick Lane: Was It Really Like That?' *Kyoritsu International Culture*, no. 21, p. 19.

Nakamura, K. (2004) 'Beikon to Jihad: 9/11 no guwa (Hanif Kureishi 'Waga musuko kyoshin sya' kaisetsu)', *Shincho*, August, no. 101, p. 100 (in Japanese).

Rai, B. (2006) *The Last Taboo*, London: Corgi Books.

Roy, A. (2006) 'Rude and Ruder Boys', *Tehelka*, July 22.

Rushdie, S. (2010) *Imaginary Homeland*, New Delhi: Vintage, p. 16.

Visram, R. (1986) *Ayahs, Lascars and Princes*, London: Pluto Press, p. 34.

——(2002) *Asians in Britain: 400 Years of History*, London: Pluto Press, pp. 1–37.

12 Illusion and mirror

Images of China in contemporary Russian literature

Go Koshino

This chapter sheds some light on images of China in Russia today, analyzing mainly contemporary fantastic novels (*fantastika*) in which a remarkable role is allocated to the eastern neighbor. The first and second sections focus on several important topics in the imperial and early Soviet eras so as to have an understanding of the historical background. One of the key issues is the dispute between Westernizers and Slavophiles, which played a role in creating archetypal images.[1] In the main third section we compare transforming variations of images of China in contemporary Russian novels in the 2000s, and analyze the Chinese mirror in which the complicated relationship between Russia, Europe and Asia is reflected.

Images of China in imperial Russia

Russian sinological tradition is derived from the eighteenth century, when the Orthodox Mission began their activities in Beijing. However, the earliest sinologists – priests – were hardly able to play a role in the process of forming images of China for their contemporaries (Widmer, 1976, pp. 166–67). In the second half of the same century Catherine the Great and her court admired Chinoiserie, following the fashion in Paris and other European societies (Maggs, 1984; Schimmelpenninck van der Oye, 2010, Ch. 3). Most of the literary and artistic motifs of the exotic Far East came from the West, with a small number of exceptions. It was only after the appearance of Nikita Bichurin (Father Hyacinth) that Russian sinology reached an academic standard equal to that of Western orientalists.[2] Born into a Chuvash family in the multilingual and multireligious Volga region, Bichurin was able to cultivate a range of intercultural understanding.

He was appointed leader of the ninth Orthodox Mission in Beijing and stayed for fourteen years in China (1808–21), collecting an enormous amount of linguistic, geographical, historical and other fundamental literature. From the end of the 1820s to the 1840s, after completing his mission in China, Bichurin, residing in St. Petersburg, continuously published many books, articles and translations on China and its neighboring nations. During this period he became acquainted with many writers and other cultural elites in

206 Culture and society

the capital city through Vladimir Odoevsky's famous salon. Alexander Pushkin, also acquainted with Bichurin, wrote such verses as: 'Let us leave, I am ready/Wherever, my friends, I'll follow you (...) to the foot of the Chinese Wall faraway/Or we'll reach the bustling Paris eventually' (Pushkin, 1959, p. 263). Early in 1830, Pushkin presented the authorities with a petition for travel to China, which was immediately rejected. Behind this seemingly capricious endeavor, the poet probably had in mind an expedition to the Russo–Chinese borderlands joined by Bichurin, which started in the same year (Alekseev, 1999, pp. 69–72).

In the 1830s and 1840s, the so-called Slavophile–Westernizer dispute arose over which model Russia should choose to follow: European modernization or old Russian traditionalism. The two parties often stood in opposition concerning evaluation of such historical figures as Peter the Great, who forcibly performed modernization following the West. Interestingly enough, we can observe a kind of mirrored shadow of this controversy in emerging images of Chinese civilization in Russia. In Westernizers' view of the world, the Qing Empire was a space of stagnation, despotism, and corruption, the reverse of the progressive model they idealized. In contrast, Slavophiles often expressed their respect for the ancient Asian civilization, preferring a multiple, divergent development of nations to a straight road of modernization. Bichurin also highly valued the Chinese cultural tradition. The following passage from his article is reminiscent of the Slavophile's typical logic, in which he criticizes contemporary Russian sinology for blind faith in European scholarship: 'If we had not been absorbed in imitating foreign authors without due thought or consideration, we could have acquired independence in various spheres of civilization long ago' (I.B., 1844, p. 170). On the other hand, Vissarion Belinsky, a standard-bearer of Westernization, was critical of Bichurin, who regarded the legal and educational systems in China as equal to European counterparts. To Belinsky, the West was the only place which deserved the name of 'the scene of historical development' in the world. Chinese traditional social institutions, although praised by Bichurin as such, actually had degraded due to corrupt practices among government officials and fallen into a status of 'stagnation', having squandered 4,000 years of history (Belinskii, 1982, pp. 595–98).

We will now look into two nineteenth-century novels in which China and Russia appear to be the great powers in the future world. The writer Vladimir Odoevsky, acquainted with Bichurin, adopts a complicated stance in between Slavophiles and Westernizers. He blames contemporary European societies for fatal corruption, but simultaneously admires an enlightened monarch, Peter the Great, who promoted policies of Westernization. In his work *The Year 4338: Petersburg Letters* (1839), one of the earliest science fiction novels, the Russian Empire becomes the center of world civilization, while the Western states have perished long ago. Moscow and St. Petersburg grow into an enormous united megalopolis, over which navigate electric airships. China is rapidly developing, awakening from a 'dead stagnation', thanks to the great reforms of the emperor Khun Gin. The novel consists of letters written by a Chinese student, Tsungiev, who travels to the Russian capital city from Beijing. It is notable that the future relationship between China and Russia appears to be a parody of Russian intellectuals' ambivalent attitudes toward the West. Odoevsky ridicules Slavophiles through such depictions, as if Chinese conservative poets find 'a kind of poesy' in some archaic out-of-date manners while he keeps Westernizers in mind, satirizing 'the extremes in the opposite direction' with which subjects of the Asian empire imitate costumes, foods, and all the ways of life of 'progressive' Russia. Moreover, the great reformer emperor Khun Gin, who chose Russia as a model of radical modernization, is obviously an Asian avatar of Peter the Great (Odoevskii, 1926).

Forty years later Gregory Danilevsky, a popular writer mainly known for historical novels, wrote the futuristic novel *A Life after One Hundred Years* (1879), which had a similar setting to *The Year 4338*. Poroshin, a young Russian, awakes to find himself in Paris after a century, hypnotized by a mysterious Armenian. In Danilevsky's future world also, Russia and China remain the only great powers. The two nations are on friendly terms with each other, but China is in a superior position, differently from Odoevsky's novel. Western countries form 'the United States of Europe' under the rule of the Chinese emperor. Possession of weapons is prohibited, and even knives and forks are replaced by chopsticks. Thanks to highly developed technology, the Anglo–French channel tunnel has long since been opened, and the Sahara Desert has turned into an inland sea, irrigated from the Mediterranean Sea. With the support of their Eastern ally, Russia has created 'the Slavo-Greco-Danube Empire', driving Turks out of the Balkan Peninsula, and has made Kolkata the third capital city of the empire (after St. Petersburg and Moscow), replacing the British in India (Danilevskii, 1901).

Although both Odoevsky and Danilevsky allocate important geopolitical status to China in the future, strangely enough they never depict the exotic Asian land itself. *The Year 4338* is set in Russia (the great capital city), and *A Life after One Hundred Years* in Paris. The authors are not particularly interested in the concrete realities of the Oriental empire, but are rather eager to reflect their own political desires on an empty image of China. In the former novel, the Chinese attitude to Russia copies the Russian view of the West. Danilevsky in turn uses the fictional role of the mighty China as a setting which would lead to contemporary international conflicts in the Balkans and Central Asia to a solution that would be advantageous for Russia.

Images of China in the Soviet period

Here we refer only to several limited topics during the early Soviet period which have high significance for our main discussion concerning the forming of images of China. In Soviet society during the 1920s, enormous sympathy and expectations arose for revolutionary trends in China. Early Soviet writers, such as Vladimir Mayakovsky, Sergei Tretyakov and Demyan Bedny, devoted

208 *Culture and society*

their pens to the Chinese people's suffering and struggle against the imperialism of the Great Powers. It was in 1926 when Odoesky's *The Year 4338*, which had been published only in fragments so far, appeared for the first time in full text. In the foreword, the compiler Orest Tsekhnovitser asserts that successors of Sun Yat-Sen's ideas certainly walk alongside the Soviet people. He also refers to the visit of Soviet pilots to Beijing during an intercontinental flight in 1925, a year before the publication, comparing it with a Chinese student's fantastic journey by airship in the far future (Odoevskii, 1926, p. 9). For the purposes of a propaganda of technological superiority and political prestige, the Great Powers of that time were competing with each other in long-distance flights across the oceans and continents for national prestige. The Soviet pilots' call at Beijing, accompanied by writers and journalists, was also widely reported in the media as a symbolic moment of Soviet–Chinese friendship. In political terms, it was revealing that their further stops in Korea and Japan during the same flight did not become a target of propaganda (Gromov, 2005, Ch. 11).[3]

It is worthy of mention here that Vasily Alekseev (1881–1951), educated in the academic tradition of St. Petersburg Orientalism, became a leading Soviet sinologist. While his research interests ranged widely from Chinese literature to its popular prints and folk religion, he was probably best known for his translation of the classic work *Strange Tales of Liaozhai*, written by Pu Songling (1640–1715). Alekseev published his translation of the book, which was composed of an enormous number of stories in several installments, the first of which appeared in 1922 as a compilation of tales featuring fox spirits, titled *The Fox Charm* (Pu 1922). This volume was published in the series of the publisher World Literature (Vsemirnaia literatura), initiated by Maxim Gorky. In the foreword Alekseev explains the ambivalent character of the fox spirit which, disguising itself as a beautiful lady, either seduces the man to absorb his energy or eagerly helps him like a devoted lover, demonstrating the translator's deep interest in this topic. Alekseev trained many disciples who would go on to form one of the cores of Soviet sinology. In the 1950s, the period of Sino–Soviet friendship, a new generation of sinologists published full translations of *Romance of the Three Kingdoms* (1954), *Water Margin* (1955), *Dream of the Red Chamber* (1958), *Journey to the West* (1959) and other classic literary works (Ma and Rongzhen, 2003, pp. 409–23). As a result, various terms from Chinese culture came to be available in Russian. In the following paragraphs, we will see how contemporary Russian writers make use of this legacy of Russian and Soviet sinology.

From the late nineteenth century Chinese immigrants increased in Russia, particularly in the Far East. At the same time, North America and Australia also accepted a large number of foreign workers from China, which stimulated the rise of the 'yellow peril' myth. During the Russian Revolution and the Civil War a number of poor Chinese immigrants fought on the side of the Red Army, which promoted a positive image of Chinese immigration, combined with the general sympathy for the revolutionary trends in China.

However, the growing population of Chinese in large cities simultaneously provoked a kind of anxiety stimulated by the increase in the crime rate. For example, Mikhail Bulgakov depicted both type of immigrants: the hero in the short piece *A Chinese Story* (1923) is a cruel but brave soldier of the Red Army, while the drama *Zoika's Apartment* (1925) features Chinese laundry workers secretly trading drugs. By the 1920s, more than 100,000 Chinese lived in Moscow and other major cities, particularly in the Far East. Over the course of the 1930s, however, their number diminished drastically, because the Soviet authorities suspected them of being Japanese spies. The myth of the Chinese menace would repeatedly appear in the late 1960s, at the time of Sino–Soviet split, and in the 1990s, when Chinese immigrants increased again in the Russian Far East.

Images of China in contemporary Russian literature

After the extended political split, the Sino–Soviet relationship had improved by the time of Mikhail Gorbachev's visit to China in 1989. Many Russians came to evaluate China's success in the economic reforms in contrast with social disorders caused by the radical reforms of perestroika. In recent years, Russia and China allegedly have often sought common interests in relation to international security issues in Eurasian regions. On the other hand, there remains a Sinophobic tendency stimulated by anxieties over increasing immigration in the Far East. Not all the anti-Western, nationalist opinion leaders support rapprochement with China. Various expectations and fears coexist, combined intricately with each other, in the contemporary Russian view of its eastern neighbor. We analyze here images of China in literary works written after the year 2000, mainly taking such fantastic novels which, set in alternative or future worlds, allocate a particular role or characteristic to China.

Images of Eurasian empire: Krusanov and van Zaichik

First, we examine *A Bite of Angel* (2000) by Pavel Krusanov, and a series of novels, *The Eurasian Symphony: There is No Bad Person* (2000–) by Kholm van Zaichik, both of which depict a parallel world in which two Eurasian powers ally with each other (Koshino, 2008). With a setting reminiscent of Odoevsky's and Danilevsky's novels, these works show more complicated composition, for example, partly adopting Eurasianist viewpoints. Krusanov is a Petrograd writer known for fantasy novels with an Oriental exoticism, often presenting controversial works that seemingly praise imperialism. Van Zaichik is a fictitious figure created by famous science fiction writers Viacheslav Rybakov and Igor Alimov. It is worth mentioning that both authors are sinologists who continue the Alekseev and St. Petersburg tradition of Chinese studies.

In the parallel world of *A Bite of Angel*, the socialist revolution of 1917 did not take place, and the Russian Empire has survived even in our time. The novel belongs to the genre of 'alternative history', which speculates what

210 *Culture and society*

would have changed in the course of time if certain events had developed differently at crucial moments of history. The hero of the novel, Ivan Nekitaev (which suggestively means 'non-Chinese') was born to a daughter of a Chinese bandit and a Russian army officer. As a boy, Ivan saw a vision in which the medieval Russian hero Alexander Nevsky had his throat bitten by an angel. This strange vision meant that Ivan was destined to come to the throne of the great empire. He enters the army and successfully builds his career, cruelly suppressing a rebellion by Caucasian people against the Russian Empire and competing with the British agency led by James Bond in Africa. Eventually, Ivan becomes emperor of Russia, as was foreseen, supported by the masses who have long been looking forward to someone with absolute power. He launches on an endless war of aggression, allied with China, against the Western states, which would bring about the end of the world.

Van Zaichik's *Eurasian Symphony* series is also an alternative history in which Russia and China have formed an enormous, united empire. The Mongol invasion never occurred in this parallel world. Sartaq Khan, a great-grandson of Genghis Khan (of Orda – the Golden Horde), concluded an equal alliance with Prince Alexander Nevsky (of Rus), which, subsequently joined by the Ming dynasty of China, developed into a Eurasia-wide power named 'Ordus'. The empire today consists of three capital cities and seven autonomies (ulus), with a descendant of the Zhu family of Ming China invited to take the throne. The series has a gentle intellectual, Bogdan Rukhovich Ouiantsev Siu, and a master of martial arts, Bagatur Lobo, as its two main heroes. Both are working in the judicial system and cope with difficult cases together, following the plotlines of detective stories. For example, in the first volume, *The Case of a Greedy Barbarian* (2000), an American billionaire conspires to steal away items of Ordussian cultural heritage. The second book, *The Case of Independent Dervishes* (2001), depicts a plot involving the pseudo-independent movement of the Aslaniv people from the empire and the treasures hidden in their mountainous land.

The original text of *The Eurasian Symphony* was seemingly written by a Dutch Orientalist, van Zaichik, in Chinese. The foreword by its alleged translators even gives details of his turbulent life, according to which he served as a Dutch diplomat committing espionage for the Soviet Union and cooperated with the Soviet secret agent Richard Sorge in Japan during World War II. He subsequently came to China and contributed to the victory of the Communist Party in the Civil War, enjoying Mao Zedong's friendship. Van Zaichik eventually left for Shandong Province to live with five wives in the countryside, writing the manuscript of *The Eurasian Symphony*. Grieving over the Sino–Soviet conflict in 1969, he fell into a life of drunkenness, which hastened his death. In fact, the dramatic figure of Holm van Zaichik was created together with the Ordussian stories as a kind of parody of the Dutch detective writer Robert van Gulik and his Judge Dee mysteries, which were set in seventh-century China.

In the novels by Krusanov and van Zaichik we can see an identical plan that shows Russia and China in a kind of union or close alliance, standing against the West. It is notable that both works refer to the name of the medieval Russian hero Alexander Nevsky, who drove back the Western aggressors, the armies of Sweden and the Teutonic knights, at the same time bending his knee to the Eastern power of the Mongolians. Sergei Eisenstein's film *Alexander Nevsky* (1938) also has the same plot: war against the West, avoiding conflict with the East. The hero of *A Bite of Angel* saw a vision of the prince Nevsky that proved indistinguishable from the actor playing his part in Eisenstein's movie. On the other hand, Alexander Nevsky in *The Eurasian Symphony* accepted not one-sided subordination, but an allegedly equal union with Mongolia. This kind of viewpoint was apparently suggested by the theories of such Eurasianists as George Vernadsky and Lev Gumilev in a symbiotic history between Russians and peoples of Central Eurasia. A peculiar point is that van Zaichik includes China in this Eurasian multinational community.

Krusanov's novel employs images of China combined with elaborately refined violence. For example, Ivan Nekitaev's subordinate, Petr, losing the patronage of his master, begins to visualize the scene of his execution 'in a somewhat Chinese taste', in which he was prepared alive. 'His skull appears lanced tidily like an anatomic exhibit, revealing a fissure in his brain. He is still alive, but unable to pronounce a word since the poisonous sting of a scorpion fish has been driven into the root of his tongue' (p. 254). Of Russian and Chinese parentage, the hero of the novel is attributed a preference for a similar kind of esthetic violence which would thoroughly emerge during the cruel war against the West.

In contrast, images of China in *The Eurasian Symphony* are mostly depicted in relation to cultural tolerance in the Ordussian Empire. Although Confucianism occupies an exceptional position because of the close connection with the imperial dynasty, Christianity (Eastern Orthodoxy), Islam, Buddhism, Taoism, and Judaism coexist without any discrimination, but syncretized with the Chinese philosophical religion. Any inhabitants of Ordus are able to easily quote from the Analects of Confucius. The fifth book of the series, *The Case of Judge Dee*,[4] is mainly set in the city of Khanbalyk (Beijing), the Chinese part of the empire. One of the heroes, Bagatur, visits the traditional Chinese residence Siheyuan converted into 'the museum of toilets in use' and finds imperial greatness in the rich diversity of exhibits, such as the Central Asian lavatory with an indicator of the direction of Mecca, or the Far Northern toilet simplified due to the extreme cold. The cultural tolerance in van Zaichik's series appears to be in contrast to the violence in Krusanov's novel, but both function as a means of governing the enormous multiethnic territory by the use of images of China.

Fox spirits and gender viewpoint: Pelevin and van Zaichik

In post-socialist Russia, Buddhism, Taoism and occultism of Oriental origin enjoy popularity alongside a revival of the traditional religion. In this context

212 *Culture and society*

the exotic figure of the Chinese fox spirit, once introduced by Alekseev to Russia, plays a remodeled role in *The Sacred Book of the Shapeshifter* (2004) by Victor Pelevin and *The Case of Fox Spirits* (2001), the fourth book of the *Eurasian Symphony* series.

Pelevin is a famous writer of the post-modernist trend, known for his preference for motifs of Oriental philosophy. The main plot of *The Sacred Book of the Shapeshifter* develops around a strange romance between the fox spirit A Khuli and the werewolf Alexander. The word shapeshifter (*oboroten*) in Russian folklore means a person transformed into an animal (usually a wolf) by supernatural forces, or a sorcerer who has the ability to shapeshift. It includes not only werewolves, but also Chinese fox spirits in Pelevin's novel. A Khuli was born in China more than a thousand years ago and moved to Russia in relatively recent times. She works as a prostitute in Moscow, depriving clients of their vigor through sexual illusions produced by her hypnotizing tail. Alexander the werewolf serves the FSB of Russia with his talent for locating oil deposits. They hypnotize each other by means of their mystic tails, which leads to a joint sexual illusion blissfully shared by the couple. At that time rumors were circulating among shapeshifters about the coming of an über-shapeshifter, a sort of parody of Nietzsche's concept of the superman or *Übermensch*. Their love breaks down because of their opposite understandings of the über-shapeshifter. Triggered by the affection of his fox lover, Alexander loses his wolf figure and metamorphoses into a shabby black dog. However, this dog proves to be a mythical monster able to eradicate everything in the world, so he believes that he has become the über-shapeshifter. In contrast, A Khuli understands that it should be a transcendent being which can release itself from illusory 'simulacra' realities. The Russian werewolf, however, has no interest in such metaphysical matters and rather dreams of reforming the real society with his monstrous power. After failing to persuade Alexander of her post-modern viewpoint of emptiness, A Khuli alone decides to throw herself into the nirvanic 'current of rainbow color'. She has left behind 'the sacred book of shapeshifter' which shows a means of deliverance from superficial realities.

The hero of van Zaichik's novel *The Case of Fox Spirits*, Bogdan, distressed after one of his beloved wives (polygamy is common in Ordus) leaves him, decides to go on a pilgrimage to the far northern sacred place, the Solovetsky islands (Solovki). In the world of van Zaichik, the islands are not dominated by the Russian Orthodox Church, but both a Christian monastery and a Buddhist temple exist there side by side. The religious space of Solovki represents the pluralism of the empire. Bogadan finds a remote hermitage in the woods in which to abandon himself to meditation, while a fox spirit visits him every night who takes the very image of his divorced wife. Moreover, dead foxes are found killed by someone in the woods nearby. The other hero Bagatur, at the same time, investigates cases of unnatural deaths of infants, whose parents have taken a popular aphrodisiac named 'the fox charm'.[5] Eventually he discovers the fact that the love potion was made from the insides of foxes slaughtered in Solovki. The Ordussian Empire is inhabited by descendants of those who were married to fox spirits. Such cases are easy to find in Chinese classical literature. Once the parents of distant 'fox' origin use the fox charm, their babies must be born to die immediately according to the law of retribution that is applied in the empire.

In both Pelevin's and van Zaichik's novels the familiar order of reality is defamiliarized, and unexpected aspects of human society are revealed with the appearance of the exotic Asian spirit. In particular, the motif of fox spirits in female disguise depriving males of energy functions in places as a satire on gender and sexual matters. For example, the fox spirit in van Zaichik's novel hypnotizes men by kissing, the sexual power of which is physically explained as deriving from the fox's saliva. Consequently, it is possible to extract the essence from the internal organs into a tablet. The love potion of Oriental origin is, ironically enough, mostly required by the European and American 'barbarians' in van Zaichik's world. A significant number of males in Western countries have lost their sexual potency due to the conditions of working long hours generated by harsh economic competition, and the disappearance of gender differences with the rise of feminism. There is even a case of 'sexual abuse' in which a husband is forced to take an aphrodisiac by his sexually aggressive wife. Although traditional gender roles are preserved in Ordus, some people under the influence of the Western way of life come to use the fox charm. In this way the sexual motif of the fox spirit serves as a means of satirizing capitalist or feminist globalization from the standpoint of traditional values.

The Chinese fox spirit in Pelevin's *The Sacred Book of the Shapeshifter* appears to be the main heroine and narrator of the novel. The motif of sexual charm is attributed to the heroine's character and never materializes as a love potion. A Khuli, who is of Chinese origin, female, and non-human, takes a stance of Otherness outside the multiple borderlines. Russian contemporary society, energetic and chaotic, together with a pedophile foreign investor, a masochist intellectual, werewolf-officer of the secret police, is depicted from her foxy and ironic viewpoint. She falls in love with the werewolf Alexander who, a macho patriot, embodies a kind of Russian national character in her opinion. For example, his hateful prejudice toward homosexuals, viewing them as a 'seedless watermelon', is regarded as an extrapolated characteristic of Russian society in general. According to A Khuli's assumption, male Russians had to turn to the ethical values of the criminal world, since all other traditional communities had collapsed without appropriate alternatives due to the Revolution and forced radical modernization. That is to say, the widespread homophobia in contemporary Russia comes from the norms of the underworld society.

It is noteworthy that Bagatur, the hero of *The Case of Fox Spirits*, also considers homosexuality unnatural, while deeply respecting the cultural diversity of the empire. Giving an example of animal behavior, he asserts that reproduction of the species should continue forever as nature aspires to it.

214   *Culture and society*

Bagatur's claim coincides with Alexander the werewolf's criticism of 'the seed-less watermelon'. The utopian coexistence of diverse nationalities in the Ordussian Empire rests on the premise that each ethnic group would be repro-duced continuously thanks to the dominance of heterosexuality. For example, there are only three remaining descendants of the Tangut people, whose empire was ruined by Genghis Khan. They strive to survive as a nation by having intercourse with fox spirits. After all, the 'diversity' of Ordus means diversity of role distribution, which would contribute to the continuous pros-perity of the empire. It applies to the distribution of gender roles, too. Con-sequently, feminism of Western origin cannot be popular in Ordus since it aims to homogenize and decrease diversity.

In contrast, the heroine of *The Sacred Book of the Shapeshifter* is much more radical in her sexual views. In her and Alexander's joint illusion evoked by their mystic tails, she proposes not only to play the roles of homosexual lovers, but even to experience a sexual act of space creatures whose oral and generative organs are united with each other (and is immediately refused by Alexander, who is loyal to the conservative macho norms). While cultural tolerance and diversity in van Zaichik's world makes the otherness even more invisible, the absolute otherness attributed to Pelevin's heroine reveals paradoxes in the intolerant world with its subversive irony.

In *The Sacred Book of the Shapeshifter,* like Pelevin's other novels such as *Chapaev and Void*, reality and illusion often appear replaceable, or, in other words, the realities consist of multiple dimensions. A Khuli is aware of the fact that her own figure and personality are arbitrarily constructed of some female stereotypes and post-modern discourses. She believes that being the über-shapeshifter means deliverance from transmigration of simulacra realities. Pelevin's favorite philosophy of Oriental emptiness here functions as a kind of post-modern criticism of Western-centered modernization. Contrastingly, the Russianness of Alexander the werewolf is rather reminiscent of pre-modern or even pre-civilized primitivism, which aims at violent transformation of realities. A Khuli and Alexander, each obtaining the key to becoming the über-shapeshifter, fail to find any point of agreement in their opposite under-standing of it. Although Russia and the Orient meet and join with each other at one time, they are eventually to be separated in Pelevin's novel. Chinese motifs in van Zaichik's series are also used to criticize modern Western values, but from the viewpoint of conservative traditionalism, as contrasted with Pelevin's case. It is revealing that Bogdan in *The Case of Fox Spirits* is able to recover from the great sorrow of losing his beloved woman, spending the night with a fox spirit, and returns to the order of everyday life.

The two writers differ in how they understand the characteristics of the Chinese shapeshifter. While the fox spirits in Pelevin's novel are usually engaged in seducing and depriving men of sexual energy, van Zaichik gives them the role of a single-minded lover, sincerely supporting their beloved men. His book contains as an appendix to *The Case of Fox Spirits* a Chinese story, *The Surprising Encounter in Western Shu*, written in the period of the

Song dynasty. The heroine of the story is also a fox spirit who helps her husband with her literary talent and the art of sorcery. Both types of fox spirit, whether deceitful or faithful, derive from Chinese classical literature. Such an ambivalent character is based on Chinese literary images of the courtesan, or possibly one of the female archetypes imagined by males in general. It can be said that van Zaichik and Pelevin differently represent the Russo–Western and Russo–Eastern relationships in light of the gender perspective, borrowing the Chinese traditional figure of the fox spirit.

Rubanov and Sorokin: the myth of yellow peril returns

In the first half of the 1990s a large number of Chinese began to visit the Russian Far East, mainly for the purposes of small trade and manual labor across the border, which was opened for them in 1992. The population of the Far East region is about 7 million, while there are more than 100 million inhabitants of Northeast China. It was feared that Chinese immigrants would occupy the underpopulated border regions. This perceived menace is growing partly because there are strong voices in China claiming that the territory of Outer Manchuria, including Khabarovsk and Vladivostok, was taken away by unequal treaties in the middle of the nineteenth century. Here we compare two novels featuring the motif of 'Yellow Peril' and a Sinicized Russian Far East, *Day of the Oprichnik* (2006) by Vladimir Sorokin and *Chlorophyllia* (2009) by Andrey Rubanov. Sorokin is a well-known writer, a maestro of Russian post-modern literature, while Rubanov is a representative of new trends that emerged after post-modernism. Both of their works, however, present a similar setting of Russia in the near future under the influence of a rising China.

In his previous novel *Blue Salo (Fat)* (1999) Sorokin had already depicted 'Euro-Asian people' who speak in a fantastic Chinese–Russian mixed language. Compared to this, the Chinese motif is introduced into the major plot in *Day of the Oprichnik*. The novel is set in Russia of the year 2027, where the imperial regime has been revived through the time of troubles (*Smuta*). The state borders are closed by the Great Wall of Russia. The majority of national revenue comes from the export of natural gas to Europe and the levy of customs duties on Chinese products. Russian traditional culture is superficially valued, while China has such an enormous impact on the society that people use a strange language in which archaic Russian phrases and Chinese terms are mingled. Colonizers from the East reach even Novosibirsk, Krasnoyarsk and other Western Siberian regions.

Russian society of the near future is ruled violently by the Oprichniks, members of the armed organization (*oprichnina*) loyal to the tsar, the name of which derives from the reign of terror by Ivan IV. The story is narrated by Komiaga, an elite of the Oprichniks, describing a workday in which he encounters various incidents. Through his eyes we can look over a cross-section of the bizarre Russian future. After sobering up by taking a pure Russian

216 *Culture and society*

breakfast, Komiaga with his colleagues executes a family of allegedly traitorous aristocrats. In the meantime they enjoy a group trip on high-quality drugs made in China, which Komiaga has extorted from a noblewoman. During a day-trip he cheats Chinese traders out of their money at the Orenburg customs, and visits a female prophet in Tobolsk as an unofficial messenger of the Empress. A dinner feast after the workday joined by his Oprichnik colleagues turns into an orgy of homosexual tastes, by which the circle of a day is to be closed.

In Rubanov's *Chlorophyllia*, 200 million Chinese migrants who have lost their homeland due to global warming are now living in Siberia. Almost the entire population of 40 million Russians has been concentrated in Moscow. They are able to live a comfortable, easy life, sharing the enormous amount of land rent from China. In the middle of the twenty-first century, huge 'grass' suddenly appears to cover the buildings of the capital city so that only the privileged residing in the upper floors can enjoy the sun. Most of the inhabitants of lower floors come to depend on this narcotic 'grass', with which people never need to suffer from hunger.

Saveliy Gerts, a capable journalist, is promoted to chief editor of a quality magazine in Moscow. After successfully having settled in the 88th floor, an elite residential area, he falls into the habit of secretly taking highly refined 'grass', as many of the upper-floor residents do. While collecting news sources, he accidentally finds out that people who regularly take 'grass' often produce a green, plant-like baby. Moreover, a habitual user like Saveliy will, sooner or later, be transformed into a vegetable. He decides to settle in a colony for addicts, far removed from Moscow. Negotiating with decivilized 'barbarians' living in the wild natural area around the colony, Saveliy feels a burning desire to genuinely work and live as a human being. Meanwhile, due to the sudden halt of the land rent from China, the inhabitants of Moscow go hungry and eat up all the 'grass' in the city. As a result, the sunshine comes back.

Although both Sorokin and Rubanov imagine a future Russia under Sinicization, this does not mean that they agree with perceptions of the Chinese 'menace'. The very setting in which, allied with Chinese global power, Russia appears predominant over the West, is reminiscent of Danilevsky's novel. However, in this case the ideal world from the Slavophile viewpoint is grotesquely distorted into a dystopia. Western powers have been declining, in contrast with the rising China. In *Day of the Oprichnik* Russia exercises a great influence on Europe by means of rich natural resources. Sorokin projects in his future novel an exaggerated picture of the real situation, in which the importing of oil and gas is closely linked with contemporary Russian diplomacy and politics. For example, Oprichnik Komiaga inspects a new play, *You Shan't Have It!*, which deals with the 'gas' issue in a preview at the concert hall inside the Kremlin. European countries suffer from the winter cold and a disrupted gas supply, and decide to send saboteurs across the border-wall to stealthily open a valve of the pipeline without permission. However, brave border guards exterminate the invaders and then press their hips to the valve to release their own 'gas'. A scream is heard from the West, that is, from the wings of the stage. In *Chlorophyllia* the fall of the Western world is depicted even more drastically. New York, London, Tokyo and other major cities in developed countries have sunk into the sea due to global warming, while Moscow, Beijing, and Delhi flourish, located in inland Eurasia. Europe has turned into 'a huge old-fashioned museum', under whose historical monuments strut immigrants from Africa. It is noteworthy that Petersburg, once called 'the window to Europe' also has gone under the water. Only curious divers visit the ruined building of the Hermitage.

The two novels have a common point in that Russia's prosperity is guaranteed by the Chinese presence. It might be considered a kind of reversed relationship of the Sino–Soviet friendship of the 1950s, but it is more feasible that China would take the part of the West, toward which Russia has a long history of ambivalent attitudes as a model of imitation and a target of antipathy. In an ode to the emperor of Russia cited in a scene in *Day of the Oprichnik*, he is praised for having 'learned Chinese and written off guojia (state) in the ideogram' besides his ability to pilot a yacht and a helicopter (p. 36). The role of French as a language of the elite of nineteenth-century Russia is displaced by Chinese in Sorokin's future novel. In *Chlorophyllia*, many Russian girls dream of being the wife of a Chinese millionaire. Saveliy Gerts is once consulted about the profitable publication of a book titled *How to get Married to the Siberian Chinese* (p. 11). It is obvious here that the longing of contemporary Russian youth for Western wealth is ironically reversed toward the East.

In both Sorokin's and Rubanov's novels, all sorts of Chinese goods predominate the market in future Russia. In *Chlorophyllia* even all daily necessities are imported from China, since Russians have given up working in preference for a life of idleness. Even spaceships and spacesuits are made in China, although Russia still maintains a lunar base. The stereotypical notion of Chinese products as illegal copies or cheap inferior articles is also inverted. For example, Komiaga in *Day of the Oprichnik* receives high-quality Chinese drugs as a bribe, which are emphasized not to be cheap American- or Dutch-made (p. 28). In *Chlorophyllia*, when there appears a Chinese Maybach, Chinese Ford, or Chinese Cadillac, the epithet 'Chinese' does not convey any negative connotations. Some complaints are voiced against the overwhelming Sinicization of Russian society, which is reminiscent of Slavophile discourses against Westernization in nineteenth-century Russia. In Sorokin's novel, for example, the Oprichniks moan and groan at the dinner feast: 'How long should our great Russia bow and scrape before China!? As we used to submit to the pagan America, now we bow down before the Celestial empire!' However, they cannot deny the fact that their lives are totally dependent on Chinese products, from food to the toilet bowl. Saveliy in *Clorophyllia*, who is also disgusted with the Sinicized way of life, feels glad in a café to find that he can order coffee made in Brazil (p. 147).

218 *Culture and society*

In contrast with the Chinese language and Chinese products often referred to in the novels, the Chinese people seldom appear. Most are depicted only as a part of a mob in the background. There are no scenes such as in Pelevin's novel, in which the Russian werewolf and the Chinese fox spirit have a philosophical dialogue, or as in van Zaichik's series, whose characters possess both Russian and Chinese characteristics inside themselves. In this way, the empty image of the Chinese in Sorokin's and Rubanov's works is closely combined with the image of China as a barrier between Russia and the outside. In *Day of the Oprichnik* a Russian imitation of the Great Wall of China closes the state border horizontally, while in *Clorophyllia* the 100th floor of high-rise buildings vertically separates the upper residential area exclusively for Chinese inhabitants. Supposedly, the focus here is on the closeness of the society which faces only toward the inside, remaining unaware of the outside on which it is strongly dependent in reality. The future Russia is supported by China as the outside, and shut down from the outside by China.

We would like to compare not only similarities, but differences in both novels. The near-future society depicted in *Day of the Oprichnik*, given the organization of archaic names as *prikaz* or Oprichinik for example, imitates the old Russia before the Westernization of Peter the Great. The old-fashioned ideal of Slavophile Russia has been partly realized, since the influence of the West is excluded in spite of the influx of Chinese elements. This purified Russianness, however, accompanies a kind of pre-modern violence such as the Oprichniks' assault on the residence of a nobleman deprived of favor, which is nothing less than a dystopia for readers outside the text. Compared with this, Rubanov's *Chlorophyllia* presents a more peaceful near-future than Sorokin's vision. However, it also proves to be a kind of dystopia where society is controlled with the more sophisticated system of the panoptic watch, such as microchips put inside peoples' bodies and a reality show in which all inhabitants participate, observed by ubiquitous microcameras. Differing from Sorokin's anti-utopian state which aims at the Slavophile ideal of purified Russianness, people in *Chlorophyllia*, released from working thanks to rent paid by the Chinese, value 'individual psychological comfort' most of all. It is possible to interpret that the novel focuses on the idleness of those who have lost their purpose or ideology. The overwhelming 'grass' growing in Moscow, providing inhabitants with necessary nourishment and narcotic pleasure, eventually turns them into plant-like beings. We even see here the traditional character of the 'superfluous man' of nineteenth-century Russian literature, the idle noblemen or intellectual elites depicted typically in Goncharov's novel *Oblomov*, projected onto the fictional future society.

Images of China in Russia demonstrate a complicated process of evolution, since they are closely connected with Russians' own self-identification, traditionally divided between Europe (Westernizers) and Russia (Slavophiles), now with the addition of Asia. Russian eyes toward China imitate the European way of viewing the Oriental world (which includes Russia). In other words, for Russia, viewing China is inseparable from being viewed by the West. When Russians refer to China positively, this favorable viewpoint is often supported by their own desire to appreciate the self-image of Russia. On the contrary, comments critical of China are linked to criticism of their own state.[6] A rich vocabulary has been supplied for the evolution of various images of China through the development of sinology and the translation of Chinese literature. Vladimir Sorokin, Viktor Pelevin, Pavel Krusanov, Kholm van Zaichik and other writers create various kinds of mirror images, intentionally reversing and grotesquely distorting traditional representations of the Celestial Empire. We can observe a sense of inferiority or superiority toward the West (or even toward the East), a 'megalomaniac' self-image of Eurasian power, a homophobic machismo mentality, anxiety over the energy-dependent economy, and various other aspects of Russian culture and society, reflected in the fantasy mirrors of China.

Notes

1 For a historical overview of images of China in Russia, see Lukin (2003). The first chapter refers to the dispute between Westernizers and Slavophiles.
2 Concerning the history of nineteenth-century Russian sinology, see Skachkov (1977). For the historical evaluation of Bichurin, see Skachkov (1977, pp. 90–123) and Tikhvinskii and Peskova (1997).
3 For more on this topic, see Koshino (2009).
4 Judge Dee 狄仁傑 is a real historical figure from the Tang era, who became a hero of traditional crime fiction, *Gong'an* 公案小说 and the series of detective stories by Robert van Gulik. Here, it is a name which the hero picks up for his pet cat in honor of the legendary Chinese judge.
5 The fox charm (*lis'i chary*) was initially used by Alekseev when he translated *Strange Tales of Liaozhai* (Pu, 1922).
6 Rozman argues that part of the anti-Chinese discourse produced at the time of the Sino–Soviet conflict was a veiled criticism of the similar socialist system of the Soviet Union as a kind of mirror image (Rozman, 1985).

References

Alekseev, M. P. (1999) 'Pushkin i Kitai' [Pushkin and China], in E. P. Chelyshev, ed., *Pushkin i mir vostoka* [Pushkin and the Eastern World], Moscow: Nauka (in Russian).
Belinskii, V. G. (1982) *Kitai v grazhdanskom i nravstvennom otnoshenii. Sochineniie monakha Iakinfa* [China in Civil and Moral Relations. Work by the Monk Hyacinth], Collection of works in nine volumes, vol. 8, Moscow: Khudozhestvennaia literatura, pp. 595–98 (in Russian).
Danilevskii, G. P. (1901) *Zhizn' cherez sto let* [A Life after One Hundred Years], Collection of works in twenty-four volumes, vol. 19, St. Petersburg: A. F. Marks, pp. 12–34 (in Russian).
Gromov, M. M. (2005) *Na zemle i v nebe* [On the Earth and the Sky], Moscow: Glasnost' AS (in Russian).

220   Culture and society

I. B. [Iakinf Bitiurin] (1844) 'Zamechaniia na tret'iu i posledniuiu stat'iu o Srednei Azii, pomeshchennuiu v 11 numere Otechestvennykh Zapisok na 1843 god' [Some Remarks on the Third and the Last Articles concerning Central Asia Published in the 11th Issue of *Otechestvennye Zapiski*], *Moskvitianin*, vol.3, p. 170 (in Russian).

Iwashita, Akihiro (2004) *A 4,000 Kilometer Journey along the Sino-Russian Border*, Sapporo: Slavic Reserach Center, Hokkaido University.

Koshino, Go (2008) 'Obraz imperii v 'al'ternativnykh istoriiakh' sovremennoi Rossii' [Images of Empire in 'Alternative History' of Contemporary Russia], in Tetsuo Mochizuki, ed., *Beyond the Empire: Images of Russia in the Eurasian Cultural Context*, Sapporo: Slavic Research Center, pp. 391–408 (in Russian).

——(2009) 'Images of Empire and Asia in the Contemporary Science Fictions of Russia', *Acta Slavica Japonica*, no. 26.

Krusanov, P. V. (2001) *Ukus angela* [A Bite of Angel], St. Petersburg (in Russian).

Lukin, Alexander (2003) *The Bear Watches the Dragon: Russia's Perception of China and the Evolution of Russia-Chinese Relations since the Eighteenth Century*, Armonk, NY: M. E. Sharpe.

Ma, Zuyi and Ren Rongzhen (2003) *hanji waiyishi: xiudingben* [History of World's Translations of Chinese Writings: Revised Edition], Wuhan: Hubei Jiaoyu Chubanshe (in Chinese).

Maggs, Barbara W. (1984) *Russia and 'Le Rêve Chinois': China in Eighteenth-Century Russian Literature*, Oxford: The Voltaire Foundation.

Odoevskii, V. F. (1926) *4338-i god* [The Year 4338], Moscow: Ogonek (in Russian).

Pelevin, V. O. (2005) *Sviashennaia kniga oborotnia* [The Sacred Book of Shapeshifter], Moscow: Eksmo (in Russian).

Pu, Sunlin (1922) *Liao-Chzhai. Lis'i chary* [Liaozhai. The Fox Charm], Petrograd: Vsemirnaia Literatura (in Russian).

Pushkin, A. S. (1959) *Poedem, ia gotov; kuda by vy, druz'ia* [Let us leave, I am ready; Wherever, my friends], Collection of works in ten volumes, vol. 2, Moscow: Academy of Sciences of the USSR (in Russian).

Rozman, Gilbert (1985) *A Mirror for Socialism: Soviet Criticism of China*, Princeton, NJ: Princeton University Press.

Rubanov, A. V. (2011) *Khlorofiliia. Zhivaia zemlia: romany* [Chlorophyllia. The Living Earth: Novels], Moscow: AST: Astrel', pp. 5–314 (in Russian).

Schimmelpenninck van der Oye, David H. (2010) *Russian Orientalism: Asia in the Russian Mind from Peter the Great to the Emigration*, New Haven, CT: Yale University Press.

Shlapentokh, Vladimir (2007) 'China in the Russian Mind Today: Ambivalence and Defeatism', *Europe-Asia Studies*, vol. 59, no. 1, pp. 1–21.

Skachkov, P. E. (1977) *Ocherki istorii russkogo kitaevedeniia* [Studies in the History of Russian Sinology], Moscow: Nauka (in Russian).

Sorokin, V. G. (2006) *Den' oprichnika* [Day of the Oprichnik], Moscow: Zakharov (in Russian).

Tikhvinskii, S. L. and G. N. Peskova (1997) 'Vydaiushiisia russkii kitaeved o. Iakinf (Bichurin)' [The Distinguished Russian Sinologist Father Hyacinth (Bichurin)], in S. L. Tikhvinskii, ed., *Istoriia rossiiskoi dukhovnoi Missii v Kitae* [History of the Russian Ecclesiastical Mission in China], Moscow: Sviato-Vladimirskoe obshchestvo, pp. 165–96 (in Russian).

Van Zaichik, Khol'm (2004a) *Delo sud'i Di* [The Case of Judge Dee], St. Peterburg: Azbuka (in Russian).

——(2004b) *Delo lis-oborotnei* [The Case of Fox Spirits], St. Petersburg: Azbuka (in Russian).

——(2005) *Plokhikh liudei net: Evraziiskaia Simfoniia. Delo zhadnogo varvara. Delo nezalezhnykh dervishei. Delo o polku Igoreve* [There Is No Bad Person: Eurasian Symphony. The Case of a Greedy Barbarian. The Case of Independent Dervishes. The Case of The Lay of Prince Igor], St. Petersburg: Azbuka. (in Russian)

Widmer, Eric (1976) *The Russian Ecclesiastical Mission in Peking during the Eighteenth Century*, Cambridge, MA: East Asian Research Center/Harvard University Press.

13 UNESCO World Heritage and the regional powers

Changing representations of religious cultural heritage

Sanami Takahashi, Noriko Maejima, and Hiroshi Kobayashi

UNESCO World Heritage: a view from the periphery

In this chapter, we analyze religious items of cultural heritage that are listed on the UNESCO World Heritage List, and consider problems of their representation and management systems in India, China, and Russia. Today, sacred sites are discussed with a focus on their complex nature. The dichotomy of the sacred and the profane is not always available. Eliade's hierophanies, for example, are not enough to understand contemporary phenomena in sacred sites where 'the sacred does not manifest itself' (Eliade, 1987, p. 11). Sacredness and tradition woven into a place are normalized and materialized, and then consumed. Under these circumstances, the boundary between religion and culture, between pilgrimage and tourism, becomes more and more blurred. A striking example of this fusion is demonstrated in the religious properties registered on the UNESCO World Heritage List.

Each of the three regional powers has its own religious tradition and culture, which may be represented by Orientalism. Today, their religious cultural resources are considered as a symbol of regional or national identity, which is often manipulated for political and economic purposes. We consider one property from each country as a case study: Bodhgaya, a Buddhist religious and pilgrimage site, Fujian *tulou*, a type of traditional dwelling of the Hakka, and Solovki (Solovetsky) Monastery, a famous old Russian Orthodox pilgrimage site and notorious concentration camp in the 1920s and 1930s under the Soviet regime. While these three loci share the same social problems with other regions in the use of World Heritage properties, the regional powers are faced with certain particular issues resulting in their peripheral position concerning the protection of cultural and historic properties. There is a discrepancy in the understanding of cultural heritage between these regions and the World Heritage Committee. When a property is recognized for its *outstanding universal value*, its global status creates a dilemma for the regional society in question.

World Heritage Sites are cultural and natural properties registered on the World Heritage List, based on the Convention Concerning the Protection of the World Cultural and Natural Heritage (the World Heritage Convention) adopted by UNESCO in 1972. According to the UNESCO website, the List includes 981 properties (759 cultural, 193 natural, and 29 mixed properties) located in 160 countries as of July 2013. When the Convention was signed, buildings constructed by secular and religious authorities in European culture supposedly provided an image of a standard property, which should be preserved under the title of 'World Heritage'. In 1994, the World Heritage Committee recognized that:

> the World Heritage List lacked balance in the type of inscribed properties and in the geographical areas of the world that were represented. Among the 410 properties, 304 were cultural sites and only 90 were natural and 16 mixed, while the vast majority is located in developed regions of the world, notably in Europe.[1]

The List did not reflect various cultural properties such as constructions made of wood, earth, and other deformable materials, folk culture resourses, intangible cultural properties, and cultural landscapes. The World Heritage Committee launched its Global Strategy in 1994 in order to redress the situation.

At the same time, the global standard for evaluating heritage sites does not necessarily coincide with the individual policies of protection and preservation of cultural properties in various regions. In other words, each country and region should preserve and exploit its cultural properties according to the global standard, taking into account local political and cultural circumstances and the lifestyle of the inhabitants living around the site. World Heritage registration also causes economic issues and problems of regional development, such as balancing exploitation and preservation, and the issue of turning a cultural property into a tourist site. We explore the interpretation and representation of World Heritage in India, China, and Russia in each local context, considering the common problems of heritage in a global context. Furthermore, we focus on the various actors who aim to preserve, exploit, or represent heritage sites for their own advantage.

Another important issue in this chapter is the correlation between traditional religious and cultural properties. Many properties included on the World Heritage List are concerned with the world's traditional religions.[2] In India, China, and Russia, state power controls the representation and use of religious heritage sites to a substantial extent. In India, it has been feared that claiming religious identity might evoke antagonism, because a religious split is a serious obstacle for the unification of the state. In China, any public religious activities had been prohibited since 1949 and only after the Chinese economic reform were 'official' religious organizations permitted. And in Russia under communist rule, even religious properties with historic and artistic value were often destroyed or disregarded, which cast a dark shadow

224 *Culture and society*

on the use and ownership of such properties. We illuminate the representation of heritage sites, historical memory, and antagonism and dialogue between the stakeholders in each of the three regional powers.

India: the politics of World Heritage: the case of Bodhgaya

Bodhgaya (state of Bihar, India) is widely known as a place where Buddha attained his enlightenment. Bodhgaya has been worshiped as a sacred place by Buddhists around the world. In 2002, the Mahabodhi Temple (the Mahabodhi Maha Vihar) in Bodhgaya was put on the World Heritage List. Considering the popular image of the place as a sacred site of Buddhism, registration of the temple might appear to be essentially (if not solely) based on the recognition of the place for its Buddhist element. We examine the actual confrontation and negotiations among strategists from a variety of social, political, and religious backgrounds related to the registration of the Mahabodhi Temple as a World Heritage Site.

Historical value of archaeological remains in Bodhgaya

In 2009, the Archaeological Survey of India (ASI) reported that there are 3,669 archaeological sites recognized as national treasures in India,[3] among which twenty-three are registered on the World Heritage List.[4] Buddhism was initiated and prospered in north India and archaeological remains related to Buddhism are spread along the Ganga River area across the states of Uttar Pradesh and Bihar. Among these sites, places related to the life of Buddha are recognized as sacred sites of Buddhism. Most of these sites lost their original shapes and remained abandoned after the thirteenth century, mainly because of the decay of Buddhism, until the nineteenth century when they were rediscovered by British archeologists. However, the Mahabodhi Temple of Bodhgaya at the point of archeological rediscovery avoided destruction and was preserved. At present, archaeological remains such as the Mahabodhi Temple and Vajrasana, one of the famous and the oldest historic places of Bodhgaya, on which Buddha meditated and earned his enlightenment, are recognized for their historical value and, as a result, have contributed to the registration of the archaeological sites in Bodhgaya as World Heritage by UNESCO in 2002. With that registration, the historic sites of Bodhgaya gained worldwide attention not only from Buddhists but also from tourists.

Stance of the Indian government on the preservation of Cultural Heritage

The current system of the management of the Mahabodhi Temple and Vajrasana was established by the Indian government, liberated from British rule in 1947. This system, compared to other cases of preservation of various historic remains, is unique. Archaeological discoveries of historic sites including those related to Buddhism took place under British rule in India. Most of these sites are designated as historical remains to be preserved according to the Ancient Monument and Archaeological Sites and Remains Act (AMASR) enacted in 1958 and are under the management of the ASI.

However, the historic remains of Bodhgaya are not designated to be preserved by AMASR. A special law, the Bodhgaya Temple Management Act, was enacted in 1949, by which the Bodhgaya Temple Management Committee (BTMC) was organized. The Indian government took the initiative of designing the law in order to ease the tensions and negotiate the differences between Hindus and Buddhists.

The tensions between Hindus and Buddhists were mainly caused by the question of ownership of Mahabodhi Temple. Before 1949 the temple had been under the sovereignty of the Hindu Shiva sect, i.e., under the control of a Hindu *mahant*,[5] and this triggered Buddhists' demand for ownership of the temple to be returned to them. To resolve the impasse, Buddhists requested that the British intervene, but the colonial government kept to a non-intervention policy.

This problem was put on the table at the general meeting of the All India National Congress Party in 1922 and continued to be debated. At that time, Jawaharlal Nehru, who would become the first prime minister of India, and Rajendra Prasad, the future first president of India, played a leading role in the National Congress Party. A task force, headed by Rajendra Prasad, was organized to examine ownership of Mahabodhi Temple and concluded that the temple should be under the joint management of Hindus and Buddhists. The Bodhgaya Temple Management Act was established based on this conclusion, and the BTMC was organized.

The representation of Mahabodhi Temple was changed by the National Congress Party. Many of India's political leaders were educated in the West and they accepted the Western image of Buddha as a great historical figure in India. Besides, the resolution of this problem basically influenced a political decision of the new independent India, which aimed to give appropriate consideration to neighboring Asian countries and put forward land ownership reform as a step towards India's modernization (Doyle, 1997).

Confrontation: concerning the legitimacy of management of the historic site

According to the Bodhgaya Temple Management Act, Art. 1 Sec. 10, the main responsibility of the BTMC is specified as the maintenance and restoration of the temple, which is similar to the role of the ASI. Besides this, the BTMC was expected to adjust various religious activities in the temple.

However, that the BTMC membership consisted of both Buddhists and Hindus caused conflict again. When the New Buddhists[6] started a movement for the return of Mahabodhi Temple to Buddhists in 1992, they criticized the fact that the management was not fully given to Buddhists and was still under the influence of Hindus, despite the fact that Bodhgaya is a sacred Buddhist site.

The New Buddhists' campaign aggravated local Hindu nationalists[7] and resulted in religious antagonism. For Hindu nationalists, Buddha is the ninth

226 *Culture and society*

incarnation of Vishnu and the Buddhists' call for Hindus to be expelled from the Mahabodhi Temple was unacceptable.

When it was decided at the twenty-sixth meeting of UNESCO held in Budapest that the Mahabodhi Temple would be put on the World Heritage List, the New Buddhists immediately demanded UNESCO's intervention in the religious conflict in Bodhgaya, revision of the Temple Management Act, and reform of the management organization, among other things.[8]

After the inscription of Mahabodhi Temple, the BTMC announced on their website in 2004 that they would strive for the preservation and exhibition of Bodhgaya and take responsibility for passing on the heritage to the future world.[9] In other words, the BTMC identified itself not as an organization responsible merely for the restoration and preservation of the historic site, but one that would guarantee mutual respect for Hinduism and Buddhism and convey the heritage of humanity to future generations.

By the inscription of Mahabodhi Temple, yet another problem surfaced concerning the development surrounding the site. An article in the newspaper *Dainik Jagran* reported on the development project of the Bihar state government,[10] which produced two different responses. One positively recognized the economic consequences of the project, while the other saw the development negatively in terms of its effect on the life of local society. The project aroused extensive anxiety among the local people, because it meant that their community might be expelled from the historic site.

An anti-development movement was organized by the local inhabitants in 2005 and several demonstrations were held until 2006. The opposition of the local people was not directed against the fact that Bodhgaya is a Buddhist site and has historical/religious value. They questioned why and for whom the development was necessary.

Leaders of the anti-development movement claimed that the historic site was an ancestral living space for the local people. It was the inhabitants who protected the site; therefore, it was unacceptable for the local people to be forced to leave the temple. They alleged that the enlightenment of Buddha would have been impossible without their ancestors. Furthermore, in their understanding, any development project that would expel the local people from the temple underestimated the role of their vigilance against theft, homicide, and rape, and that such a development project would make the sacred site dangerous for pilgrims and tourists (Maejima, 2010).

Management of Buddhist sites as a symbol of national identity

In conclusion, we illuminate several points. First, with the launch of the BTMC, the management of the historic site in Bodhgaya was designated to agents who have different religious backgrounds. The establishment of the BTMC itself reveals a definite respect for the fact that Bodhgaya is a religious site for both Buddhists and Hindus.

Since India's independence the BTMC has played a leading role in the management of Bodhgaya. However, as the actions of the New Buddhist movement in 1992 show, the legitimacy of the BTMC as the sole agent of temple management in Bodhgaya has always been contested. Against these doubts, its legitimacy is based on its appointment by UNESCO as the organization responsible for the temple management of Bodhgaya that is committed to preserving the heritage of humankind for future generations. At this point, it should be noted that, as an immediate reaction to the development project around the temple, local people were roused to become new voices in the series of events in Bodhgaya. Through their anti-development movement they showed themselves to be not passive bystanders but rightful participants in the social process that constructs the identity of the temple in Bodhgaya.

Second, after the Temple of Bodhgaya was designated a World Heritage Site, joint action between the BTMC and other organizations including the ASI began concerning the management of the site, and mobilization against the development committee has been observed. We can consider these movements as the consequences of confrontation, dialogue, and negotiation beyond the boundaries of institutions and organizations. Lastly, we discuss the situation of Bodhgaya again in the general context of India. The engagement of the Indian government in the management of Bodhgaya started with a special law enacted in 1949, which was earlier than the policy of separation of religion from politics stipulated in the Indian Constitution. In other words, the engagement of the Indian government with the situation of Bodhgaya can be construed as a necessary step toward the national policy of separating religion from politics. Furthermore, considering the fact that the engagement of the Indian government, as exemplified in the appointment of plural agents from different religious backgrounds, was based on its recognition of the religious nature of the historic sites in Bodhgaya, the engagement of the Indian government differs radically from that of the colonial government and its non-intervention policy.

Independent India uses Buddhist symbols to establish its national identity: the Buddhist wheel of truth is set on the national flag and the stone pillar of King Asoka is incused on the national bill. In 1956 the government celebrated the 2,500th anniversary of Buddha's achievement of nirvana and invited guests from all over the world. At the ceremony, Prime Minister Nehru called for (1) the construction of an international Buddhist society in Bodhgaya, and (2) the center-staging of Bodhgaya as a symbol of peace and international harmony for all humankind. An article in the *Indian Express* of November 27, 1956 explained why the secular Indian government had taken the opportunity on the celebration of the Buddhist anniversary to announce that Buddhism is not a purely religious phenomenon, but that it also has important academic and cultural aspects.[11]

This episode provides a window through which one can imagine the challenge of the new Indian government after liberation that held 'unity in diversity' to be a guiding ideal of a liberated India. This ideal reflects the nature of

228 Culture and society

the challenge that India faces: confrontations and contradictions rooted in differences of religion, ethnicity, and caste.

The very organization of the BTMC consisting of agents from different religious backgrounds is testimony to various interpretations of the situation and commitment to resolving the difficulties therein, which filled the newly born government of India with agony after liberation. In other words, the design of the BTMC implies a rather narrow and difficult path for 'unity in diversity' among contenders such as a government that promotes modernity in the Indian context, Hindus with a traditional background, and Buddhists from outside with international support.

China: politics of representation of the Fujian *Tulou* as World Cultural Heritage

In this section, we consider China's cultural properties in regard to their cultural representation. Since the Communist Party of China (CPC) established the People's Republic of China (PRC) in 1949, religious activities have been politically repressed. Inscription on UNESCO's World Heritage List is closely related to the question of how to accommodate the religious aspects of cultural properties to the CPC's political correctness. This section explores the politics of representation in China, taking as a case study the inscription of the Fujian *tulou* on the World Heritage List.

From Kejia tulou *to Fujian* tulou

Fujian *tulou* are located in Fujian Province on the southeast of China. They were incorporated onto the World Heritage List in July 2008. A *tulou*'s exterior is made of earth and it looks like a big earthen fort; hence it is known as *tu* (earth) *lou* (building). Most *tulou* are circular or square in plan, and some of them are three to four stories high and sixty to eighty meters wide with hundreds of rooms. Tens of families and hundreds of people are able to live together in a single building. Most *tulou* were built by the Hakka (Kejia in Chinese) people, who are a sub-ethnic group of the Han Chinese, and they have lived in *tulou* in clan units as a standard abode.

When we discuss cultural representation, the most important point is 'who represents whom?' This vernacular architecture was called just *tulou* for the past hundreds of years in local society, but the local government decided to call it *Kejia tulou* because they planned the tourism development of *tulou* as a part of Kejia (Hakka) culture.[12] After UNESCO registered it on the List, however, the architecture came to be called *Fujian tulou*. It means that *tulou* habitation is not only for the Hakka people but also for other ethnic groups. The various discourses surrounding *tulou* were not created by the people who live in them, but by the local government, global media, or academic institutes. Thus, the official explanation of Fujian *tulou* differs from the local context.

UNESCO appreciated the significance of *tulou* in terms of the 'harmonious relationship with their environment'. They especially valued the fact that the buildings truly embodied local folk-knowledge such as ancestor worship and *fengshui* thought.[13] However, if we shift our ground to the point of view of local society, these cultural customs had been regarded as remnants of feudalism by the CPC, and were even the subject of punishment a few decades ago. Even now, religious activities in Chinese society are conducted under certain restrictions; therefore, the religiosity of the heritage site, as evaluated by UNESCO, is also considered to be under political influence. In the following section we illuminate the historical background to two key-words, 'ancestor worship' and *fengshui*, which are applied to *tulou* by UNESCO, and consider how these keywords have been regarded in Chinese society.

Religiosity of cultural property in Chinese society

Religious organizations and activities have had negative connotations since the CPC took power in 1949. Traditional religion and folk customs were regarded as bad habits of feudalism, and local governments considered that they must be strictly managed. On most *tulou* registered on the Heritage List one sees the Communist Party of China's logo on the upper part of the entrance and a CPC political slogan on an outer wall. *Tulou* habitants were forced to adopt an attitude that eliminates religious aspects and folklore.

However, since the CPC adopted the 'reform and open door policy' in 1978, former 'superstitious' activities, including ancestor worship and *fengshui* activity, are gradually being reevaluated. According to Bruun, the practice of discovering burial grounds and performing ancestral rituals boomed among the ordinary people, and many exhumed their ancestors for reburial, based on *fengshui*, since they were not able to bury them in this style previously because of the political situation of that time (Bruun, 2003, p. 105). The *People's Daily*, the official newspaper of the CPC, on June 22, 1999, criticized the spread of religious activities in an article entitled 'Respect Science and Knock Down Superstition'. It referred to the fact that some CPC leaders believe in superstitions such as *fengshui*, fortune-telling, astrology, and divination lore for the sake of self-interest, and have fallen into spiritualism. Thus, religious activities or religious movements have been consistently denied on the surface, but have been activated again since 1978.

Mao Zedong (Chairman Mao)'s former residence in Shaoshan City, Hunan Province provides us with a good example of how religious activity has changed in the last decades. The most popular tourist spots in Mao's former residence are the house in which Mao Zedong was born and Dishui Cave, where the grave of his grandfather is located (Han, 2008, pp. 225–61). The government developed tourism here as a part of its patriotic education program, and it regarded the place as a sacred site of the Communist Revolution. However, in recent years, sightseeing at Dishui Cave has become popular for

230 *Culture and society*

religious reasons. Many tourists come there to share Mao's good luck. It means that people think that the success of Mao was a result of great *fengshui* power from his grandfather's grave. It seems ironic that a sacred place of the Communist Revolution is becoming more and more popular, not because its visitors sympathize with communist ideology, but because they want the *fengshui* or spiritual power of Mao, who famously repressed religious activities. Thus, there have been various discourses surrounding cultural property because of diversification and changes of subject of representation. However, when the government needs to give an official comment on a cultural property, it uses a discourse in line with its religious policy. In what follows, we discuss the official representation of Fujian *tulou*, which differs from the folk knowledge of the local context.

The tourism development project and the creation of hyperreality

In discussing the cultural representation of *tulou*, the most important point is the significance of the 'ancestral hall'. As a matter of fact, that hall is not recognized as an ancestral hall by the locals. Hakka people have a well-known folk history which tells how their Hakka ancestors lived in the ancient capital of China located around the Yellow River. They had to take refuge in the south because they were attacked by barbarians. When Hakka people talk about Hakka history, they always emphasize that they are the legitimate descendants of the aristocracy of the Han Chinese, and that the Hakka have a rigid patrilineal system. Therefore, it has generally been considered that a *tulou's* central hall represents their genealogical history, and that the hall embodies their patrilineal concept.[14] In addition, the hall also has a significant meaning in terms of *fengshui*. According to *fengshui* thought, if people give good *fengshui* power to their patrilineal ancestors, all their descendants will be successful. Based on *fengshui*, the most important place in a *tulou* is the center of the building and most *tulou* have a hall in this position. Many people think that the central hall is the Hakka people's 'ancestral hall', because this is a place that can receive strong *fengshui* power, and where residents pray to their ancestors for the well-being of their clan (Jiang, 2001, p. 123). To sum up, we can see two concepts in the hall of *tulou*: one is ancestor worship, and the other is *fengshui*. And these two concepts emphasize the cultural property of folkloric values and promote the tourist development of *tulou* as Hakka culture. And, finally, UNESCO gave a favorable assessment of the historical background of *tulou* and their harmonious relationship with the surrounding environment.

According to a survey by the author, however, there are no 'ancestral halls' at all in *tulou*. Because of space constraints, we cannot discuss this aspect in detail, but in short the local people do not recognize the hall as their ancestral hall. This hall has been used for the rituals of various gods and for ceremonial occasions of the clan. Besides, their ancestral hall is located outside the *tulou* and it is there that they practice ancestor worship (Kobayashi, 2012, pp. 97–127). So,

UNESCO World Heritage 231

why has the notion of an 'ancestral hall', which should not exist, appeared in the official explanation? There are two possible reasons. The first is that some academic researchers and various mass media have provided *tulou* with a monolithic Hakka image. In Meizhou City, Guangdong Province, there are so many vernacular architectural styles that incorporate an ancestral hall, and the city is well known for being the capital of Hakka ethnicity. So it is easy for Meizhou's 'Hakka culture' to set the standard of Hakka culture, and some people have applied the city's 'Hakka culture' to other Hakka residences. The *tulou* area was originally a peripheral aspect of Hakka culture, but as it has become famous, it has been adopted as standard 'Hakka culture'. As a result, the 'ancestral hall' appears in *tulou* as a hyperreality. The second reason is that most of the academic researchers who have created an official explanation of *tulou* are not local people. Among them, Japanese architectural researchers have contributed to fudging the discourse on the hall through a critical misunderstanding of it. They decided that the hall was an 'ancestral hall,' and so this became the official explanation, as it was subsequently cited by many other researchers. Thus, the official explanation of *tulou*, established by the local government and overseas researchers, was uncritically accepted by UNESCO.[15]

Experience of the insider and discourse of the outsider

Before the growth of tourism, most people around the *tulou* area were engaged in agriculture. As the number of tourists grew, their occupations began to change. Some opened guest houses, restaurants, and souvenir shops. Some of the men became bike-taxi drivers for tourists, and some women became tour guides to earn cash. In such ways the local people communicate with lots of tourists every day, and so they need to be able to speak about Hakka culture. On the one hand, the narratives are based on their own experience, but on the other hand, they are made up by others such as travel companies, the mass media, or UNESCO.

If a woman wishes to be a tour guide, she must pass a written test prepared by a travel company. The questions are selected from an official guidebook whose publication is limited. The guidebook is written in dialogue format for the tourists; when a tourist group arrives at a *tulou*, the book says that a guide should explain that 'this is the ancestral hall of the residents'.[16] Depending on their experience, local tour guides will not present the hall as an 'ancestral hall', but they are a little hesitant to differentiate between their own folk knowledge and the guidebook's explanation. They do not accept the explanation of 'ancestral hall' now, but one day they may change the way they describe the hall. In fact, a few of them are already calling it an 'ancestral hall' rather than just a 'hall'. In this sense, we can see that the local people are playing the role of agents representing a Hakka culture that has not been created by insiders, but by outsiders.

232   *Culture and society*

Russia: significance of the inscription on the World Heritage List and destiny of religious properties in the case of the Solovki Islands

In the Russian Federation, fifteen cultural and nine natural heritage sites have been put on the World Heritage List since 1988, when the Soviet Union ratified the World Heritage Convention. In spite of the considerable number of registered heritage sites, Russian society is not very interested in UNESCO World Heritage. For example, the first academic publication on World Heritage in Russian was the reference book *World Heritage* published in 2000 (Maksakovskii, 2000, pp. 5–6); since then there has been little research focusing on World Heritage in general. Furthermore, TV, journals, and other media rarely report news and events related to UNESCO World Heritage. The inscription on the World Heritage List does not play a significant role in the promotion of tourism, and the brand 'World Heritage' does not have commercial influence. However, these circumstances do not mean that the political and social influence of the World Heritage Committee can be ignored. We explore a certain role of UNESCO's assessment regarding the problem of preserving and exploiting cultural heritage of religious interest.

On the management of religious heritage

Cultural heritage sites in Russia include many religious properties. Every listed cultural heritage site except for the Curonian spit and the Struve geodic arc include religious elements, which consist mostly of Russian Orthodox buildings with the exception of the citadel, ancient city, and fortress buildings of Derbent, located in the Republic of Dagestan.

The management of religious and cultural properties is considered to be one of the most complicated problems in post-socialist Russia. Under the rule of the Communist Party, especially during the religious repression of the 1920s and 1930s and Khrushchev's anti-religious campaign from the late 1950s to 1964, a considerable number of religious buildings were destroyed or closed. Many religious buildings not used for worship or other religious purposes were converted to barns and stables and suchlike, or turned in to cultural halls and libraries. After World War II, Soviet Russia began to preserve and exploit its cultural and historic properties (*parmiatniki kur'tury i istorii*), taking into account the historical importance of architecture and landscape. At that time, state museums were established at former monasteries and churches whose cultural and historic significance was highly valued. Such museum tourism had been semi-officially encouraged since the mid-1960s. Whereas when the Russian Orthodox Church (ROC) began to develop its public and social activities at the end of the 1980s, not only those that were closed and neglected, but also former religious buildings now used for secular purposes were transferred (*peredat'*) to the ROC. Most bishops, clergymen, and believers consider the transfer as 'restitution' (*vozvrashchenie*). In other words, they think the ROC has a legitimate right to take back the former church estates, and this has led to serious conflict between the Church and the secular institutions, mainly museums. For example, Valaam Monastery, which has spiritual and historic significance, declared that the non-Orthodox inhabitants should leave the Valaam Islands.[17] The Ryazan Eparchy demanded complete restitution of the Ryazan Kremlin, and the exclusion of the museum from the site.[18]

The Russian government adopted a new federal law, 'On the Transfer of State or Municipal Properties of Religious Origin to Religious Organizations' in November 2010;[19] the state and municipalities were now obliged to transfer to religious organizations any unused church buildings and other religious artifacts of little cultural or historic significance. Museums, libraries, and other academic and cultural institutions are exempt from the law. Thus, the law should bring a degree of resolution to the conflict over the possession of former religious items.

The process of the inscription of the Solovki Islands on the List

The Solovki (Solovetskii) Islands and monastery in the Archangel region is also a locus of confrontation concerning the management of the properties, as with Valaam Monastery and Ryazan. The Solovki Islands are an archipelago in the White Sea, located in the northern part of European Russia (at latitude 65° north and longitude 35° east). Solovki Monastery was founded in the first half of the fifteenth century and became the largest monastery and pilgrimage site in northern Russia. Under communist rule, the monastery became a notorious labor camp, in use from 1923 to 1939, where many political prisoners were sent and executed. In 1967, the Solovki State Historical, Architectural and Natural Museum-Reserve, which worked to research and restore the historic building, was established. The museum, the Orthodox heritage and the rich natural life of the area attracted many tourists, whose number reached 35,000. After the monastery resumed its religious activities in 1990, it further developed its activities and has now become one of the most famous pilgrimage sites in Russia.

The cultural and historic ensemble of the Solovki Islands was put on the World Heritage List in 1992, and it was a fairly early registration process, since it was the sixth Russian heritage site to be listed. The Ministry of Culture of the Soviet Union began the process by which A. Martynov, a director of the museum (1986–94), was to prepare the necessary documents to be considered by the World Heritage Committee. The museum's director and curators considered that not only should the churches, chapels, and other monastery buildings be protected, but also the original ecosystem of the Solovki Islands (Martynov, 2008, pp. 264–67). They claimed Solovki was worth protecting as a 'historical, cultural, and natural complex'. Screening the proposal, the International Council on Monuments and Sites (ICOMOS) gave unanimous approval for Solovki's inclusion on the World Heritage List, although because they thought that 'the historical and cultural importance of

234   *Culture and society*

Solovetskii far outweighs its natural interest',[20] Solovki was registered as a 'historical and cultural complex'.

The museum and the monastery: cooperation and confrontation

Solovki Monastery was reestablished in 1990 and some of the buildings were conveyed to the Russian Orthodox Church. As of May 1991, there were only two monks and four novices (*poslushniki*);[21] thus, the monastery had no part in the management of the islands. When Father Iosif (secular name: Bla-tishchev; his term as *namestnik* 1992–2009) came to the island as a *namestnik* or abbot, he became popular with the inhabitants and museum staff. At that time, the condition of the monastery buildings was poor and the museum strived to acquire a larger budget for conservation and restoration. According to the director, Martynov, Father Iosif petitioned Patriarch Alexy II to ask President Yeltsin for more money. Furthermore, the inscription on the World Heritage List served as a great incentive; as a result, the jurisdiction of the museum was transferred from the regional administration to the direct control of the Russian Federation (Martynov, 2008, p. 287).

While the Russian economy was suffering from a serious economic crisis during the 1990s, the situation regarding restoration works, the number of visitors, and the management of properties appeared to go through no significant change. However, when the Russian economy recovered, the museum received a huge amount of federal budget; thus, it began to exert influence not only on the cultural problems, but also the economy and politics of the islands. In October 2000, the regional government of Archangel changed the political status of the Solovki Islands to that of an independent district (*raion*) that needed special preservation as a World Heritage Site, and it directly appointed a district governor (*mer*) (Ekologiia kul'tury, 2000, pp. 5–9),[22] M. Lopatkin (2000–2009), who assumed the post of director of Solovki Museum at the same time. He took the initiative of concluding a 'general agreement on interaction and collaboration' with the monastery, and the museum thus took advantage of the conservation of cultural and historic properties and the management of tourism (Takahashi, 2009, p. 516). During this period, Solovki's airport was improved, a new luxury hotel was opened, and Solovki became one of the most popular tourist destinations in Russia.

However, its management by the museum, focusing on the economic development of the islands, did not continue for very long. On July 25, 2005, a federal cultural institute held a conference about the problem of the development of the islands, and the representatives of the Moscow Patriarchate exaggerated the historical significance of Solovki Monastery, concerned that the sacred place would turn into an entertainment center, and suggested the possibility of expanding the monastery's territory (Stoliarov, 2006, p. 287). By the end of 2007, several internet sources reported that Solovki Museum would be closed in the near future and tourists and non-believer inhabitants would be kept out of the islands. In the autumn of 2008, the Solovki Islands were transferred to the jurisdiction of Solovki Monastery. One year later, Archimandrite Porfirii was appointed as a *namestnik* of the monastery and it was he, not as Christian Porfirii, but as Russian citizen Shutov, who assumed the position of director of the museum at the same time.[23] However, the monastery has not expelled the non-Orthodox inhabitants and the museum has continued its work under the leadership of Assistant Director Martynov.

Cultural heritage, preserved by the Church

In Russia, management by the ROC of cultural and historic properties is a 'new' trend. In many cases, specialists and professional institutions, such as state museums, are concerned about the appropriate conservation and usage of heritage with adequate understanding of its value. In response, the Church takes in historians and restorers of religious pictures and architecture and aims to be a responsible heritage manager. The ROC claims that because the Church is able to play the role of museum-reserve, there remain no problems with the transfer of cultural properties. In May 2012 the Ministry of Culture of the Russian Federation made an agreement with the ROC on the preservation and use of cultural and historic sites and the training of specialists.

Thus, Solovki's inscription on the World Heritage List strengthened the position of the museum, which received federal funding in the first half of 2000, and the museum conserved and used the heritage site from a secular viewpoint. However, with the expansion of the authority of the ROC in Russian politics, the monastery is beginning to take control of the management, conservation, restoration, and use of the site. Furthermore, the World Heritage Committee recognizes management by religious organizations. In May 2013, an international seminar was held in Moscow which underlined the ability of religious communities to be administrators of World Heritage Sites.[24]

It was monks who overcame the harsh natural conditions of the area and created its impressive architecture over many centuries. It stands to reason that the historic ensemble be restored to its original owner. However, the restoration is being carried out according to a certain standardized trend without adequate consideration of the historical background of each site or of the influence of religious and secular institutions on local society. Besides, there appears to be close cooperation between the ROC and the government in post-socialist Russia. The contemporary system of heritage sites of religious origin still arouses suspicion about diversity and openness among the secular and non-Orthodox population and the original managers.

For whom and for what purpose is heritage? Toward an open discussion

All three regional powers have a huge number of heritage sites and they have at the same time dealt with cultural and historic properties in a unique way that differs from the practice in Western Europe. Inscription on the World

236 *Culture and society*

Heritage List brings a change in the situation surrounding the heritage, and the significance of the properties also changes, which sometimes results in conflict and confusion in management and representation of the heritage sites.

For a further consideration of cultural heritage of religious interest, we need to pay more attention to the principle of the separation of politics and religion in each country. The confusing and ill-defined definition of politics and religion, religion and culture, makes the principle of separation more complicated. The conservation and use of cultural properties of religious origin are not exclusively religious issues. Religious antagonism might raise many problems concerning national identity, and religious activities have been substantially repressed or restricted under socialism. In these regional powers, religious life is considered to be the spiritual basis of the unique and traditional lifestyle of local people and, ultimately, the cultural aspects of religion are exaggerated, which makes easier the official representation and conservation of religious heritage. Religious heritage is often exploited and destroyed as an important symbol of a certain social strata. Religious communities sometimes confront the authorities, sometimes leaving center stage and at other times reinterpreting the official context in order to continue their religious practices and beliefs. Besides, not only are they an embodiment of traditional values, but they also aim to gain an advantage from tourism and other secular changes.

Registration on the List is often considered to be a neutral evaluation of the cultural properties beyond local conflict. In November 2010 the World Heritage Center organized a seminar in Kyiv on 'The Role of Religious Communities in the Management of World Heritage Properties', which discussed for the first time in the history of the World Heritage Convention joint management of religious properties at the international level.[25] The World Heritage Committee regards religious value and sanctity as an indivisible part of *the outstanding universal value* of heritage. It also exaggerates the significance of the spiritual role played by religious communities, made up of believers and traditional and indigenous peoples, in living religious properties and sacred sites. The religious communities are expected to participate in the preservation and use of the properties as an important stakeholder. Thus, the World Heritage Committee is beginning to pay great attention to the religious elements of cultural properties and is reviewing the multi-joint-management system and dialogue between various stakeholders. We should observe the influence of the direction of the Committee on the management and conservation of cultural heritage of religious interest in the future. At each heritage site, we need to listen to the voices of various stakeholders and explore the representation and story of the site.

Notes

1 UNESCO World Heritage Center, 'Global Strategy', http://whc.unesco.org/en/global strategy/.
2 Approximately 20 percent of the properties on the World Heritage List have some sort of religious or spiritual connection. UNESCO World Heritage Center, Initiative on Heritage of Religious Interest, http://whc.unesco.org/en/religious-sacred-heritage/.

3 Archeological Survey of India, 'Alphabetical List of Monuments', http://asi.nic.in/asi_monu_alphalist.asp.
4 'The number of nominated world heritage by nationality', http://unesco-worldheritage.com/000/005_1/.
5 In 1727, Shah Alam, the Muslim emperor who ruled over India, had given ownership of Mahabodhi Temple to a *mahant*, meaning a priest in a *math* (monastery) of the Hindu Shiva sect (Banerjee, 2000, Preface).
6 New Buddhists are those former low caste Hindus who were converted to Buddhism by Ambedkar, who appealed to the lower castes to improve their state and be released from the caste system. Ambedkar himself is from a low caste and participates in the social reform movement to abolish social customs that discriminate according to caste. The people belonging to the lowest caste are deep-rootedly repressed and discriminated against by other castes.
7 This conflict can be compared with Ayodhya, which is known as a Hindu sacred place and which caused serious religious tensions between Hindus and Muslims in the same years.
8 'Buddhist Monks Demanding Control of BodhGaya Temple Seek UN Intervention', *Rediff.com*, August 22, 2002.
9 BTMC, 'Buddhagaya – The World Heritage Site', www.mahabodhi.com/en/worldheritage.html (August 26, 2004).
10 'Mahabodhi Temple Draft Development Plan Ready', *Dainik Jagran*, July 13, 2002.
11 'Message of Buddha Commended', *Indian Express*, November 27, 1956.
12 Becoming a UNESCO World Cultural Heritage Site has brought big changes to local people's lives. But they never thought that their houses should be represented as a symbol of Hakka because they believe the place where they live is an area surrounded by Hakka culture.
13 UNESCO, Fujian *Tulou* – UNESCO World Heritage Centre, http://whc.unesco.org/en/list/1113.
14 UNESCO, Fujian *Tulou*-Nomination File (84.669Mb), p. 27, http://whc.unesco.org/uploads/nominations/1113.pdf.
15 For example, UNESCO's nomination file indicates that the ancestral hall, which is the most important part of the whole *Tulou*, is on the central axis line of the rear building (UNESCO, Fujian *Tulou*-Nomination File (84.669Mb), p. 38, http://whc.unesco.org/uploads/nominations/1113.pdf.
16 Fujian *tulou*'s tour guide teaching materials also regard their central hall as an ancestral hall (Yongding xian lvyou shiye ju [Yongding province travel business division], 2010, pp. 69, 76).
17 Various journals and internet news sources began to expose the problem in the Valaam Islands from 2000. Some insist on the legitimacy of the monastery from a patriotic viewpoint (for example, see Polushin, 2002, pp. 24–25), while others criticize the policy of the monastery (Vasil'ev, 2004, p. 19).
18 The Ryazan Eparchy began to claim complete ownership of the site in 2006. See Burdo and Filatov, 2009, p. 229 and 'RPTs protiv muzeev: osada Piazanskogo kremlia', http://scepsis.ru/library/id_2939.html.
19 Federal'nyi zakon Rossiiskoi Federatsii ot 30 noiabria 2010 g. no. 327-FZ 'O peredache religiozhym organizatsiiam imushchestva religioznogo naznacheniia, nakhodiashchegosia v gosudarstvennoi ili munitsipal'noi sobstvennosti', www.rg.ru/2010/12/03/tserkovnoedobro-dok.html.
20 UNESCO, Advisory Body Evaluation, ICOMOS, October 1992, http://whc.unesco.org/archive/advisory_body_evaluation/632.pdf.
21 Solovetskii gosudarstvennyi muzei-zapovednik nauchnyi arkhiv, f. 2, op. 2, d. 75, l. 9.
22 The designation of the Solovki Islands was changed to 'municipal district' (*munitsipal'nyi raion*) in 2004. In December 2004, an assistant director of the museum was elected as *mer*. In 2006, the Solovki *raion* was abolished and the territory

238 *Culture and society*

acquired the new position of 'rural habitation' (*sel'skoe poselenie*), belonging to the Primorskii *munitsipal'nyi raion*.
23 Father Porfirii was born in Sarov in 1965. He majored in economics in Moscow. The 1,000th anniversary of the Christianization of Rus' aroused his spiritual interest in Orthodoxy. He began to serve as a novice (*poslushnik*) in Sergiev posad in 1994 and became a monk in 1997 (Matonin *et al.*, 2010, pp. 210–13).
24 See the word file document, titled 'Moscow resolution', at page 2 on the site 'The International Seminar for religious representatives involved in the management and use of the World Heritage properties', http://whc.unesco.org/en/events/1056/.
25 'Initiative on Heritage of Religious Interest', http://whc.unesco.org/en/religious-sacred-heritage/.

References

Banerjee, N. (2000) *Gaya and Bodhgaya: A Profile*, Delhi: Inter India Publications.
Bruun, O. (2003) *Fengshui in China: Geomantic Divination between State Orthodoxy and Popular Religion*, Man and Nature in Asia series, no. 8, Singapore: NIAS Press.
Burdo, M. and S. Filatov, eds (2009) *Atlas sovremennoi religioznoi zhizni Rossii* [Atlas of the Contemporary Religious Life in Russia], vol. 3, Moscow: Letnii sad (in Russian).
Doyle, T. N. (1997) *BodhGayā: Journeys to the Diamond Throne and the Feet of Gayāsur* (Ph.D. thesis, Harvard University).
Ekologiia kul'tury: informatsionnyi biulleten' [Cultural Ecology: An Information Bulletin] (2000) vol. 4, no. 17, Archangel: Severo-Zapadnoe knizhnoe izdatel'stvo Komiteta po kul'ture i turizmu administratsii Arkhangel'skoi oblasti (in Russian).
Eliade, M. (1987) *The Sacred and the Profane: The Nature of Religion*, New York: Harcourt Brace Jovanovich.
Han, M. (2008) 'Shozan no seichika to Mo Takuto hyosho' [Creating a Sacred Site of Shaoshan City and Representation of MaoZedong], in Shigeyuki Tsukada, ed., *Minzoku hyosho no poritikusu: Chugoku nanbu ni okeru jinruigaku rekishigakuteki kenkyu* [Politics of Ethnic Representation: Anthropological and Historical Studies in Southern China], Tokyo: Fukyosya, pp. 225–61 (in Japanese).
Jiang, C. (2001) '"YiJing" yishi zai Yongding tulou zhong tixian' [Yongding Tulou Embodied YiJing Thought], in Dehui Yu, ed., *Yongding kejia tulou congshu: Lunwenji* [Yongding Kejia Tulou Cultural Series: Collected papers], China: Zuozhe Press (in Chinese).
Kobayashi, Hiroshi (2012) 'Fukken doro karamiru hakka bunka no saisosei: Doro naibu ni okeru "sodo" no kijutsu wo meguru gakujutsu hyosho no bunseki' [Fujian Tulou and Re-Creation of Hakka Culture: Analysis of Academic Representation surrounding the Description of Tulou's Ancestral Hall], in Masahisa Segawa, ed., *Hakka no sosei to saisosei: Rekishi to kukan karano sogoteki saikento* [Creation and Re-Creation of Hakka Culture: Comprehensive Reconsideration from the Point of View of History and Space], Tokyo: Fukyosya, pp. 97–127 (in Japanese).
Maejima, N. (2010) 'Rokaru na bunmyaku ni okeru 'seichi' no basyosei: Indo Buddagaya ni okeru "bukkyo seichi" wo jirei ni' [The Significance of Local Context for the Formation of 'Sacred Place': The Social Formation of 'Sacred Place' in BodhGaya, India], *Nihon Toshi syakai gakkai Nenpo* [Annals of the Japan Association for Urban Sociology], no. 28, pp. 167–81 (in Japanese).

UNESCO World Heritage 239

Maksakovskii, V. P. (2000) *Vsemirnoe kul'turnoe nasledie: nauchno-populiarnoe spra-vochnoe izdatel'stvo* [The Curtural World Heritage: A Popular-Scientific Handbook], Moscow: Agenstvo 'izd. servis' (in Russian).

Martynov, Aleksandr Ia. (2008) *Zapiski provintsial'nogo arkeologa* [Notes of a Rural Archaeologist], Archangel: Solti (in Russian).

Matonin, V., A. Laushkin, D. Levedev and S. Rapenkova (2010) 'Solovki: delo dlia sobornogo tvorchestvo: interv'iu s arkhimandritom Porfiriem' [Solovki: An Issue for the Collective Creation: An Interview with Archimandrite Porfirii], *Solovetskoe more*, no. 9, pp. 210–13 (in Russian).

Polushin, A. V. (2002) 'Doroga na Varaam: o vzaimootnosheniiakhi poselka' [A Way to the Valaam: About the Relationship with the Local Community], *Russkii dom*, no. 4, pp. 24–25 (in Russian).

Stoliarov, V. P. (2006) 'Kratkii ocherk istorii osvoenie Solovetskogo arkhipelaga' [A Short History of Pioneering of the Solovetskii Archipelago], *Solovetskie ostrova. Dukhovnoe, kul'turnoe i prirodnoe naslediia* [Solovetskii Islands. The Spiritual, Cultural and Natural Heritage], Moscow: Rossiiskii nauchno-issledovatel'skii institut kul'turnogo i prirodnogo naslediia, pp. 456–639 (in Russian).

Takahashi, S. (2009) 'Church or Museum?: The Role of State Museums in Conserving Church Buildings, 1965–85', *Journal of Church and State* (Oxford University Press), vol. 51, no. 3, pp. 502–17.

Vasil'ev, S. (2004) 'Perestroika "po-monastyrski"' [Perestroika in the 'Monastery Way'], *Ogonek*, no. 31, pp. 18–19 (in Russian).

'Yongding xian lvyou shiye ju' [Yongding Province Travel Business Division] (2010) *Fujian tulou Yongding kejia: Jiangjieyuan peixun jiaocai* [Teaching Materials for Tour Guide], Fujian: Yongding xian lvyou shiye ju (limited publication, in Chinese).

Index

abolition of agricultural taxes 97, 100
Abkhazia 4, 166
Af-Pak 140, 147
agro-firms 97
Alekseev, Vasily 208–9, 212, 219
Algeria 5, 172, 177–80, 182–85
Ali, Monica 192, 196
ancestor worship 229–30
Andhra Pradesh (AP) 88, 101
Anglo-Muhammadan law 176
anti-bourgeois liberalism 126
Archaeological Survey of India (ASI)
   224–25, 227
automobile industry policy 39

Balasa's revealed comparative advantage
   (RCA) 16–18, 25
Belinsky, Vissarion 206
Bichurin, Nikita 205–6, 219
Bo Yibo 127, 135
Bodhgaya 222, 224–27; Bodhgaya
   Temple Management Committee
   (BTMC) 225–28, 237
Bogd Khan 164–65
Bolshevik 162–66
Bosnia 129, 183
BRICS 144
British Asian literature 5, 191–93, 200
   see also immigrant literature; migrant
   literature
British East India Company 174–75, 177
British Empire see empire
Bukhara 164
Bulgakov, Mikhail 209

caste 73, 76, 90, 92, 174, 228, 237
Civil Nuclear Agreement 140
Communist Party: China (CCP, CPC) 3,
   69–75, 80–81, 89–90, 95–96, 98, 100,

111, 120–24, 126–28, 131–32, 135,
228–29; Soviet Union (CPSU) 30,
68–69, 71, 75, 108, 110–15, 118–19,
121, 130–31
comparative advantage 15–17, 41, 45
competitive authoritarianism 74
Confucianism 211
Congress of Berlin 156
Congress Party 90, 92–93, 101, 225
Congress system 72, 90–91, 100
Connectionism 100
Cossack 161
Crimea 14, 131, 166, 176, 178, 180
current account 30–31, 47, 49–51, 53,
   56–61

Dalai Lama 123–25, 127
Danilevsky, Gregory 207, 209, 216
Dhaliwal, Nirpal Singh 198–203
democratic consolidation 107, 116
Deng Xiaoping 2, 9–12, 14, 22, 74,
   124–28, 130–35
dominant party 3, 6, 67–75, 77, 79–80,
   90: definition of 80; typology of 68–70
dual trade system 2, 31–35, 39, 44, 45
Dzhivelegov, A. K. 160

economic opening policy 29–31
Eliade, Mircea 222
empire: British 155, 157, 160, 163–64;
   German 156; Russian 155–57,
   159–65, 176, 206, 209–10; Ottoman 5,
   155–57, 160, 172–74, 178, 180,
   182–84; Habsburg 155–56, 167; Qing
   163–64, 206; post-4, 134
enclave economy 32
EPZ (export processing zones) 31–34
exchange rate 2, 24, 47–49, 55, 57–60,
   62

Fang Lizhi 122
Father Hyacinth *see* Bichurin, Nikita
FDI (foreign direct investment) 10, 12, 15–16, 23, 28, 30–33, 49–51, 56, 58, 133, 141, 146
fengshui 229–30
foreign reserves 2, 24, 29–30, 47–51, 53–62
fox spirits 208, 211–14
free trade zone 33
Fujian tulou 222, 228, 230, 237

Galicia 156, 158, 162
Gandhi, Indira 13, 76
Gandhi, Mahatma 72, 76, 137
Gandhi, Rajiv R. 142
Ganga River 224
Gansu 96, 101
German Empire *see* empire
Gerschenkron, Alexander 9–12
global financial crisis 2, 47–48, 57–60
global imbalance 2, 47, 56–57, 60–62
Gorbachev, Mikhail 11–15, 20, 30, 75, 108–16, 118–19, 122–23, 125–28, 130–32, 134–35, 209
Gram Panchayat (GP) 87–88
Grand Duke Nikolai Nikolaevich 159–60
Guangdong 32–33, 95, 231

Habsburg Empire *see* empire
Hakka 222, 228, 230–31, 237
Henan 95, 101
Hohenzollern 155, 160–61
homeland 191, 195–96, 199, 201–3, 216
Hu Jintao 122, 125
Hu Yaobang 123, 125–26, 128
hyper-reality 231

Ichas, Martynas 160
IMF (International Monetary Fund) 13, 29–30, 48, 54, 58–59, 62
immigrant literature 5, 191, 195, 202
Indian National Congress (INC) 67, 69–70, 72–74, 76, 79–80, 91
Indo-Soviet Treaty of Peace, Friendship and Cooperation 144
infant industry protection 41
International Council on Monuments and Sites (ICOMOS) 233, 237
Irish Home Rule Bill 157

Jiang Zemin 125, 131–32
Jiangxi 96, 101

Kaliningrad 34–35
Kandla 33
Kashmir 140, 144, 146–47, 192
Khiva 164
Khrushchev, Nikita 232
knock-down assembly 42–43
Kovalevskii, Maksim 160
Krusanov, Pavel 209–10, 219
Kurd 158, 162
Kureishi, Hanif 192, 195–96, 200, 203

Lewisian turning point 14, 16
Li Peng 122, 132
Local Area Development (LAD) funds 92
local content 42–43
localization policies 42–44
Lok Sabha 87–88

McFaul, Michael 106–7
Malkani, Gautam 197, 201
Mao Zedong 111, 120, 124–25, 132–33, 135, 210, 229–30
marketization 3, 97, 106–10, 114–15, 116, 118
Mecelle 182–83
Medvedev, Dmitrii 77–79
Member of Legislative Assembly (MLA) 87, 91–92
Member of Parliament (MP) 87
migrant literature *see* immigrant literature
Monoculture 28
Mahalanobis, P. C. 13
Mufti 173, 175–79, 181, 183
Mumbai attacks 146
Muslim Ecclesiastical Assembly 177, 179, 181

national self-determination 157, 159–60, 166
Nehru, Jawaharlal 13, 72, 137, 225, 227
Nevsky, Alexander 210–11
New Buddhists 225–27, 237
New Rural Construction 96
non-alignment 137–38
non-tariff barrier to trade 36, 39, 41, 45
Nuclear Suppliers Group (NSG) 138, 140, 143, 145, 147–48

ODA (official development assistance) 29, 31
Odoevsky, Vladimir 206–7, 209
Orientalism 208, 222

242 *Index*

Orissa 87–88, 90–92, 101
Ottoman Empire *see* empire

Palestine 183–84
Panchayat Samiti 87–88, 92, 102
Patriarch Alexy II 234
Pelevin, Victor 5, 211, 212–15, 218–19
People's Daily 131, 229
Pilgrimage 212, 222, 233
People's Liveration Army (PLA) 123,
    125–27, 131, 138, 143
poverty alleviation project 98
processing trade 32–33, 39
Pu Songling 208
Pushkin, Alexander 206
Putin, Vladimir 12, 73–74, 78–79, 93,
    99, 102–3, 116, 145

qadi 173, 175–83
Qian Qichen 121, 128, 132
Qing dynasty 155, 164–66; Qing Empire
    see empire

Rai, Bali 199–200, 203
Rajendra Prasad 225
Rasmussen's index of power of
    dispersion (IPD) 18–23
Rasmussen's index of sensitivity of
    dispersion (ISD) 18–23
rate of import tariff burden 33–36
religiosity 229
revived Bretton Woods system 2, 56–57, 67
Revolution of 1848 (1848 Revolution)
    156
RIC (Russia, India, China) 144–49
Rubanov, Andrey 215–18
Rushdie, Salman 191–92, 202
Russian Empire *see* empire
Russian Orthodox 212–2, 232, 234
Russian Revolution (Revolution of
    1917) 156, 164–66, 208–9
Russo-Turkish War 170
Ruthenia 156

Santa Cruz 33
sarpanch (village chief) 88–89, 92, 94,
    99, 102
savings and investment balance (S-I
    balance) 51–53, 58; imbalance 57
şeyhülislâm 173, 176, 181–84
SEZ (special economic zones) 10, 15, 23,
    29, 31–32, 34, 132–33
Shanghai Cooperation Organization
    (SCO) 144, 146, 148

shari'a 4–5, 171–77, 179–85; shari'a
    court 173–75, 178, 181
Shenzhen 133
Shevardnadze, Eduard 130
Singh, Manmohan 140–41, 144
SITC classification 16
Slavophile-Westernizer dispute 206
Solovetsky islands *see* Solovki
Solovki 212–13, 222, 232–35, 237
Sorokin, Vladimir 5, 215–19
sterilization 54, 56, 59, 61–62
strategic autonomy 138, 142
strategic partnership 4, 138, 140, 142,
    145–46, 149; omnidirectional 4, 138,
    148–49
string of pearls 143
Suehiro, Akira 12, 15

trade openness index 38–39
Tambov 88–89, 93–94, 101
Tiananmen incident 121, 127, 132
Treaty of San Stefano 156–57
TRIM agreement 42–43
triple transformation 106, 108, 114, 119
Tuva 164–66

'ulama 173, 176–80, 183–84
UNESCO 6, 222–24, 226–32, 236–37
Ungern-Sternberg, Baron 165
United Nations Framework Convention
    on Climate Change (UNFCCC)
    142–43, 146–48
United Nations Security Council
    (UNSC) 138, 140–41, 144, 146–48
United Russia (UR) 3, 67, 70, 73–74,
    76–81, 86, 93–94, 100

Vajpayee, Atal Bihari 139–41, 149
Van Gulik, Robert 210, 219
Van Zaichik, Kholm 5, 209–15, 218–19
village chief *see* sarpanch (village chief)
Volga-Ural regions 5, 172, 176, 180,
    183–84

Wei Jingsheng 126
Wen Jiabao 143
Wilson, Woodrow 157
workers' remittances 16, 22, 24
World Bank 30, 45
World Heritage 222–24, 227, 232,
    234–38; List 222–24, 226, 228,
    232–36; Committee 5, 222–23,
    232–33, 235–36; Convention 223,
    232, 236

World War I 4, 155–58, 162, 164–67, 183

World War II 13, 69, 94, 165–66, 195, 210, 232

WTO (World Trade Organization) 24, 29, 34, 41–43, 45, 68, 142–43, 146–48

Xinjiang 4, 125, 131

Yan Jiaqi 124

yellow peril 208, 215

Yeltsin, Boris 11, 13, 30, 112–16, 118–19, 130–31, 134, 234

Zhao Ziyang 123–27

Zhou Enlai 124

Zhu Rongji 132

zhuanchang (inter-firm transaction) 32–33

Zilla Parishad 87, 92

eBooks
from Taylor & Francis
Helping you to choose the right eBooks for your Library

Add to your library's digital collection today with Taylor & Francis eBooks. We have over 50,000 eBooks in the Humanities, Social Sciences, Behavioural Sciences, Built Environment and Law, from leading imprints, including Routledge, Focal Press and Psychology Press.

Free Trials Available

We offer free trials to qualifying academic, corporate and government customers.

Choose from a range of subject packages or create your own!

Benefits for you
- Free MARC records
- COUNTER-compliant usage statistics
- Flexible purchase and pricing options
- 70% approx of our eBooks are now DRM-free.

Benefits for your user
- Off-site, anytime access via Athens or referring URL
- Print or copy pages or chapters
- Full content search
- Bookmark, highlight and annotate text
- Access to thousands of pages of quality research at the click of a button.

eCollections
Choose from 20 different subject eCollections, including:
- Asian Studies
- Economics
- Health Studies
- Law
- Middle East Studies

eFocus
We have 16 cutting-edge interdisciplinary collections, including:
- Development Studies
- The Environment
- Islam
- Korea
- Urban Studies

For more information, pricing enquiries or to order a free trial, please contact your local sales team:

UK/Rest of World: **online.sales@tandf.co.uk**
USA/Canada/Latin America: **e-reference@taylorandfrancis.com**
East/Southeast Asia: **martin.jack@tandf.com.sg**
India: **journalsales@tandfindia.com**

■ www.tandfebooks.com